THE BUSINESS TRAVELER GUIDE TO
WASHINGTON, DC

WITHDRAWN

Jason R. Rich

Ep Entrepreneur. Press

Editorial Director: Jere L. Calmes
Cover Design: Brand Architects Inc. and Desktop Miracles, Inc.
Production and Composition: Eliot House Productions

© 2007 by Entrepreneur Media Inc.
All rights reserved.
Reproduction or translation of any part of this work beyond that permitted by Section 107 or 108 of the 1976 United States Copyright Act without permission of the copyright owner is unlawful. Requests for permission or further information should be addressed to the Business Products Division, Entrepreneur Media Inc.

This publication is designed to provide accurate and authoritative information in regard to the subject matter covered. It is sold with the understanding that the publisher is not engaged in rendering legal, accounting or other professional services. If legal advice or other expert assistance is required, the services of a competent professional person should be sought.

City Factoid icon: © Ilkka Kukko
Money saver icon: © Miguel Angel Salinas Salinas
Time saver icon: © Miguel Angel Salinas Salinas
Tip icon: © Carston Reisinger
Warning icon: © Miguel Angel Salinas Salinas

Library of Congress Cataloging-in-Publication Data
    Rich, Jason R.
        Business traveler guide to Washington D.C. / by Jason R. Rich.
        p.   cm.
        Includes bibliographical references and index.
        ISBN-13: 978-1-59918-142-4 (alk. paper)
        ISBN-10: 1-59918-142-8 (alk. paper)
        1. Washington (D.C.)—Guidebooks. 2. Business travel—Washington (D.C.)—Guidebooks. I. Title.
    F192.3.R53 2007
    917.5304'4—dc22   2007016072

Printed in Canada
12 11 10 09 08 07   10 9 8 7 6 5 4 3 2 1

CONTENTS

Acknowledgments ix
Preface xi

SECTION I
Welcome to Washinton, DC 1

Getting to Washington, DC 2
Contacting the Airlines Directly 2
Online Travel Services......................... 7
Airport Security Considerations and Tips 11
Curbside Check-In at the Airport 14
Navigating Your Way through
   Washington Dulles International Airport 14
Navigating Your Way through
   Ronald Reagan Washington National Airport ... 22
Navigating Your Way through
   Baltimore/Washington International
   Thurgood Marshall Airport 28
Ground Transportation Options 33
Frequent Flier Miles—A Business Traveler's
   Best Friend 39

SECTION II
Packing for Your Business Trip............. 43

Shopping for the Perfect Luggage 44

Packing Tips................................... 47
Washington, DC Weather...................... 48
Packing for Your Trip 49
Before-Leaving-Home Checklist 54

SECTION III
Where to Stay While in Washington, DC 55

Choose Your Accommodations
  Based on Amenities and Services Offered....... 57
The *Business Traveler* Top 15 Business-Friendly
  Hotels in Washington, DC 60
Major Hotel Chains in the Washington, DC Area.. 85
Need Additional Help Finding a Hotel? 86
Take Advantage of Concierge Services
  Offered at Your Hotel 87

SECTION IV
Getting Around Town 89

Taxis 90
Rental Cars.................................... 92
Chauffeured Limousines and Town Cars 96
Public Transportation—
  The Metrorail and Metrobus 97
Shuttle and Charter Buses 102
DC Circulator Bus 103
Water Shuttle................................ 104
Scooter Rentals 104
Walking 104

SECTION V
Where to Dine in Washington, DC.......... 105

The *Business Traveler* Top 15 Fine-Dining
  Restaurants in Washington, DC............... 106
Theme and Specialty Restaurants 123
Ordering Room Service 127

SECTION VI
Entertainment in Washington, DC.......... 131

Washington, DC Tours........................ 132
Theater and Stage Performances............... 137

Professional Sporting Events 140
How to See Sold-Out Shows, Concerts,
   and Sporting Events....................... 143
Golf Courses 144
The *Business Traveler* Top 15 Tourist
   Attractions in Washington, DC 145
Shopping Opportunities for
   Busy Business Travelers.................... 157
Media Listings for Washington, DC 160

SECTION VII
Attending a Business Meeting or Convention . 163
   The Washington Convention Center 164

SECTION VIII
Business Services 179
   Audiovisual Equipment Rentals 180
   Balloons 181
   Banking and Financial Services............. 181
   Boxes and Shipping Supplies 182
   Bus Charters 182
   Car Rentals................................ 183
   Caterers 183
   Cell Phone Services and Accessories........ 184
   Computer Rentals, Repairs, and
      Technical Support 184
   Credit Card Companies 186
   Dry Cleaning and Tailoring 186
   Embroidery and Screen-Printing Companies ... 188
   FedEx Kinko's Locations.................... 188
   Florists 189
   Foreign Currency Exchange Services 190
   Full-Service Banks......................... 191
   Golf Courses 192
   Jet Charter Companies...................... 192
   Lawyers.................................... 192
   Limousine and Town Car Services 192
   Locksmiths 192
   Malls and Shopping 193
   Meeting and Banquet Room Rentals 193

Messenger Services 194
Modeling Agencies and Temporary
　Trade Show Personnel..................... 195
Office Supply Superstores 195
Photography Services 196
Secretarial and Temporary
　Employment Services 197
Shipping and Freight Services 197
Ticket Brokers 197
Trade Show and Private Security Services 198
Trade Show Exhibit Sales, Installation,
　Repair, and Dismantling 198
Translators and Interpreters................... 199
Traveler's Checks............................ 199
U.S. Post Office Locations 200
Video Production Services and
　Equipment Rental 200
Western Union Electronic
　Money-Transfer Services (Worldwide) 201

SECTION IX
Personal Services 203

Airline Directory............................ 204
Alcoholics Anonymous....................... 204
Chiropractors 204
Dentists 205
Department Stores 205
Eyewear Stores and Optometrists 206
Fitness Centers and Gyms 207
Florists and Balloon Delivery.................. 209
Hairstylists, Hair Salons, and Barbers........... 209
Hospitals 209
Limousine and Town Car Services 210
Massage Therapists and Day Spas.............. 210
Nail Salons................................. 211
Personal Shopping Services 215
Pharmacies 215
Rental Cars................................. 217
Shoe and Luggage Repair and Luggage Sales 217
Tailors and Clothing Alterations 218

Tuxedo Rentals 218
Wheelchair and Scooter Rentals 219

SECTION X
Help for Travel-Related Problems and Emergencies 221

Making Last-Minute Changes to
  Your Travel Itinerary 222
Dealing with Travel and Weather Delays 223
Lost Luggage 225
Lost or Stolen Credit Card, Driver's
  License, and/or Passport 228
Lost, Stolen, or Damaged Laptop Computer 229
Buying a New Outfit Fast or Removing a Stain ... 230
Prescription Refills 230
Replacing Prescription Eyewear................ 231
Medical or Dental Emergencies................ 231
Cell Phone-Related Problems 233

APPENDIX
Travel Charts and Worksheets 235

Tipping Recommendations 236
Tip Calculation Chart........................ 237
Travel Itinerary Worksheet.................... 238
Expense Tracker Worksheet 240
Trade Show Meeting Planner.................. 241
Frequent Traveler Program Worksheet.......... 242

Index 243

ACKNOWLEDGMENTS

Thanks to Jere Calmes, Karen Thomas, Leanne Harvey, Stephanie Singer, Courtney Thurman and Ronald Young at Entrepreneur Press for inviting me to work on this project, as well as to Karen Schopp at McGraw-Hill for her help marketing this travel guide series.

My never-ending love and gratitude goes out to my life-long friends—Mark, Ellen (as well as Ellen's family) and Ferras, who are all extremely important people in my life, as well as to my other close friends—Garrick Procter, Christopher Henry, and Chris Coates.

My gratitude also goes out to all of the public relations and marketing people who work for the various Washington, DC-area hotels, restaurants, shows, and attractions. These people were extremely helpful as I gathered information for this guide. A special thanks goes out to Rebecca Pawlowski at the Washington, DC Convention and Tourism Corporation, as well as to Heather, Lindley, and Megan at Heather Freeman Media and Public Relations for their support on this project.

I'd also like to thank my family for all of their support and give a shout-out to my Yorkshire terrier "Rusty" (www.MyPalRusty.com). Yes, he has his own web site, so please check it out! To visit my web site, point your web browser to www.JasonRich.com.

PREFACE

Finally, a Washington, DC travel guide exclusively for business travelers! Whether you're a frequent business traveler who spends several weeks every month on the road and considers an airplane seat to be as familiar as your own bed, or you have the occasional need to travel for business, you have very different needs than vacationers and people who travel for pleasure. *Entrepreneur Magazine's Business Traveler* series consists of city-specific travel guides designed to meet your needs head-on and provide you with a comprehensive, convenient, and single source of important travel-related information.

From booking your travel reservations to packing, navigating your way around the city, attending conventions or meetings, entertaining important clients, choosing the best restaurants, relaxing after a long day, and dealing with travel-related problems or emergencies, this guide offers you resources, phone numbers, web sites, addresses, and information that will help to make your trip a total success.

The best way for a business traveler or convention-goer to utilize the information within this guide is to read (or skim) it in its entirety. This will give you an overview of Washington, DC (and the surrounding areas), and what you can expect from your trip. Then, as you plan or experience each phase of your trip, refer to the appropriate section of this guide for more detailed information. Throughout the guide, you'll find helpful Tip, Warning, Money Saver, and City Factoid icons that are accompanied by tidbits of information you'll find particularly useful.

The trick to experiencing the most enjoyable, stress-free, and successful business-related trip is to plan ahead. Not only will this save you (or your business) money, but it'll save you time later and help you avoid the many hassles associated with making last-minute travel plans.

As the nation's capital and home of the United States federal government, Washington, DC has become a center for business, culture, and tourism. As you're about to discover, the DC area offers something for everyone when it comes to fine dining, entertainment, shopping, world-class day spas, and luxury hotel accommodations.

For business travelers in particular, the city offers thousands of available meeting rooms equipped for any need; full-service business centers within virtually every upscale hotel; high-speed internet access (often wireless) at most hotels and meeting spaces; the Washington Convention Center (a state-of-the-art trade show,

The Washington Convention Center is where many conferences, trade shows, and business gatherings are held. It's located in downtown DC.

banquet, and convention facility); plus countless ways to entertain important clients, customers, or business associates—day or night.

As you are making your travel, meeting, or convention plans, the Washington, DC Convention and Tourism Corporation (202-789-7000, 800-635-MEET, www.washington.org) and the DC Chamber of Commerce Visitor Information Center (866-324-7386, www.dcchamber.org) can be excellent resources. The Convention and Tourism Corporation's services team can help you select the ideal location for a function, trade show, banquet, conference, meeting of any size, or any other event and then assist you with every aspect of the event or meeting planning process.

TIP

To track down almost any type of business-oriented service associated with trade shows, banquets, meetings, or conventions in the DC area, visit www.dcises.org/event_resource_directory.shtml. Also, refer to Section VIII, "Business Services."

A BIT OF WASHINGTON, DC HISTORY

The original inhabitants of the area were the Piscataway Indians, a branch of the Algonquin Indians. The tribe settled in the region in the early 17th century. At the time, much of what is now Washington, DC was considered uninhabitable wetlands. However, the nearby cities of Georgetown and Alexandria, which are also located along the Potomac River, eventually evolved and began growing by the mid-1700s. This brought attention to the region.

Washington, DC was founded in 1791. It was named after President George Washington. At the time, it was referred to as Federal City. The *DC* in Washington, DC stands for District of Columbia, which is named after Christopher Columbus.

Washington, DC is not a state unto itself, nor is it a part of any other state within the United States. The District of Columbia is a federal district, which was specifically created to be the home of the United States government.

In 1790, Congress passed the Residence Act, which granted President George Washington the ability to select a site for a new federal district, which would become the nation's capital. At the time, the nation's capital was in Philadelphia, Pennsylvania. President Washington owned property in Mount Vernon, which is also located along the Potomac River, so he was familiar with the region.

The White House is home to the President of the United States and one of the most recognizable landmarks in the world. It's located at 1600 Pennsylvania Avenue NW.

The first building to be constructed in the DC area was the White House. Groundbreaking for the construction took place on October 13, 1792, which coincided with the very first celebration of Columbus Day. In 1800, the seat of government was officially moved to Washington, DC. On February 27, 1801, the District of Columbia was formally placed under the jurisdiction of Congress.

CITY FACTOID
As of mid-2007, Washington, DC had a population of about 572,000. In 2006, more than 15.4 million people (including 7 million business travelers) visited the DC area.

As the nation's capital, in addition to being home to the White House and the U.S. Capitol, along with many other government offices, Washington, DC is also home to dozens of historical monuments and memorials, museums (including 17 Smithsonian museums), the Library of Congress, and the National Archives. It's also home to more than 150 embassies, chancelleries, and diplomatic residences. Many of these embassies offer guided tours. For a list of embassies, visit www.embassy.org.

TIP
Information about visiting many of the popular attractions in Washington, DC can be found in Section VI, "Entertainment in Washington, DC."

WASHINGTON, DC GEOGRAPHY 101

Washington, DC is located south of Maryland, north of Virginia, and about 233 miles south of New York City. The city runs along the Potomac River and encompasses about 68 square miles. The city was created from land donated by the state of Maryland.

Today, Washington, DC is divided into four quadrants—northwest (NW), southwest (SW), northeast (NE), and southeast (SE). The center of these four quadrants is where the U.S. Capitol building is located. Within these quadrants, the city is further divided into many unique neighborhoods, including Georgetown, Dupont Circle, Adams Morgan, Capitol Hill, and Anacostia.

For the purposes of this book, the Washington, DC area, which is also commonly referred to as the Washington, DC metropolitan area, refers to the District of Columbia, plus seven counties in neighboring Maryland (Anne Arundel, Charles, Calvert, Frederick, Howard, Montgomery, and Prince George), five counties in neighboring Virginia (Arlington, Fairfax, Loudoun, Prince

Just as the Capitol is a centerpiece in the U.S. government system, from a geographic standpoint, it's also located in the center of the DC area.

William, and Stafford), and five cities in Virginia (Alexandria, Falls Church, Fairfax City, Manassas, and Manassas Park).

CITY FACTOID
As of 2007, the Washington, DC sales tax rate was 5.75 percent. Total hotel tax, including sales tax, however, was 14.5 percent. The food and beverage tax (applicable in restaurants) was 10 percent. The sales tax in nearby Maryland was 5 percent. The hotel tax varied by county (between 5 and 8 percent). In Virginia, the sales tax was 4.5 percent. The hotel tax varied by county (between 9.5 and 10 percent).

As you're navigating your way around Washington, DC, remember that numbered streets go north to south. Lettered streets run east to west. (There is no J, X, Y, or Z Street.) As you travel outward, the street names continue alphabetically using two- and later three-syllable names the farther from the center of the city you travel. Avenues named for U.S. states (such as Pennsylvania Avenue) run diagonally.

TIP
The telephone area code for Washington, DC is 202. When calling outside of the DC area, dial 1 + area code + phone number. For directory assistance within the DC area, call (202) 555-1212. For directory assistance outside of the DC area, dial 1 + area code + 555-1212.

One of the most economical, safe, efficient, and convenient ways to get around the city is the Metrorail public transportation system, which is described in Section IV, "Getting Around Town."

CITY FACTOID
The average hotel room rate in the Washington, DC area is about $200 per night. Throughout the year, the area hotels enjoy about a 74 percent occupancy rate. Hotel usage is the highest during March, April, and May.

PREFACE ·· xvii

MAP OF WASHINGTON, DC AREA

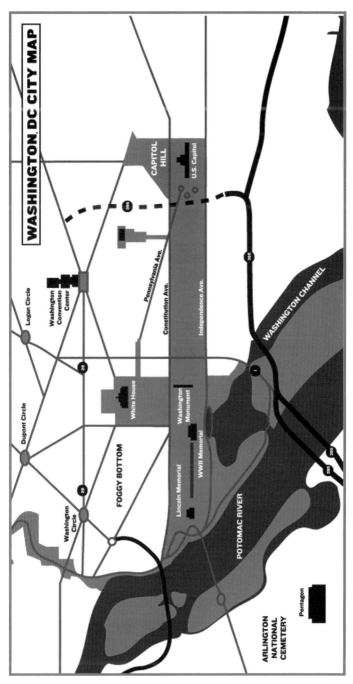

Map of Washington, DC area adapted from www.mapnetwork.com/mapspages/washington/DC_visitor_map_screen.pdf. Illustration by Amy Thomas.

MAP OF WASHINGTON, DC REGIONAL AREA

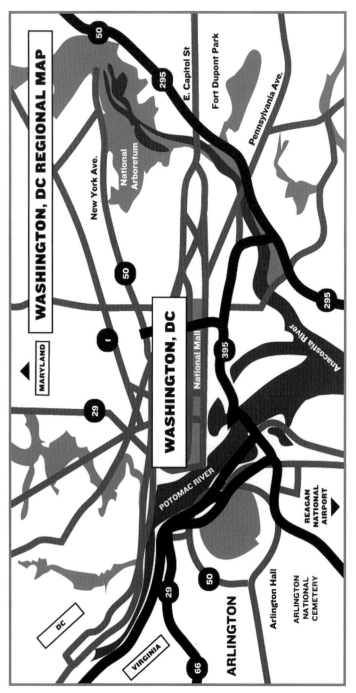

Map of regional area adapted from http://map.mapnetwork.com/destination/dc/.
Illustration by Amy Thomas.

CITY FACTOID
One of the most celebrated events in the DC area each year is the Cherry Blossom Festival. It takes place between mid-March and mid-April, during the peak time when the cherry blossom trees throughout the city are in full bloom. A variety of special events take place during this period.

LET'S GET STARTED PLANNING YOUR TRIP

As you'll discover, this guide is divided into ten sections to help you plan and experience your trip. Section I, for example, will help you book your airfare and then navigate your way around the three popular DC area airports upon your arrival.

Section II will help you pack for your trip. In Section III, you'll read about DC area hotels and discover which hotels made it onto the *Entrepreneur Magazine's Business Traveler* Top 15 Business-Friendly Hotels list. In Section IV, you'll discover all of the different ways of getting around town, while Section V focuses on the top restaurants in the DC area. Section VI offers all of the information you need to entertain yourself and your most important clients during your trip. In Section VII, you'll read all about attending a trade show or event at the Washington Convention Center.

Sections VIII and IX will help you track down any business-related or personal services you might need during your visit to the DC area. Finally, Section X will help you efficiently deal with any travel-related problems or emergencies that might arise. At the very end of this guide, you'll find a collection of travel worksheets and charts, which are excellent tools to help make your travel more organized and efficient.

TIP
Within this guide, you'll discover a handful of full-color maps that'll assist you in navigating around Washington, DC and surrounding areas.

If you find this book useful, additional city-specific travel guides covering popular business travel destinations, such as Las Vegas, New York City, Los Angeles, Chicago, and Orlando will also be available in 2007, with additional guides slated for publication in 2008. For details, point your web browser to www.jasonrich.com or www.entrepreneurpress.com.

TIP
If you utilize a wireless Palm-OS or Pocket PC Smartphone device, you can use the Pocket Express service (http://express.handmark.com/index.php) to access up-to-the-minute news, weather, 4-1-1 Directory Assistance, maps, and other information of interest to business travelers for a small monthly fee. You can also use your cell phone to obtain referrals to restaurants, shops, health services, and travel news by accessing Infospace (www.mobile.infospacefindit.com). For Palm OS PDAs and Treo Smartphones, the SplashTravel software ($19.95, www.splashdata.com/splashtravel/index.htm) offers a handful of useful applications of interest to business travelers, including an expense tracker, packing list manager, and enhanced scheduler application. To download a detailed and interactive map of the Metrorail subway system for your iPod, visit www.wmata.com/ipodMap/default.cfm. All of these applications can be used while on the go to help better organize your trip and make your travels more efficient.

SECTION I

Photo © L Fink

WELCOME TO
WASHINGTON, DC

The easiest and best way to ensure a stress-free journey to Washington, DC, is to invest the time to plan your trip in advance. This will help ensure you're able to book the most convenient flights and obtain reservations at your first-choice hotel. This section provides the information you need to make your travel reservations, find the lowest airfares, and navigate your way through the airport upon your arrival to the nation's capital.

GETTING TO WASHINGTON, DC

While plenty of people drive or take a bus from nearby cities, in order to reach Washington, DC, the majority of business travelers and convention-goers fly to this favorite destination. Another popular option is Amtrak, especially if you're traveling from a nearby city, such as New York City, Boston, Philadelphia, Hartford, Wilmington, Alexandria, or Providence. Information about Amtrak trains is offered later in this section.

Washington, DC, is serviced by three major airports—Washington Dulles International Airport, Ronald Reagan Washington National Airport, and Baltimore/Washington International Thurgood Marshall Airport—which are conveniently located a short distance outside of the nation's capital.

For domestic flights (incoming or outgoing), Ronald Reagan National Airport is the closest and most convenient to Washington, DC. Once at the airport, you can reach the city via car, taxi, or Metro (the city's mass-transit subway and bus system).

When it comes to making your travel arrangements and then booking your reservations (airline, hotel, and rental car), you have four primary options:

1. You can shop for the best airline, hotel, and rental car rates by calling each company or service provider directly or visiting its web site.
2. You can use one of the popular travel-related web sites (described in this section) and book all of your travel arrangements online simultaneously.
3. You can utilize the services of a local travel agent. A travel agent will do a lot of the busywork associated with making travel reservations for you.
4. You can schedule your travel through your company's corporate travel department (if applicable). Or, for those attending a convention or trade show in Washington, DC, the convention coordinator typically offers travel services with special discounts. In many cases, this option allows you to make changeable travel arrangements and choose accommodations at or close to the convention or meeting you'll be attending.

CONTACTING THE AIRLINES DIRECTLY

As you'll discover, not every major airline services every city or flies into each of the popular Washington, DC area airports. The

Unless you're a foreign dignitary, top-level government official, or personal friend of the president, chances are you'll need to find sleeping accommodations outside of the White House.

following charts list the major airlines that service each Washington, DC area airport. (This list is subject to change.) Based on these lists, you'll need to choose an airline that also services your home city and that offers convenient flights to and from the DC area. Keep in mind, direct flights might not always be available.

The following charts list the major airlines that service each airport, along with contact information for making travel reservations.

 MONEY SAVER
A new discount airline, called Virgin America (a sister company to Virgin Atlantic), began offering service between Washington, DC and places such as Los Angeles, New York City, Las Vegas, and San Francisco in mid-2007. Expect this airline to expand its coverage and compete head-on with JetBlue, Southwest, and AirTran—offering discounted air service between many major U.S. cities. For details, visit www.virginamerica.com or call (877) FLY-VIRGIN.

MAJOR AIRLINES SERVICING WASHINGTON DULLES INTERNATIONAL AIRPORT (IAD)

Aeroflot (888) 686-4949	Concourse D, Baggage claim 15 — www.aeroflot.ru/eng
Air Canada (888) 247-2262	Concourse C, Baggage claim 1, 2, 3, 4 — www.aircanada.ca
Air France (800) 321-4538	Concourse B, Baggage claim 15 — www.airfrance.com
AirTran Airways (800) AIR-TRAN	Concourse B, Baggage claim 6, 7 — www.airtran.com
ANA (All Nippon Airways) (800) 235-9262	Concourse B, Baggage claim 15 — www.ana.co.jp/eng
American Airlines (800) 433-7300	Concourse D, Baggage claim 13, 14 — www.aa.com
American Eagle (800) 433-7300	Concourse D, Baggage claim 13, 14 — www.aa.com
America West Airlines (part of U.S. Airways) (800) 2FLY-AWA	Concourse Z, Baggage claim 11, 12 — www.usairways.com/awa
Austrian (800) 843-0002	Concourse D, Baggage claim 15 — www.aua.com/us/eng
British Airways (800) 247-9297	Concourse D, Baggage claim 15 — www.britishairways.com
Continental Airlines (800) 525-0280	Concourse B, Baggage claim 11, 12 — www.continental.com
Continental Express (800) 525-0280	Concourse B, Baggage claim 11, 12 — www.continental.com
Delta Airlines (800) 221-1212	Concourse B, Baggage claim 13, 14 — www.delta.com
Delta Connection (800) 325-5205	Concourse B, Baggage claim 13, 14 — www.delta.com
Ethiopian (800) 445-2733	Concourse D, Baggage claim 15 — ww.ethiopianairlines.com
JetBlue (800) 538-2583	Concourse B, Baggage claim 10 — www.jetblue.com
Korean Air (800) 438-5000	Concourse B, Baggage claim 15 — www.koreanair.com
Lufthansa (800) 645-3880	Concourse B, Baggage claim 15 — www.lufthansa.com
MAXJet (888) 435-9626	Concourse B, Baggage claim 15 — www.maxjet.com
Northwest Airlines (800) 225-2525	Concourse B, Baggage claim 13, 14 — www.nwa.com
Saudi Arabian Airlines (800) 472-8342	Concourse H, Baggage claim 15 — www.saudiairlines.com/index2.jsp
South African Airways (800) 722-9685	Concourse B, Baggage claim 15 — ww2.flysaa.com/saa_home.html
Southwest Airlines (800) 435-9792	Concourse B, Baggage claim 13, 14 — www.southwest.com

MAJOR AIRLINES SERVICING WASHINGTON DULLES INTERNATIONAL AIRPORT (IAD)

SAS	Concourse B, Baggage claim 15
(800) 221-2350	www.flysas.com
Sun Country	Concourse B, Baggage claim 11, 12
(800) FLY-N-SUN	www.suncountry.com
Grupo TACA	Concourse B, H, Baggage claim 15
(800) 535-8780	www.taca.com
Ted	Concourse C, Baggage claim 1, 2, 3, 4
(800) 225-5833	www.flyted.com
United Airlines	Concourse C, D, Baggage claim 1, 2, 3, 4
(800) 241-6522	www.united.com
United Express	Concourse A, B, C, Baggage claim 1, 2, 3, 4
(800) 241-6522	www.united.com
U.S. Airways	Concourse Z, Baggage claim 11. 12
(800) 428-4322	www.usairways.com
U.S. Airways Express	Concourse Z, Baggage claim 11, 12
(800) 428-4322	www.usairways.com
Virgin Atlantic	Concourse B, Baggage claim 15
(800) 862-8621	www.virgin.com-atlantic.com

MAJOR AIRLINES SERVICING RONALD REAGAN WASHINGTON NATIONAL AIRPORT (DCA)

Air Canada	Terminal B, Gates 10-22, Baggage claim 1-6
(888) 247-2262	www.aircanada.ca
AirTran Airways	Terminal A, Gates 1-9, Terminal A Baggage claim
(800) AIR-TRAN	www.airtran.com
Alaska Airlines	Terminal B, Gates 10-22, Baggage claim 1-6
(800) 252-7522	www.alaskaair.com
American Airlines	Terminal B, Gates 23-34, Baggage claim 1-6
(800) 433-7300	www.aa.com
American Eagle	Terminal B, Gates 23-34, Terminal A Baggage claim 1-6
(800) 433-7300	www.aa.com
ATA	Terminal A, Gates 1-9, Terminal A Baggage claim
(800) 435-9282	www.ata.com
Continental Airlines	Terminal B, Gates 10-22, Baggage claim 1-6
(800) 525-0280	www.continental.com
Delta Airlines	Terminal B, Gates 10-22, Baggage claim 1-6
(800) 221-1212	www.delta.com
Delta Connection	Terminal B, Gates 10-22, Baggage claim 1-6
(800) 325-5205	www.delta.com
Delta Shuttle	Terminal B, Gates 10-22, Baggage claim 1-6
(800) 933-5935	www.delta.com

MAJOR AIRLINES SERVICING RONALD REAGAN WASHINGTON NATIONAL AIRPORT (DCA)

Frontier (800) 432-1359	Terminal C, Gates 23-34, Baggage claim 7-12 www.frontierairlines.com
Midwest (800) 452-2022	Terminal A, Gates 1-9, Terminal A Baggage claim www.midwestairlines.com
Northwest Airlines (800) 225-2525	Terminal A, Gates 1-9, Terminal A Baggage claim www.nwa.com
Spirit Airlines (800) 772-7117	Terminal A, Gates 1-9, Terminal A Baggage claim www.spiritair.com
United Airlines (800) 241-6522	Terminal C, Gates 23-34, Baggage claim 7-12 www.united.com
U.S. Airways/America West (800) 363-2597	Terminal C, Gates 23-45, Baggage claim 7-12 www.usairways.com
U.S. Airways Shuttle (800) 428-4322	Terminal C, Gates 35-45, Baggage claim 7-12 www.usairways.com

MAJOR AIRLINES SERVICING BALTIMORE/WASHINGTON INTERNATIONAL THURGOOD MARSHALL AIRPORT (BWI)

Air Canada (888) 247-2262	Terminal E www.aircanada.ca
Air Jamaica (800) 523-5585	Terminal E www.airjamaica.com
AirTran Airways (800) AIR-TRAN	Terminal D www.airtran.com
America West (800) 235-9292	Terminal D www.usairways.com
American Airlines (800) 433-7300	Terminal C www.aa.com
Continental Airlines (800) 525-0280	Terminal D www.continental.com
Delta Airlines (800) 221-1212	Terminal C www.delta.com
Frontier Airlines (800) 432-1359	Terminal C www.frontierairlines.com
Icelandair (800) 223-5500	Terminal E www.icelandair.com
Mexicana (800) 531-7921	Terminal E www.mexicana.com
Midwest (800) 452-2022	Terminal D www.midwestairlines.com
North American Airlines (800) 359-6222	Terminal E www.flynaa.com

MAJOR AIRLINES SERVICING BALTIMORE/WASHINGTON INTERNATIONAL THURGOOD MARSHALL AIRPORT (BWI)

Northwest Airlines	Terminal D
(800) 225-2525	www.nwa.com
Pan Am Clipper Connection	Terminal C
(800) 359-7262	www.flypanam.com
Southwest	Terminal A & B
(800) 435-9792	www.southwest.com
United Airlines	Terminal D
(800) 241-6522	www.united.com
USA 3000	Terminal E
(877) 872-3000	www.usa3000.com
U.S. Airways	Terminal D
(800) 428-4322	www.usairways.com

ONLINE TRAVEL SERVICES

There are dozens of popular travel-related web sites that can save you a fortune on your airline tickets, rental cars, and hotels. When booking your airfare online through any of these travel sites, however, keep in mind that your flights are usually *not* changeable or refundable. All sales are final, and you typically will not receive airline frequent flier miles for your trips. The benefit is that you can usually save up to 60 percent off published airfares simply by shopping online using one of these services.

TIP
If you're looking to fly to or from Washington, DC, via an airline's business class or first class, contact the airline directly, as opposed to booking through one of the travel-related web sites.

Here are a few tips for finding the best airfares to and from Washington, DC, online:

- Book your travel between 7 and 21 days in advance. (This rule does not apply to all the travel-related web sites. Some offer low fares with only 24 hours' advance booking.)
- Plan to leave and return on a Tuesday, Wednesday, Thursday, or Saturday. (Monday and Friday are the busiest days to travel to and from the DC area.)

- Consider accepting a red-eye flight when traveling from the West Coast to the East Coast.
- Reserve your airfare, hotel, and/or rental car at the same time as a package deal.
- Be willing to accept nondirect flights with one, possibly two stops.
- Before making a purchase (which will often be nonrefundable and nonchangeable), check two or three travel and/or airline web sites to ensure you're getting the best rates. Shop around for the best deals, even if you're traveling on a last-minute basis.

TIP
If you book through certain travel web sites, such as Travelocity, airfares and other travel can sometimes be changed, but for a fee.

WARNING
If there's a chance you'll need to change your travel itinerary at the last minute, you're better off booking your airfare directly through your desired airline. You'll pay a bit more, but typically you'll have the option to change your flight(s). When changing the flight, you'll often be charged a flat change fee of between $50 and $150 (depending on the airline), plus you'll have to pay the difference in airfare between your original flight and the new flight (if applicable). Many airlines will allow you to fly standby to avoid paying these fees, but be sure to check with the airline directly to understand the travel limitations. Optional travel insurance allows you to change your flight, but only if there's a medical emergency, not a change in your work itinerary. JetBlue and Southwest offer the most flexible policies of all airlines for changing flights without incurring high fees.

The following is information about several popular travel-related web sites:

- **Hotwire.com** *(www.hotwire.com)*. An easy-to-use web site for finding and booking airfares, hotels, rental cars, or complete travel packages. This service tends to offer the lowest fares and rates you'll find online. For flights, simply enter your departure and return dates, departure and destination cities, and the number of people traveling to see a variety of low airfare options. This web site displays the specific airline, flight numbers, travel times, and price for your travel request. The site will also suggest alternate travel times and dates if you're shopping for a lower fare.

- **Kayak.com** *(www.kayak.com)*. This web site does not offer the flashy bells and whistles found on many travel-related web sites; however, it quickly accesses hundreds of other travel-related and airline web sites in order to find the very best deals. Kayak.com is easy to use and often finds extremely competitive airfares, hotel rates, and rental car rates. Once you select an airfare, for example, Kayak.com forwards you directly to the web site offering it. This site is totally unbiased in terms of what deals are offered. No preferential treatment is given to particular airlines or service providers.
- **Nextag.com** *(www.nextag.com)*. This is a comprehensive price-comparison web site that's designed to help consumers find the lowest prices for virtually anything. The travel selection of Nextag.com allows you to shop for discounted airfares, hotels, rental cars, and travel packages. The site is advertiser based, meaning that in addition to searching other travel-related sites for the best deals, Nextag.com will also feature offers from companies that have paid to be included and compete for your business.
- **Orbitz.com** *(www.orbitz.com)*. Find and book airfares, hotels, rental cars, and complete travel packages with ease by entering your departure and return dates, departure and destination cities, and the number of people traveling. This web site displays a variety of specific airlines, flight numbers, travel times, and prices for your travel request. The site is affiliated with LastMinute.com (www.lastminute.com), which offers last-minute travel deals and discounts. Once you book travel through Orbitz, you can take advantage of Orbitz TLC Mobile, which can be accessed using your wireless PDA or Smartphone. This service allows you to obtain travel itineraries, check the status of flights, be alerted of delays, and reserve same-day hotel rooms while on the go.
- **SideStep.com** *(www.sidestep.com)*. Using this service, you can quickly search for the lowest available airfares from

more than 100 airline web sites and travel online services simultaneously. Unlike some of the other online travel services, this one also researches several of the lower-priced airlines, including JetBlue.
- ***Travelocity.com*** *(www.travelocity.com)*. Find and book airfares, hotels, rental cars, and complete travel packages with ease using this service. Simply enter your departure and return dates, departure and destination cities, and the number of people traveling. This web site displays a variety of specific airlines, flight numbers, travel times, and prices for your travel request. Detailed information about hotels and various destinations is also provided in the form of online travel guides and reviews.
- ***Yahoo! Travel*** *(http://travel.yahoo.com)*. Find and book airfares, hotels, rental cars, and complete travel packages with ease using this service. Simply enter your departure and return dates, departure and destination cities, and the number of people traveling. This web site displays a variety of specific airlines, flight numbers, travel times, and prices for your travel request.

WARNING
Check-in mistakes sometimes occur when the ticketing agent attaches the wrong destination tags to your luggage, sending your bags to the wrong city. As you check your luggage with your airline, double-check that the bags have the appropriate tags indicating what city you're flying to. In addition to your flight number, the airport code that should appear on your departure flight's tags is "IAD" for Washington Dulles International Airport, "DCA" for Ronald Reagan Washington National Airport, or "BWI" for Baltimore/Washington International Thurgood Marshall Airport. Manually confirm that the tags are correct. Don't just assume the ticket agent has done this correctly. You will receive claim checks for each piece of luggage checked with the airline. In some cases, claim check ID numbers will simply be printed on your boarding pass. Do not throw away your boarding passes or luggage claim tags until you arrive at your final destination. Before departing and prior to your return, remove all old tags from your luggage.

AIRPORT SECURITY CONSIDERATIONS AND TIPS

Since the terrorist attacks of 9/11, the security at airports has understandably become extremely tight. While this security is necessary for the most part, having to endure the hassle of long lines and the Transportation Security Administration's (TSA) regulations has become an ongoing frustration for many frequent business travelers.

Refer to Section II, "Packing for Your Business Trip," for more details about packing your carry-on and checked luggage. Additional information about the latest rules and regulations for passengers can also be found at www.tsa.gov. If you're a regular business traveler, refer to this web site monthly to learn about the latest changes in airport and airline security procedures. Being familiar with these procedures will speed up your trip through the airport and help you get through security faster and with less hassle.

WARNING
Never be rude to or disobey the TSA officers. Doing so may cause you serious delays or keep you from boarding your flight. Cooperating with their requests allows TSA officers to conduct their security-related jobs in a timely and responsible manner. To report specific violations and concerns about security, call the TSA Contact Center at (866) 289-9673 or the Office of Civil Rights at (877) 336-4872.

The following strategies will help you pass through security with the least delay and hassle possible.

- While in the airport, carry your photo ID and boarding pass with you at all times and be prepared to present them to security and airline personnel multiple times. According to the TSA, a valid photo ID consists of a driver's license, passport, or military ID.
- Avoid wearing excessive metal when traveling. All metal objects will need to be removed as you pass through airport security. Belt buckles, metal barrettes, underwire bras, large metal body piercings, and shoes containing metal should all be removed or they'll set off the metal detectors and cause delays. Small plastic bins are available to contain your personal items as they pass through security.

However, to avoid the possibility of theft, it's better to place these items within your carry-on.
- Have a credit card, debit card, or your frequent flyer program membership card for the airline with you, along with your photo ID, when you check in using an automatic kiosk at your airline's ticket counter. Most airlines now require this.

TIP
The major DC area airports are almost always crowded. Allow between 30 and 45 minutes just to get through security. Ideally, you should arrive at the airport between 90 minutes and two hours prior to your flight. This should leave ample time to return your rental car, check in with the airline, check your luggage, go through security, and make your way to the gate. You must be at your designated gate at least 30 minutes before departure for boarding, or you could lose your seat aboard the aircraft and miss your flight.

TIP
Once you arrive at the airport and pass through security, keep your boarding pass handy at all times. It likely will be checked multiple times between the time you check in with your airline and when you actually board the aircraft. After passing through the security checkpoint, you should no longer need your photo ID, unless the airport is at a heightened level of security.

- Personal electronics (cell phones and PDAs), your wallet, pens, loose change, keys, metal belt buckles, and all other personal belongings should all be removed from your pockets and placed in your carry-on and put through the airport's X-ray machine at the security checkpoint.
- As you approach the security checkpoint, remove your laptop from its case and send it through the X-ray machine separately. This is a TSA requirement. Failing to do so may cause you to undergo a more intense and time-consuming security screening procedure.
- Remove your shoes, jacket, and/or coat, and send these items through the X-ray machine separately.

- Pay attention to the latest list of items and objects that cannot be carried onto an airplane. Either place these items within your checked-in luggage (if appropriate and allowable) or ship them separately to your destination. Items that can't be carried onto aircrafts include knives, sharp objects, weapons, lighters, and hazardous chemicals (including common cleaning products). For a complete and up-to-date list of prohibited items, point your web browser to www.tsa.gov/travelers/airtravel/assistant/index.shtm or call (866) 289-9673.

TIME SAVER
Do not wrap any gifts you are carrying aboard the airplane. You need to make them available for inspection as you proceed through airport security.

- Dispose of all beverages and full-size containers of liquid (or gel) items before reaching the airport security checkpoint. You are allowed up to three ounces of liquid or gels, such as small containers of shampoo or toothpaste, in your carry-on. However, they must be enclosed in a clear plastic bag and declared when you pass through security.

TIP
If you are carrying an item that the TSA doesn't allow, instead of throwing it away or turning it over to the authorities, you can mail it back to your home or office. Prohibited items may include pocketknives, lighters, nail clippers, and any other small and/or sharp objects. Self-serve CheckPoint Mailer stations are located near the security checkpoints. Simply place the item(s) in a supplied envelope, complete the label and required form, and your items will be mailed to you for a flat fee of $8 for all domestic packages and $12 for international packages.

TIP
No matter which Washington, DC area airport you travel through, if you find yourself lost, confused, or in need of assistance, locate the nearest Travelers Aid counter at the airport (they're typically found near baggage claim). This

nonprofit organization can help if you have lost your tickets or ID, get separated from your travel companions, or require information and/or directions. These services are offered free of charge.

CURBSIDE CHECK-IN AT THE AIRPORT

Many airports and airlines offer curbside check-in as a convenience. While this service used to be free, most airlines now charge between $2 and $3 per bag, plus you're expected to tip the attendant. Instead of proceeding to the airline's ticketing counter within the airport, you can check your luggage and receive your boarding pass just outside the terminal's entrance, then go directly to security and ultimately to your departure gate.

Depending on crowds, using curbside check-in can save you time. When using curbside check-in, you should check your bags at least 45 minutes or one hour before your scheduled departure time. If the national security threat rises to Code Orange or higher, however, curbside check-in will not be available.

NAVIGATING YOUR WAY THROUGH WASHINGTON DULLES INTERNATIONAL AIRPORT

Address: Dulles, Virginia

Airport code: IAD

Web site: www.metwashairports.com/dulles

General information: (703) 572-2700

Flight tracking information: call (702) 572-6240 or www.flightview.com

Parking information: (703) 572-4500

Travelers aid: (703) 572-8296

Airport emergencies (port authority police): (703) 572-2952

Airport lost and found: (703) 572-8479

Paging: (703) 572-8296 or (703) 572-2536

TSA customer service/lost and found: (703) 661-6211

Each year, more than 27 million passengers fly into or out of Dulles International Airport, which is serviced by more than a dozen domestic and almost two dozen international airlines. The airport was named after John Foster Dulles, who was secretary of state under President Dwight D. Eisenhower from 1953 to 1959. The airport first opened in November 1962.

The airport is located about 26 miles from downtown Washington, DC. It's located along Route I-66 and the Capital Beltway. It takes between 45 and 90 minutes to travel by car to and

SECTION I / **WELCOME TO WASHINGTON, DC** ·· **15**

In 2007, Washington Dulles International Airport was in the midst of a massive renovation and expansion effort that is expected to last several years, so don't be surprised when you see a lot of construction taking place.

MAP OF WASHINGTON DULLES INTERNATIONAL AIRPORT

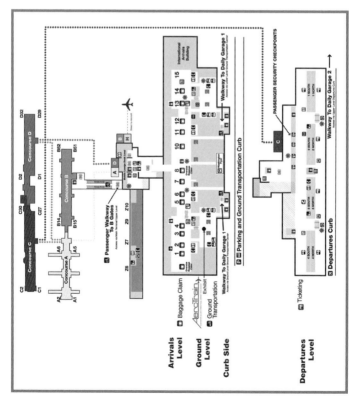

Courtesy of Metropolitan Washington Airports Authority.

These mobile lounges are used to transport travelers to and from their airline's terminal and the main terminal building, where the ticket counters and baggage claim areas are located. Allow about 15 minutes to make this trip.

from Dulles Airport and the downtown DC area. Currently, the airport has a total of 128 airplane gates, which are divided into several separate terminal areas, referred to as concourses. The airport comprises the main terminal building along with the international arrivals building and Concourses A, B, C, D, G, H, and Z.

Currently, 54-foot-long mobile lounges and moving walkways are used to transport passengers between concourses. Starting in 2009, a new underground automated train service will be used. This is part of a massive $3.4 billion expansion and modernization effort that kicked off back in 2000.

TIP
Dulles Airport features a full-service business center. It's open between 7 A.M. and 9 P.M. daily and offers foreign currency exchange, travel insurance, fax machines, photocopying, a notary public, and other services. The business center is located in the main terminal on the ticketing level. Call (703) 572-2946 for details. Private meeting rooms are not available at the airport, but there are meeting rooms available for rent at nearby hotels.

Since no vehicle waiting is allowed directly in front of the main terminal building, if you're being picked up at the airport by a private vehicle, the person picking you up can temporarily wait in a free parking lot called the Cell Phone Waiting Area. When you've arrived at the main terminal building, call your driver to let him know you are awaiting pickup. Dulles International Airport also offers more than 25,000 parking spaces (divided into short-term and long-term lots).

When departing from Dulles International Airport, to allow ample time to check in with your airline, check your luggage with the airline, go through security, and travel to the appropriate concourse to your airplane's gate, allow two hours for all domestic flights. Between the hours of 5:30 A.M. and 8 A.M., 11 A.M. and 1 P.M., and 4:30 P.M. and 6:30 P.M., arrive at the airport three hours before your airplane's scheduled departure time. This does not include additional time that's needed to return a rental car (if applicable).

TIP
To download and print a free detailed directory of all flights to and from Dulles International Airport, visit www.metwashairports.com/dulles/flight_information_3/flight_guide. This directory is updated monthly and includes all flights operated by all airlines that service this airport.

Terminal Layout and Services Offered

Once you check in at the ticketing counter for your airline within the main terminal building, you will need to reach your airplane's gate, which will be located in one of the airport's concourses. After proceeding through security, follow the signs to your designated concourse and gate. Shuttles to the concourses depart every 5 to 10 minutes, depending on the time of day. Allow up to 15 minutes just to go to and from the main terminal building and your concourse.

HOW TO REACH YOUR CONCOURSE
(FOR DEPARTING PASSENGERS)

Your airline ticket or boarding pass will show what concourse and gate your airplane will be taking off from. You can confirm this information by checking any of the flight information monitors throughout the airport. If your ticket says, "Departing from Gate B4," for example, your gate will be located within Concourse B. Follow the appropriate signs.

CONCOURSE	DIRECTIONS
Concourse A or C	Ride the shuttle that departs from the left (east) after passing through security.
Concourse B	Follow signs for the moving walkway. A shuttle is also available, but it departs every 15 minutes.
Concourse D, G, or H	Walk across the enclosed bridge (after security) to the shuttle departure area and your concourse. Follow the appropriate signs for the shuttle that travels to your departure gate.
Concourse Z	Walk across the enclosed bridge (after security), then down one flight, to the Z gates. Follow the signs, stairs and escalator are available.

More than 100 privately owned and operated food and retail shops are located throughout the main terminal building and concourses. You'll also find the following services within the airport:

- Airline ticket counters—main terminal building (departures level)
- Automated teller machines (ATM)—located throughout the airport, including all concourses
- Baggage claim area—main terminal building (ground level)
- Car rental counters—main terminal building (ground level)
- Cellular phone rentals—Concourse B (703) 572-2558
- Chapel—Concourse B
- Duty-free shopping (for international travelers only)—main terminal building, Concourses B, C, and D
- Food—a wide range of fast-food and sit-down dining options are available throughout the airport.
- Foreign currency exchange—main terminal building (departure level) and Concourses B, C, and D
- Ground transportation—outside the main terminal building (ground level)
- Hotel information desk—main terminal building (ground level)
- Passenger pick-up—outside the main terminal building (arrivals level)
- Shoe-shine service—main terminal building (departure level), Concourses A and C
- Shopping—a wide range of shops, bookstores, and newsstands are available throughout the airport. Most shops can be found in the various concourses, after passing through security.

- Smoking lounge—Concourse B (near Gate B38), Concourse C (near Gate C4), and Concourse D (near Gate D30). Smoking is not permitted anywhere else at the airport.

RETAIL SHOPPING

Throughout the airport, you'll find a wide range of retail shops, including Brooks Brothers (Concourse B), Brookstone (Concourse B), MindWorks (Concourse D), the Smithsonian Museum Store (Concourse B), Borders Books, (Concourses A, C, and D), and the Massage Bar (Concourse B). Aside from the newsstands and a few souvenir shops, many of the popular retail stores can be found in Concourse B.

FAST-FOOD DINING OPTIONS

The following are the fast-food dining options available within the airport:

- Auntie Ann's Hand-Rolled Soft Pretzels—Concourse C
- Ben & Jerry's Ice Cream—Concourse B
- California Tortilla—Concourse C
- Caribou Coffee—main terminal building (after security)
- Cinnabon—main terminal building
- Cuisine d'Avion—main terminal building and Concourse D
- Daily Grind—main terminal building (after security)
- Dunkin' Donuts—Concourses B and D
- Euro Café—Concourse A
- Famous Famiglia—Concourse A
- Fuddruckers—Concourse B
- Gaslight Bakery—Concourse B
- Guava and Java—Baggage claim 3
- Matsutake Sushi—Concourse B
- Maui Wowi Hawaiian Coffees and Smoothies—Concourse C
- Pizza Hut—main terminal building (food court)
- Potbelly Sandwich Works—Concourses B and C
- Ranch 1 Chicken Sandwiches—Concourse A
- Starbucks Coffee—main terminal building (baggage claim), Concourses B, C, and D.
- Subway—main terminal building (Z gates), Concourse D
- Villa Pizza—Concourses B and D
- Wendy's—Concourse C

SIT-DOWN DINING OPTIONS

The following restaurants offer full-service, sit-down dining within the airport:

- Brew Pub—Concourse A
- Cosi—Concourse A
- Firkin and Fox—Concourse C
- Gas Light Bakery—Concourse B
- Gordon Biersch—Concourse D
- Harry's Tap Room—main terminal building (ticketing level), Concourse B
- Moe's Grill and Bar—Concourse D
- Nelson's Bar—Concourse D
- Old Dominion Brewing Co.—Concourse B
- Tequileria—Concourse B
- Tidewater Landing—Concourse C
- Vino Volo Wine Room—Concourse C

TICKET COUNTERS (DEPARTURES) AND BAGGAGE CLAIM (ARRIVALS)

When you arrive at Washington Dulles International Airport by airplane, upon exiting your aircraft, follow the signs to the baggage claim area. It's here you can retrieve your checked luggage and access ground transportation. The ticketing and check-in counters are also located in this area for departing passengers. Follow the appropriate signs for your airline.

TIP

If you need to schedule last-minute ground transportation or have questions about your options, proceed to one of the ground transportation information counters you'll find in the baggage claim areas of the main terminal building.

AIRLINE CLUBS AND LOUNGES

The following airline clubs are located within Dulles International Airport. For a per-visit fee or by paying an annual membership fee, you can relax in the quiet, comfortable, and convenient airline clubs, lounges, and business centers.

Operated by the individual airlines and available to members, these clubs offer couches, TVs, telephones, bar service, complimentary newspapers and magazines, copiers, fax machines, internet access, clean restrooms, and other amenities, which makes them especially attractive if you have an extended wait at the airport.

AIRLINE CLUB	LOCATION
Air France	Concourse B (opposite Gate B46)
American Airlines	Concourse D (opposite Gate D26)
ANA	Concourse B (opposite Gate B46)
British Airways	Concourse D (opposite Gate D19)
Northwest Airlines	Concourse B (opposite Gate B20)
Ted Airlines	Concourse C and D (opposite Gates C8, C16, and D7)
United Airlines	Concourse C and D (opposite Gates C8, C16, and D7)
Virgin Atlantic	Concourse B (opposite Gate B32)

For an annual fee, you can join Priority Pass, which offers access to more than 500 airport lounges worldwide, regardless of what airline you're traveling with. For more information, point your web browser to www.prioritypass.com or call (800) 352-2834. Annual membership prices range from $99 to $399.

STUCK AT THE AIRPORT?

Located within a short drive from Washington Dulles International Airport are more than 50 hotels and motels. Many of these properties offer free shuttle service to and from the airport. If your flight gets canceled, or you have a last-minute change of plans, you can contact any of these hotels to arrange for nearby overnight accommodations. Following is a sampling of the nearby accommodations.

If you get stuck overnight at an airport because of a canceled flight, if the cancellation is a result of bad weather, you will be

HOTEL NAME	ADDRESS	PHONE
Comfort Inn	200 Elden Street	(703) 437-7555
Courtyard by Marriott	533 Herndon Parkway	(703) 478-9400
Crown Plaza	200 Centreville Road	(703) 471-6700
Embassy Suites	13341 Woodland Park Drive	(703) 464-0200
Fairfield Inn	23000 Indian Creek Drive	(703) 435-5300
Hampton Inn Dulles South	4050 Westfax Drive	(703) 818-8200
Hilton Washington Dulles	13869 Park Center Road	(703) 478-2900
Hyatt Hotel	2300 Dulles Corner Blvd.	(703) 713-1234
Sheraton	11810 Sunrise Valley Drive	(703) 620-9000
Super 8 Motel	7249 New Market Court	(703) 369-1700

responsible for covering the cost of your accommodations, meals, and ground transportation. If, however, the airline canceled your flight because of mechanical problems (or any reason that was the airline's fault), you're probably entitled to have the airline pay for your overnight accommodations plus provide you with vouchers for meals.

MONEY SAVER

To save money on last-minute hotel accommodations near the airport or anywhere in the Washington, DC, area, consider accessing the Hotels.com web site (www.hotels.com) or calling (800) 246-8357.

NAVIGATING YOUR WAY THROUGH RONALD REAGAN WASHINGTON NATIONAL AIRPORT

Address: Arlington County, Virginia

Airport code: DCA

Web site: www.metwashairports.com/national

General information and Travelers Aid: (703) 417-3972 or (703) 417-3974

Flight tracking information: www.flightview.com

Parking information: (703) 417-1234

Airport emergencies (port authority police): (703) 417-8560

Airport lost and found: (703) 417-0673

Paging: Contact your airline or visit any Travelers Aid information desk.

Reagan National Airport is the closest airport to Washington, DC. This airport handles domestic air travel. It's the most convenient airport to fly into and out of for domestic travelers.

MAP OF RONALD REAGAN WASHINGTON NATIONAL AIRPORT

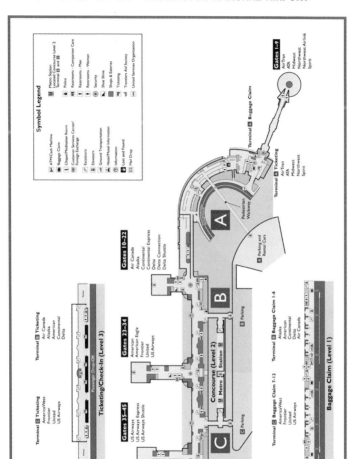

Courtesy of Metropolitan Washington Airports Authority.

For domestic travel to and from Washington, DC, the most convenient airport to utilize is Ronald Reagan Washington National Airport, which services more than 18 million passengers per year and hosts over a dozen domestic airlines. The airport, which also goes by the name Reagan National Airport or DCA, is composed of a main terminal building (containing the ticketing and check-in counters in the departures area and baggage claim in the arrivals area) as well as three main terminals (A, B, and C), which contain a total of 45 airplane gates. Because this airport is relatively small, walking between terminals and gates is easy. Moving walkways are available.

CITY FACTOID
Reagan National airport originally opened to the public in June 1941, after the site was selected by President Franklin D. Roosevelt. At the time, much of the 860 acres was under water, so 20 million cubic yards of sand and gravel were moved to the construction site. Since 1941, the airport has been expanded and modernized in order to meet the demands of today's travelers.

One extremely beneficial feature of this airport is that in addition to conveniently located rental car counters (in the main terminal, near baggage claim), there's also a Metrorail station located a very short walk from the main terminal building. Train service can take you directly into Washington, DC (or to the convention center), in a matter of minutes. The Metro also links to two nearby Amtrak train stations (one in Washington, DC, and the other in nearby Alexandria, Virginia). For Metro information and schedules, call (202) 637-7000, or see Section IV, "Getting Around Town."

Rental cars can be picked up in the Terminal A parking lot, while passenger pickup and drop-off is available outside of the main terminal. The airport is also located close to two Greyhound bus terminals, the closest of which is about four blocks away at 1005 First Street NE.

Since no vehicle waiting is allowed directly in front of the main terminal building, if you're being picked up at the airport by a private vehicle, the person picking you up can temporarily wait in a free parking lot called the Cell Phone Waiting Area. When you've arrived at the main terminal building, call your driver to let her know you are awaiting pickup.

TIP
To download and print a free detailed directory of all flights to and from Reagan National Airport, visit www.metwashairports.com/news_publications/publica tions/flight_guide. This directory is updated monthly and includes all flights operated by all airlines that service this airport.

Terminal Layout and Services Offered
Throughout the airport, you'll find more than 100 shops and dining options, plus a variety of services available to travelers, including ATMs, public telephones, Travelex foreign currency exchange

kiosks, and shoe-shine stations. There is also a full-service Chevy Chase Bank within the airport (301-987-BANK).

Some of the shops you'll find within the airport (mostly in the Terminals B and C areas) include:

- America! (souvenirs and gifts)
- Borders Books and News
- Brooks Brothers
- Brookstone
- Capital Travelmart
- CNBC Express
- Crabtree & Evelyn
- Faber News and Gifts
- Godiva
- Hudson News
- Jos. A. Bank
- Knits, Etc.
- Olsson.com Books
- PalmOne (airport wireless)
- Pen and Prose
- PGA Tour Shops
- Simply Wireless
- The Smithsonian Museum Store
- Sunglass Hut
- Taxco Sterling Co.
- Wilson's Leather

TIP
Reagan National Airport offers a full-service business center. It's open between 7 A.M. and 9 P.M. daily and offers foreign currency exchange, travel insurance, fax machines, photocopying, a notary public, and other services. The business center is located in Terminal C. Call (703) 417-3200 for details. Private meeting rooms are not available at the airport, but there are meeting rooms available for rent at nearby hotels.

FAST-FOOD DINING OPTIONS

The following fast-food dining options are available within the airport. Most can be found after proceeding through airport security.

- Allie's Deli
- Auntie Anne's Hand-Rolled Soft Pretzels

- Cinnabon
- Cosi
- Dunkin' Donuts
- Five Guys Famous Burgers and Fries
- Freshens Yogurt
- Fuddruckers
- Greenleaf Grille
- Jerry's Subs and Pizza
- Mamma Ilardo's Pizzeria
- Maui Tacos
- Mayorga Coffee Roasters
- Ranch-1 (chicken sandwiches)
- Starbucks Coffee
- Wall Street Deli

SIT-DOWN DINING OPTIONS

The following sit-down restaurants are available within the airport. Most can be found after proceeding through airport security. Reservations are not required.

- California Pizza Kitchen (takeout also available)
- DC Samuel Adams
- Foggy Bottom Brew Pub
- Legal Sea Foods (takeout also available)
- Matsutake Sushi
- Samuel Adams Brew House
- Sam's Brew House
- T.G.I. Friday's
- Tidewater Landing

TICKET COUNTERS (DEPARTURES) AND BAGGAGE CLAIM (ARRIVALS)

When you arrive to Reagan National Airport by airplane, upon exiting your aircraft, follow the signs to the baggage claim area. It's here you can retrieve your checked luggage and access ground transportation. The ticketing and check-in counters are also located in this area for departing passengers. Follow the appropriate signs for your airline.

AIRLINE CLUBS

The following airline clubs are located within Reagan National Airport. For a per-visit fee or by paying an annual membership fee,

AIRLINE CLUB	LOCATION
Air Canada	Terminal B
Alaska	Terminal B
American Airlines	Terminal B
Continental	Terminal B
Delta	Terminal B
Northwest	Terminal A
United	Terminal C
U.S. Airways	Terminal C

you can relax in the quiet, comfortable, and convenient airline clubs, lounges, and business centers.

STUCK AT THE AIRPORT?

Located within 10 miles of Reagan National Airport are more than 75 hotels. If your flight gets canceled, or you have a last-minute change of plans, you can contact any of these hotels to arrange for nearby overnight accommodations. The following is a partial listing of what's available. Also, be sure to read Section III, "Where to Stay while in Washington, DC."

HOTEL NAME	ADDRESS	PHONE
Americana Motel	1400 Jefferson Davis Highway	(703) 979-3772
Best Western Inn	724 Third Street NW	(202) 842-4466
Courtyard by Marriott	2899 Jefferson Davis Highway	(703) 549-3434
Crowne Plaza	1489 Jefferson Davis Highway	(703) 416-1600
Crystal Gateway Marriott	1700 Jefferson Davis Highway	(703) 920-3230
Doubletree Crystal City	300 Army Navy Drive	(703) 416-4100
Econo Lodge	6800 Lee Highway	(703) 538-5300
Hampton Inn Suites	2000 Jefferson Davis Highway	(703) 418-8181
Hilton	2399 Jefferson Davis Highway	(703) 418-6800
Hyatt Regency	2799 Jefferson Davis Highway	(703) 418-1234

NAVIGATING YOUR WAY THROUGH BALTIMORE/WASHINGTON INTERNATIONAL THURGOOD MARSHALL AIRPORT

Address: Anne Arundel County, Maryland

Airport code: BWI

Web site: www.bwiairport.com

General information: (410) 859-7111

Flight tracking information: www.flightview.com or www.bwiairport.com/flight_status/arrivals_departures/

Parking information: (800) 468-6294

Police/airport emergencies: (410) 859-7040

Airport lost and found: (410) 859-7387

TSA: (410) 303-7305

Paging: (800) 435-9294

Baltimore/Washington International Thurgood Marshall Airport, also known as BWI, is a medium-size airport that handles both domestic and international travel. The airport is serviced by approximately 30 commercial airlines, with Southwest Airlines being the most active. BWI is located about 30 miles from Washington, DC, and 10 miles south of Baltimore.

Since no vehicle waiting is allowed directly in front of the main terminal building, if you're being picked up at the airport by

MAP OF BALTIMORE/WASHINGTON INTERNATIONAL THURGOOD MARSHALL AIRPORT (LOWER LEVEL)

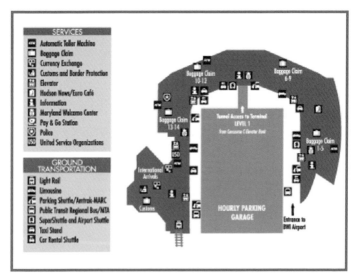

Courtesy of Maryland Aviation Administration.

MAP OF BALTIMORE/WASHINGTON INTERNATIONAL THURGOOD MARSHALL AIRPORT (UPPER LEVEL)

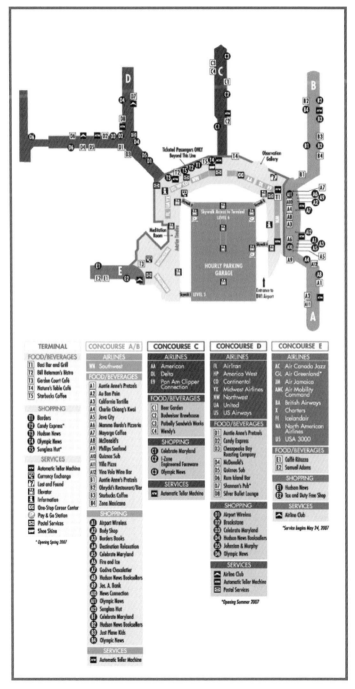

Courtesy of Maryland Aviation Administration.

a private vehicle, the person picking you up can temporarily wait in a free parking lot called the Cell Phone Waiting Area. When you've arrived at the main terminal building, call your driver to let him know you are awaiting pickup.

TIP

To download a free, printed and detailed directory of all flights to and from BWI, visit: www.bwiairport.com/airlines_schedules/flight_schedules. This directory is updated monthly and includes all flights operated by all airlines that service this airport. A digital version of this directory can also be downloaded and transferred to your Palm OS or Pocket PC-based PDA or Smartphone.

GETTING TO WASHINGTON, DC FROM BWI

Travel to and from Washington, DC, is relatively easy from the nearby BWI Rail Station, which is located about one mile from the airport. A free shuttle bus to the rail station is available. It takes about 35 minutes by train to reach the downtown DC area. A one-way ticket on the MARC Penn Line train to Union Station costs $6. Trains operate hourly throughout the day, with more frequent trains added during peak hours. Call (410) 672-6169 or visit www.marctracker.com for schedule and details.

The Amtrak train that goes from BWI Rail Station to Union Station in Washington, DC, costs between $17 and $36 each way. Call (800) USA-RAIL or (202) 484-7530 or visit www.amtrak.com for the schedule. The same train also stops in Philadelphia, Pennsylvania, Wilmington, Delaware, and Alexandria, Virginia.

Other ground transportation options include a bus service that connects to the Metro subway system as well as taxis, chauffeured limousines (or town cars), and rental cars, all of which are more costly. The rental car facility for BWI (where you can pick up or drop off a car) is located at 7432 New Ridge Road, Hanover, Maryland. Here you'll find 10 rental car agencies, including Alamo, Avis, Budget, Dollar, Enterprise, Hertz, National, and Thrifty. Free shuttle bus service to and from the airport is provided by each of the rental car companies. See the customer service desk for each rental car company located near the baggage claim area of the main terminal building, or call the rental car company directly. Phone numbers are provided later in this section.

For additional information about ground transportation options for getting to and from BWI and Washington, DC (and surrounding areas), see "Ground Transportation Options " on page 33.

CITY FACTOID
In 2006, BWI handled more than 20.7 million passengers. Construction for the airport began in 1947. It was officially opened in June 1950. Since then, the airport has undergone major expansion and modernization.

Terminal Layout and Services Offered

BWI is shaped like a large semicircle, with an hourly parking garage located in the middle. Around the semicircle, you'll find Terminals A, B, C, D, and E. (Terminals A and B are connected.) Each terminal has its own airline check-in counter and baggage claim areas. Terminal E is primarily for international arrivals and departures. If you're arriving or departing via a charter flight, it will be through Terminal E as well. Walking between terminals is relatively quick and easy. Moving walkways are available.

Throughout the airport, you'll find dozens of shops and dining options, plus a variety of services available to travelers, including ATMs, public telephones, Travelex foreign currency exchange kiosks, and shoe-shine stations. Postal services are available in the main terminal and in Terminal D.

Some of the retail shops and newsstands you'll find within the airport include:

- Airport Wireless—Terminals A/B and D
- Body Shop—Terminal A
- Borders Books—main terminal building and Terminals A/B
- Brookstone—Terminal D
- Celebrate Maryland—Terminals A/B, C and D
- Destination Relaxation—Terminal A
- Hudson News—main terminal building, Terminals A/B and D
- Jos. A. Bank—Terminal A
- Johnston & Murphy—Terminal D
- News Connection—Terminal A
- Olympic News—Terminals A/B and C
- Sunglass Hut—Terminal A

TIP
Private meeting rooms can be rented at the airport. For details, call (410) 691-2515.

DINING OPTIONS

The following fast-food and sit-down dining options are available within the airport. Most can be found after proceeding through airport security.

- Au Bon Pain—Terminal A/B
- Auntie Anne's Pretzels—Terminals A/B and D
- Beer Garden—Terminal C
- Bill Bateman's Bistro—main terminal building
- Boci Bar & Grill—main terminal building
- Budweiser Brew House—Terminal C
- Caffe Ritozzo—Terminal E
- California Tortilla—Terminal A/B
- Candy Express—Terminal D
- Chesapeake Bay Roasting Company—Terminal D
- Euro Café—main terminal building
- Garden Court Café—main terminal building
- Java City—Terminal A/B
- Mamma Lliardo's Pizzeria—Terminal A/B
- McDonald's—Terminals A/B and D
- Nature's Table Café—main terminal building
- Ortega—Terminal D
- Pizzeria Uno—Terminal D
- Quizmo's Subs—Terminal A/B
- Rum Island—Terminal D
- Samuel Adams Pub—Terminal E
- Shannon's Pub—Terminal D
- Starbucks—main terminal building
- Uncle Teddy's Pretzels—Terminal D
- Zoma Mexicana—Terminal A/B

TICKET COUNTERS (DEPARTURES) AND BAGGAGE CLAIM (ARRIVALS)

When you arrive at BWI by airplane, upon exiting your aircraft, follow the signs to the baggage claim area. It's here you can retrieve your checked luggage and access ground transportation. The ticketing and check-in counters are also located in this area for departing passengers. Follow the appropriate signs for your airline.

AIRLINE CLUBS

Airline clubs are located in Terminals D and E only and are operated by United (Terminal D), U.S. Airways (Terminal D), and British Airways (Terminal E).

STUCK AT THE AIRPORT?

Located within a short drive from BWI are a handful of inexpensive and midpriced hotels and motels. If your flight gets canceled, or you have a last-minute change of plans requiring overnight hotel or motel accommodations, call (410) 859-7111 and press number 6, followed by 2 for a listing of nearby hotels and motels that offer free shuttle bus transportation to and from the airport.

To save money on last-minute hotel accommodations near the airport or anywhere in the Baltimore or Washington, DC, area, consider accessing the Hotels.com web site (www.hotels.com) or calling (800) 246-8357.

GROUND TRANSPORTATION OPTIONS

Information about rental cars, taxis, limos, buses, and trains can be found in Section IV, "Getting Around Town." For getting to and from any of the Washington, DC area airports and any hotel, for example, a variety of shuttle bus services, shared vans, and private town car (limo) services are available. Many of these companies offer door-to-door service from the airport to your hotel or any address within the nation's capital or surrounding areas.

There is a fee for utilizing any of these ground transportation options. For more information, visit the ground transportation information desk at the baggage claim area of the airport. You can also contact any of these ground transportation providers directly. Advanced reservations are recommended, but not required.

Shuttle Bus and Other Ground Transportation Options

The Washington Flyer Coach Bus service offers comfortable, climate-controlled buses that travel between the airport and several Washington, DC area destinations, such as Metro's West Falls Church Station for just $9 each way (or $16 round-trip). For details about this bus service, call (888) WASHFLY or visit www.washfly.com.

SuperShuttle offers door-to-door, shared-van service to and from the Washington, DC area airports and any destination. (This means up to four separate parties can ride in the same van, which will make multiple stops to pick up or drop passengers off at their respective hotels.) The shuttle service operates on an on-demand basis. Look for the blue vans outside of the airport's terminal, or call (800) BLUE-VAN or visit www.shipershuttle.com to make a reservation. Prices vary based on your pickup and drop-off locations.

Like SuperShuttle, the Airport Shuttle (800-776-0323 or 410-381-2772) offers shared-van, door-to-door service from BWI to neighboring areas. Prices vary based on your pickup and drop-off locations.

From BWI, the Washington Metropolitan Area Transit Authority Bus offers ongoing bus service between the airport and the Greenbelt Metro Station. The bus runs every 40 minutes. Call (202) 637-7000 or visit www.wmata.com for details. Once aboard the Metro, you can access virtually any location within Washington, DC, and the surrounding areas.

TIP
Business travelers often find it cost and time efficient to utilize a private, chauffeured town car for their Washington, DC area airport ground transportation needs. A private town car offers more luxurious, door-to-door service that can be prearranged. Prices vary based on your pickup and drop-off locations.

Metro Train Service to and fdrom the Airport

One of the easiest, safest, most convenient, and cost-effective ways of traveling between Washington Dulles International Airport, as well as Ronald Reagan Washington National Airport, and most areas in or near Washington, DC (including the convention center), is the Metro train service.

Taxi Service

Located just outside of the baggage claim areas of each Washington, DC area airport you'll find a taxi dispatcher and designated taxi stand where you can hail a taxi to any location within the area. (Look for the sign that says "Taxi Passengers.") See Section IV, "Getting Around Town," for more information about traveling within Washington, DC, via taxi.

- For taxi service from any location in the Washington, DC area to the airport, call (703) 661-6655 to make a reservation.
- For taxi service between BWI and Washington, DC, call BWI Taxi Management at (410) 859-1100.

For more information about the Metro, see Section IV, "Getting Around Town," or visit www.wmata.com. (If you have a wireless PDA or Smartphone, you can access online Metro information, including schedules, from www.wmata.com/mobile.)

TIP
When riding in a taxi, be sure to write down the medallion number of the vehicle. If you need to file a complaint or retrieve lost items, this information will be helpful. Also be sure to ask for and keep your receipt.

Washington Flyer Taxicabs is the exclusive taxi service for Dulles Airport. It operates 24 hours per day to and from the airport. These taxis accept all major credit cards. Fares are based upon metered rates. Depending on your final destination, the average fare between Dulles International Airport and Washington, DC, will be $51 to $58. No reservation is required for taxi service.

WASHINGTON FLYER TAXICAB RATES FROM DULLES INTERNATIONAL AIRPORT

- First ¼ mile or part thereof $2.80
- Each additional ¼ mile or part thereof $.45

- Each additional passenger $1.50
- Each suitcase in excess of one per passenger $.50
- Each trunk or large-size article $2.00
- Each 77 seconds of waiting time $.45 (equaling $21.04 per hour)
- Snow Emergency Surcharge $2.50

TAXI RATES FROM REAGAN NATIONAL AIRPORT

For additional information about taxi service from Reagan National Airport, call (703) 417-0981. No advance reservations are required. Simply proceed to the designated taxi stand located outside of the airport's main terminal.

- Airport departure fee $1.75
- First mile $4.15
- Additional miles $1.80 each
- Extra passengers $1.50 each
- Luggage $.50 per piece (beyond one per passenger)
- Trunks and footlockers $2.00 each
- Morning weekday surcharge (between 7 A.M. and 9:30 A.M.) $1.00 per trip
- Evening weekday surcharge (between 4 P.M. and 6:30 P.M.) $1.00 per trip

SAMPLING OF AVERAGE TAXI FARES BETWEEN LOCATIONS

LOCATIONS	APPROXIMATE FARE	DISTANCE
BWI and Baltimore	$23.00	10 miles
BWI and Washington, DC	$63.00	30 miles
Dulles International Airport and Andrews Air Force Base	$86.00	41 miles
Dulles International Airport and BWI	$115.00	57 miles
Dulles International Airport and Capitol Hill	$54.00	26 miles
Dulles International Airport and Reagan National Airport	$58.00	27 miles
Dulles International Airport and the Pentagon	$51.00	26 miles
Dulles International Airport and White House	$51.00	25 miles
Reagan National Airport and Andrews Air Force Base	$28.00	14.5 miles
Reagan National Airport and BWI	$72.00	40 miles
Reagan National Airport and Capitol Hill	$10.00	4.5 miles
Reagan National Airport and the Pentagon	$8.00	3 miles

TIP
Private car and chauffeured limousine service is available from multiple companies to and from the Washington, DC area airports. For service to and from BWI, for example, contact RMA Limo at (800) 878-7743 (www.rmalimo.com). Listings for additional limousine and town car services can be found in Section IV, "Getting Around Town."

Car Rental

Many of the popular rental car companies have customer service counters located near the baggage claim area at each DC area airport. While it's best to reserve your car in advance in order to ensure availability and get the best rates, you can often rent a car simply by approaching one of these counters.

The following rental car companies are located on airport property (or nearby) at all Washington, DC area airports:

- Alamo—(800) 832-7933
- Avis—(800) 230-4898
- Budget—(800) 527-0700
- Dollar—(800) 800-4000
- Enterprise—(800) 736-8222
- Hertz—(800) 654-3131
- National Car Rental—(800) 227-7368
- Thrifty—(800) 367-2277

TIP
While the rental car customer service counters are located on-site, you may need to board a complimentary shuttle bus and be driven to the car rental parking lot where you will actually pick up your vehicle. Allow between 20 and 45 minutes for the check-in and car pickup processes, depending on crowds. When applicable, shuttle buses board directly outside the baggage claim area. Follow the appropriate signs.

Amtrak Service to and from Washington, DC

Phone number: (800) USA-RAIL
Web site: www.amtrak.com

Yet another popular, convenient, efficient, and cost-effective way to travel to Washington, DC, from various nearby cities, including New York City, Boston, Hartford, Providence, New London, New Haven, Stamford, Newark, Baltimore, Wilmington, Alexandria, and Philadelphia, for example, is via Amtrak train.

In addition to regular train service offered throughout much of the United States, Amtrak offers its high-speed Acela train along what's referred to as the Northeast Corridor. This is an ideal alternative to flying or driving to Washington, DC, for business travelers. The Acela train travels up to 150 mph and offers coach, first-class, and business-class seating. Each Acela train seat is equipped with an electrical outlet for your laptop, cell phone, or a DVD player, plus meals and snack services are available. The trains are also equipped with conference tables, restrooms, and other amenities. Travel time is typically equivalent to flying between cities (including airport travel time) but requires much less hassle.

TIP
In addition to being an Amtrak train station and Metro station, Union Station is also an indoor mall and offers numerous restaurants and cafés.

While the train fare for the Acela service is comparable with the cost of flying between popular East Coast cities and Washington, DC, travelers do not have to deal with airport security, costly airport parking, traffic, or the commute to and from busy airports. Reservations are highly recommended. The Amtrak train station in the DC area is located within Union Station, in the heart of Washington, DC.

MONEY SAVER
Amtrak offers discounts to AAA and AARP members.

Bus Service to and from Washington, DC

In addition to driving, taking the train, or flying to Washington, DC (from nearby cities), another option is to take a bus. This is one of the least expensive travel options, but it is also often one of the least convenient and slowest forms of travel.

For more information about bus service to Washington, DC, call Greyhound Bus (800-231-2222), Bonanza Bus (800-556-3815), Grayline Bus (212-397-2620), or Peter Pan Lines (800-343-9999) directly.

FREQUENT FLIER MILES—A BUSINESS TRAVELER'S BEST FRIEND

If you find yourself doing a considerable amount of personal and/or business travel, one of the best perks offered by airlines, hotels, rental car companies, and some major credit card issuers is the ability to accrue frequent flier miles. Simply by flying with the same airline, staying at the same name-brand hotels, or utilizing the same rental car company when you travel, for example, you can acquire miles or points that can later be redeemed for free airline tickets, upgrades, free accommodations at hotels, or other perks.

Virtually every major airline offers its own frequent flier program, which you can register for, free of charge, by filling out a form online (by visiting the airline's web site) or at the airport (speak with an airline representative at the ticket counter). Contact your favorite airline for details. In addition to earning miles by flying, you can also earn miles by doing business with the airline's promotional partners, which include specific credit card companies, hotels, rental car companies, and a wide range of other businesses.

Once you accrue a predetermined number of frequent flier miles with each airline, you'll also receive preferred status, which entitles you to additional perks, such as the ability to use special airport check-in counters (with much shorter lines), special toll-free reservation numbers (which don't require you to wait on hold), and complimentary upgrades to first class when you travel using a coach ticket.

Many hotel chains and rental car companies offer their own frequent traveler programs that allow customers to earn free accommodations, upgraded rooms, free meals, and other benefits, or automatic upgrades to their rental car. The points you receive from these programs can also often be redeemed for airline frequent flier miles and used for free travel.

Savvy business travelers learn how to maximize their frequent flier points by doing the majority of their travel with one airline (and then utilizing their favorite airline's partners to earn extra miles). Simply by charging everyday business expenses to a specific credit card that awards frequent flier miles, for example, is another quick way to build up additional mileage.

TIP

As you travel for business or pleasure, be sure to register the frequent flier program of each airline that you travel with plus register for frequent traveler programs offered by the hotel chains and rental car companies you utilize. Be sure to keep a list of your membership numbers handy so you can receive credit for all of your travels and earn rewards faster. You can use the worksheet on page 242 to organize this information.

To help manage all of your frequent flier and frequent traveler memberships, or to obtain details about the various special offers from airlines, hotels, and rental car companies, visit the FrequentFlier.com web site (www.frequentflier.com). From this free site, you can review the terms of each popular frequent flier or traveler program, learn how to maximize your mileage or point collection by utilizing travel partners and affiliates associated with each program, and subscribe to a free newsletter.

It's important to understand that when you join any of these programs, the ultimate goal is not to collect the miles or points themselves, but to ultimately trade in or redeem the points for the most valuable perks and benefits possible—whether it's free travel or upgrades, for example. One way to earn extra miles is to carefully read the membership newsletter published by their airline or hotel chain, to learn about special promotions that allow you to quickly earn miles or points. If you utilize certain flights, travel dates, or promotional partners, you could earn double or triple miles for your travel, for example.

WARNING

Every airline's frequent flier program has various rules and limitations. For instance, most airlines won't award frequent flier miles for airline tickets purchased through a discounted online travel service. Also, it is possible for accrued miles or points to expire after a predetermined period. To avoid losing the points or miles you've collected, be sure to redeem them in a timely manner.

The following is a list of the popular frequent flier or frequent traveler programs offered by the major airlines and hotel chains. Ideally, you want to join the appropriate rewards program prior to booking your travel reservations; however, you can also be credited for miles or points if you join after completing your travel.

Once you join one or more of these programs and begin accruing miles or points, you will see how much fun and addictive it can be, especially when you get to reap the benefits of your frequent traveling and start to receive free travel, perks, and rewards.

POPULAR FREQUENT TRAVEL PROGRAMS

AIRLINE	PROGRAM NAME	WEB SITE
Air Canada	Aeroplan	www.aeroplan.com/home.do
AirTran	A Plus Rewards	www.aplusrewards.com/a_rewards_more_rewarding.aspx
Alaska Airlines	Mileage Plan	www.alaskaair.com/mileageplan/
American Airlines	AAdvantage	www.aa.com/apps/AAdvantage/AAdvantageHome.html
ATA	Travel Awards	www.ata.com/awards/index.html
Continental	OnePass	www.continental.com/web/en-US/content/onepass/default.aspx
Delta	SkyMiles	www.delta.com/skymiles/index.jsp
Independence Air	iClub	www.flyi.com/iclub/iclub_home.jsp
JetBlue	TrueBlue	www.jetblue.com/trueblue/
Northwest Airlines	WorldPerks	www.nwa.com/freqfly/
Southwest Airlines	Rapid Rewards	www.southwest.com/rapid_rewards/rapid_rewards.html
United Airlines	Mileage Plus	www.united.com/page/middlepage/0,1454,1136,00.html
U.S. Airways	Dividend Miles	www.usairways.com/awa/content/dividendmiles/default.aspx
Virgin America	eleVAte	www.virginamerica.com
AmeriHost, Days Inn, Howard Johnson, Knights Inn, Ramada, Super 8, Travelodge, Villager, Wingate Inn	TripRewards	www.triprewards.com
Best Western	Gold Crown Club	www.goldcrownclub.com/
Hilton	HHonors	http://hhonors.hilton.com/en/hhonors/index.html
Hyatt Hotels	Hyatt Gold Passport	http://goldpassport.hyatt.com/gp/en/index.jsp

AIRLINE	PROGRAM NAME	WEB SITE
InterContinental, Crowne Plaza, Holiday Inn, Holiday Inn Express, Staybridge Suites	Priority Club Rewards	www.ichotelsgroup.com/h/d/pc/1/en/home
Marriott, Renaissance, Courtyard, Residence Inn, Fairfield Inn, TownePlace Suites, Ritz-Carlton, Ramada	Marriott Rewards	http://marriott.com/rewards/rewards-program.mi
Westin, Sheraton, Four Points, St. Regis, Luxury Collection, W Hotels	Preferred Guest	www.starwoodhotels.com/preferredguest/index.html
Wyndham, Summerfield Suites	ByRequest	www.wyndham.com/wbr/wbr_signin.wnt?

Donate Your Miles and Help a Worthy Cause

Many of the major airlines, including American Airlines, Continental, Delta, Midwest Express, United, and Virgin Atlantic, allow frequent fliers to donate their accrued miles to charities, such as the Make-A-Wish Foundation, the United Way, the Red Cross, the Special Olympics, the Adam Walsh Children's Fund, and CARE. When you donate your miles, free airlines tickets and other benefits are granted to people who need them. In many cases, the airline will match your miles donation. For details about these programs, contact your airline's frequent flier membership office.

Manage Your Miles

To help you keep track of your frequent flier and frequent traveler memberships, use the worksheet in the Appendix. Otherwise, you'll need to travel with and keep all of your individual membership cards handy.

SECTION II

©Norman Pegso

PACKING FOR YOUR
Business Trip

When you're traveling for business, preparation is one of the keys to enjoying a stress-free trip. One way to prepare is to select the most suitable luggage and then carefully pack everything you'll need. Finding suitable luggage that's rugged, well-built, and designed for what you are transporting is important, but not always as easy as it may seem. As you start shopping for luggage, you'll quickly discover many similar-looking bags at vastly different price points.

SHOPPING FOR THE PERFECT LUGGAGE

The first step to choosing appropriate luggage is to determine your needs. Figure out what you'll be carrying and how long you typically travel (from one to three days, from three to five days, or a week or longer). In your checked luggage, will you be packing several business suits that can easily get wrinkled, or more casual attire? Knowing this will help you determine the size, design, and number of bags you should purchase to meet your unique needs.

TIP
Many pieces of luggage designed for business travelers by high-end companies, such as Zero Halliburton (www.zerohalliburton.com) and Tumi (www.tumi.com), have special compartments designed to hold suits and other clothing that you want to remain wrinkle free. The Zero Halliburton 24-inch Expandable Upright with Suiter, for example, is made from extremely durable material and has a separate compartment for two or three business suits, as well as built-in wheels and an expandable handle. It is ideal for a trip of between three and seven days. Similar designs are also available in 20-, 22-, 27-, and 29-inch sizes to accommodate a wide range of packing needs. You can mix and match bag styles to create a luggage set that's ideal for you.

The luggage you select should be easy to transport. After all, you'll need to navigate your way through busy airports, down long hotel hallways, and in and out of cars or taxis. Doing this with poorly designed luggage can put added stress on your back, neck, and arms. Plus, you don't want your luggage to fall apart midtrip.

Soft-sided luggage with durable wheels is often ideal for businesspeople on the go. This type of luggage tends to weigh less than most old-fashion, hard-case luggage, which is important, since all major airlines now have strict weight restrictions for checked luggage. Bags weighing more than 50 pounds are each subject to a surcharge of $25, $50, $100, or more, depending on the airline.

Passengers are also limited to checking only two or three bags (depending on the airline). Each additional bag is subject to a fee of $50, $100, or more. It's important that the luggage you choose be able to hold everything you'll need to have with you yet meet your airline's requirements.

The construction of a bag is as important as its design. Ideally, you want luggage designed to take a beating, yet remain strong.

You'll pay a bit extra for bags with strong and padded handles, durable wheels that glide smoothly, well-sewn seams, and heavy-duty zippers, and that are made from extra-strong material, such as ballistic nylon or napa leather. But over the long term, these bags will last much longer and keep their contents safer.

TIP

When evaluating luggage, consider the interior design of each bag. Does the luggage have enough pockets and compartments to accommodate your needs? Will it allow you to keep your toiletries separate (in case of spillage)? Also, is the bag comfortable to carry or pull? Are the handles durable, padded, and located in the best possible places?

By visiting a specialty luggage store or high-end department store, you'll be able to see top-quality, name-brand luggage from a variety of manufacturers. Remember, when it comes to the price of the bag, make sure you're paying for top-quality construction, not just for a designer name. Each popular luggage manufacturer typically offers several product lines with different looks, color schemes, designs, and levels of construction quality. If you take only one business trip per year, you may be able to purchase less expensive and lower-quality luggage. However, if you travel often, you should invest in durable luggage that will last.

TIP

If you're buying luggage with wheels, make sure the wheels are well-made, spin smoothly, are quiet when they roll, and don't wobble. Remember, when the bag is full, you'll be pulling or carrying up to 50 pounds. Also, focus on the durability of the bag's handles and zippers, as well as the material used for the bag's overall construction.

The last factors to consider are the look of the bags and the color scheme, as well as how the various bags in the set interconnect for easy transport. Many larger bags on wheels have hooks that allow you to easily attach smaller bags. Just because the manufacturer offers a set of luggage with five or six bags in different sizes and styles, doesn't mean you need all these bags. Pick and choose the bag styles that best meet your needs.

TIP

As soon as you've purchased your luggage, make sure you fill out and securely attach luggage tags with, at least, your full name and phone number. (Listing your address and cell phone number is optional.) It's also important to place your contact information *inside* each checked bag. This will make it easier to recover your belongings if the bag gets lost in transit or the luggage tag falls off.

When shopping for luggage, check out luggage sets by several manufacturers. Be sure to ask about the luggage's warranty and determine the process for getting bags repaired. Some luggage companies charge a minimum of $100 per bag (plus shipping), even for a basic repair. Remember, many bags from different manufacturers look very similar but have very different construction quality and overall value. It's important to carefully evaluate luggage firsthand to make sure it fits your needs before purchasing it.

Zero Halliburton (www.zerohalliburton.com) and Tumi (www.tumi.com) are two manufacturers that offer multiple lines of high-end, well-constructed, and extremely well-designed luggage that's ideal for business travelers. Both offer pieces created from durable ballistic nylon (also used to create bulletproof vests), as well as premium-quality, ultrasoft, yet very durable napa leather.

TIP

Because many pieces of luggage look similar, creative travelers often use brightly colored luggage tags or place colorful ribbons around their bags' handles to set them apart. This will help ensure the wrong person doesn't accidentally retrieve any of your luggage at an airport's baggage claim area, for example.

Some of the other popular luggage manufacturers that offer designs for frequent business travelers include:

- American Tourister (www.americantourister.com)
- Delsey (www.delseyusa.com)
- Hartmann (www.hartmann.com)
- Kipling (www.kipling.com)
- Samsonite (www.samsonite.com)

- Skyway Luggage Company (www.skywayluggage.com)
- TravelPro USA (www.travelpro.com)

WARNING
Because of heightened airport security, it is no loner advisable to lock your luggage, even with TSA-approved luggage locks. If your luggage is hand searched, the locks will be cut off and discarded by security personnel. Never pack any valuables in your luggage that could be lost or stolen. Valuables should be kept in a carry-on bag or shipped in advance. In addition, when staying at a hotel, instead of locking your luggage, take advantage of the in-room safe available at most high-end hotels to protect your valuables.

PACKING TIPS

Now that you've selected the ideal luggage for your trip, you want to ensure that you pack everything you'll want and need while you're away. This section offers useful packing tips and a detailed packing list.

Most business travelers have one or more large pieces of luggage that will be checked with the airline plus one carry-on bag (and a personal item, such as a laptop case or purse).

In your carry-on, be sure to pack anything and everything you'll need during your flight or immediately after you land. If you are landing at your destination and immediately attending an important meeting, have everything with you for that meeting. It's become an all-too-common occurrence for checked luggage to get lost or temporarily delayed, and you don't want this to affect your meeting.

As a general rule, refrain from overstuffing your bags to the point where they're difficult to close or, when opened, your belongings spill out. When TSA officers search your bags, they should be easy to open and close.

WARNING
Be mindful of the changing list of items the TSA does not permit within checked or carry-on luggage. For an up-to-date list of prohibited items, point your web browser to www.tsa.gov/travelers/index.shtm.

When packing casual clothes, rolling them (as opposed to folding them) helps save space and prevent wrinkles. For your business attire, use luggage with a special "suiter" compartment. For items you want to keep wrinkle free, learn how to properly fold them, then place them within the bag in an area where they won't be crushed. Be sure to place any toiletries that could leak in a sealable bag, separate from your clothing. As an added precaution, consider wrapping liquid or gel items (such as shampoo, perfume, toothpaste, or liquid cosmetics) in individual sealable plastic bags or in sealable plastic containers, like Tupperware®.

Shoe polish or dirt from your shoes can easily rub off onto your clothing and create permanent stains. Wrapping your shoes in a soft shoe bag, separate from your clothing, can help prevent this. To help maintain the shape of your shoes and keep them from getting crushed, insert a wooden shoe tree or stuff rolled socks into each shoe.

TIP
If you're packing books, printed brochures, or other heavy paper-based items, spread them out in your luggage. Don't pile them in a corner, for example. You want to keep the weight evenly distributed within your luggage.

WASHINGTON, DC WEATHER

The weather in Washington, DC, can be unpredictable and varies greatly by season. During the spring, summer, and fall months, the climate in the nation's capital tends to be very pleasant. Winters, however, can get very cold, although you can generally expect more rain than snow. In January, for example, the temperature will range anywhere from a chilly 30° to 44° F, with occasional rain or snow, so bundle up and wear waterproof shoes if you'll be walking around the city. In July, the average temperature will probably be anywhere from a comfortable 69° F to a warm 87° F, with occasional rain possible.

Before packing, obtain an extended weather forecast for Washington, DC, and if necessary, pack an extra sweater, gloves, hat, scarf, or rain gear. For up-to-date weather forecasts, point your web browser to www.weather.com or www.cnn.com/weather. The following chart lists the average temperatures in Washington, DC, throughout the year.

YEARLY AVERAGE TEMPERATURES FOR WASHINTON, DC

Month	High Temperature (Fahrenheit)	Low Temperature (Fahrenheit)
January	44	30
February	46	29
March	54	36
April	66	46
May	76	56
June	83	65
July	87	69
August	85	68
September	79	61
October	68	50
November	57	39
December	46	32

PACKING FOR YOUR TRIP

The following is a comprehensive list you can use when packing for your trip. Don't forget to pack any additional work-related items not already listed here.

Remember: Never pack any personal electronics, a laptop computer, a camera, important business papers, jewelry, eyeglasses, antiques, business equipment, or other expensive items within your checked luggage. These items are *not* covered by the airline if they're lost, damaged, or stolen.

PACKING CHECKLIST

Packed	Item/Garment	Quantity Needed
❏	Airline tickets, travel itinerary, confirmation letters	
❏	Allergy medication	
❏	Bathing suits and poolwear	
❏	Batteries	
❏	Belt(s)	
❏	Blouses	
❏	Books and magazines	
❏	Boots	
❏	Business cards	
❏	Business organizer	
❏	Camera and film (or memory cards and batteries)	

PACKING CHECKLIST

Packed	Item/Garment	Quantity Needed
❏	Casual shirts	
❏	Cell phone (including charger and headset)	
❏	Coat	
❏	Cufflinks	
❏	Data CDs	
❏	Day planner/appointment book/address book	
❏	Deodorant	
❏	Dress shirts	
❏	Dress shoes	
❏	Dresses and gowns	
❏	Eyeglasses and contact lenses	
❏	Golf clubs	
❏	Hair care products	
❏	Hairbrush and grooming products	
❏	Hat or cap	
❏	Health insurance card	
❏	ID (driver's license or passport)	
❏	iPod (MP3 player) and headphones	
❏	Jacket or windbreaker	
❏	Jewelry and fashion accessories	
❏	Laptop and accessories (including charger)	
❏	Lingerie	
❏	Makeup and cosmetics	
❏	Moisturizer	
❏	Nail care items	
❏	Neckties	
❏	Over-the-counter medications and vitamins	
❏	Perfume or cologne	
❏	Personal digital assistant (including charger)	
❏	Prepaid calling cards	
❏	Prescription medications	
❏	Product brochures, press kits, and sales literature	
❏	Purses	
❏	Scarf	
❏	Shaver (razor) and blades, shaving cream, etc.	
❏	Shorts	
❏	Sleepwear	
❏	Sneakers	
❏	Socks (white and colored)	
❏	Sport coat	
❏	Suits (formal business attire)	
❏	Sunglasses	
❏	Tampons and sanitary napkins	
❏	Toothbrush, toothpaste, and dental floss	
❏	Travel alarm clock	

SECTION II / PACKING FOR YOUR BUSINESS TRIP ·· 51

PACKING CHECKLIST		
Packed	Item/Garment	Quantity Needed
❏	Trousers (pants, jeans, etc.)	
❏	T-shirts	
❏	Undershirts	
❏	Underwear	
❏	Video camera (including charger and accessories)	
❏	Walking shoes	
❏	Wallet (credit cards, cash, traveler's checks)	
❏	Watch	
❏	Workout clothes	
❏	Work-related papers, reports, proposals, and files	
❏	Other:	
❏	Other:	
❏	Other:	

TIP

If you have multiple pieces of consumer electronics that will need to be charged, such as your laptop, cell phone, headset, PDA, and iPod, consider packing your own power strip. Few hotels offer an ample number of conveniently located and accessible electrical outlets to meet the needs of most business travelers.

TIP

Regardless of the temperature outside, inside the hotels, restaurants, theaters, and convention centers, you'll encounter air-conditioning or heating, depending on the season. So pack accordingly.

Whether you're attending a convention or exploring the nation's capital, you'll be doing a lot of walking! You'll want to wear extremely comfortable walking shoes or sneakers.

Packing Checklist for Your Carry-On Bag

Remember, anything you may want or need during the flight should be placed in your carry-on and brought with you onto the aircraft. Use the checklist below to help you make sure you have all you might need.

TIP

Business meetings, conventions, and seminars are all excellent networking opportunities. Don't forget to pack a large supply of your business cards and carry a nice business card holder. The business card holder should also have a pocket for storing the business cards you collect from others. If you need business cards printed quickly while in Washington, DC, refer to Section VIII, "Business Services."

WARNING

The TSA has imposed restrictions on bringing more than three ounces of liquids or gels aboard flights. This includes everything from drinks to shampoo. (Prescription medications can still be carried onto the aircraft but are subject to inspection.) Other items—such as lighters, chemicals, and any sharp instruments (including pocketknives, scissors, and tools)—continue to be prohibited. See the TSA's web site (www.tsa.gov) to learn about the latest restrictions. Drinks, including bottled water, may be purchased at the airport *after* you pass through security.

CARRY-ON BAG PACKING LIST	
❏	Airline tickets, boarding passes, and your travel itinerary
❏	All personal electronics (iPod, PDA, etc.)
❏	Business equipment
❏	Business papers and work-related items
❏	Camera
❏	Cell phone (and charger)
❏	Change of clothing
❏	Eyeglasses or contact lenses
❏	Headphones
❏	Jewelry
❏	Keys
❏	Laptop (including DVDs you might want to watch during the flight)
❏	Paper and pen
❏	Photo identification
❏	Prescription medications
❏	Reading material (books and/or magazines)
❏	Wallet (money, credit cards, traveler's checks, etc.)

Optional Items

To make a long flight more relaxing, consider investing in a pair of noise-canceling headphones. These headphones can be connected to your iPod, laptop, or the aircraft's in-flight entertainment system to reduce most outside noise, such as babies crying and the roar of the aircraft's engine.

Noise-canceling headphones may allow you to sleep better during a flight or better enjoy whatever in-flight entertainment you have planned. The cost of noise-canceling headphones is between $100 and $400. They're available from companies such as Bose (www.bose.com), Shure (www.shure.com), Sharper Image (www.sharperimage.com), and Brookstone (www.brookstone.com). This is a must-have accessory for frequent business travelers.

Several different models of Shure Sound Isolating Earphones are now available. Each offers superior sound quality and allows you to truly enjoy what you're listening to. These Shure products are also lightweight and extremely comfortable to wear. Similar products from Bose, for example, are more cumbersome to travel with because of their size and shape.

TIP
If you find your ears getting clogged during flights, EarPlanes by Cirrus Air Technologies (800-EAR-6151 or www.cirrushealthcare.com) offer an inexpensive solution. These reusable earplugs are designed to regulate air pressure in your ears naturally. They sell for about $5 per pair and are available from pharmacies nationwide. They're particularly useful if you're suffering from a cold, flu, or allergies.

Keeping Healthy

Worried about catching a cold or getting sick while traveling? One way to help prevent this is to take Airborne, an all-natural herbal supplement designed for business travelers. Simply add one of these orange-flavored tablets to a glass of water and drink. You can take Airborne every three hours, as needed, as a dietary supplement. It's an excellent tool if you're starting to feel the onset of cold- or flu-like symptoms, or as a preventive measure. For more information, point your web browser to www.airbornehealth.com.

Travel Wellness (866-823-5072 or www.travelwellness.com) offers a variety of herbal, all-natural, antiviral, and antibacterial products for travelers, including Vira-Eze, which is available as a

100 percent organic throat spray or in the form of patented, disposable wipes. The company also offers its Travel Relaxation Kit ($14.99), which includes a salt bath packet, a lavender linen spray, tea sticks, an eye mask, and an herbal product called Serenity. Travel Wellness' web site offers health tips for business travelers.

BEFORE-LEAVING-HOME CHECKLIST

The following are some tasks you may want to complete before leaving on your business trip:

BEFORE-LEAVING-HOME CHECKLIST	
Completed	Task
❑	Adjust the thermostat
❑	Arrange for the care and feeding of your pet(s)
❑	Call a taxi or limo service to schedule ground transportation to and from the airport
❑	Contact the post office and put your mail on hold
❑	Discard any refrigerated items that will spoil while you're away
❑	Double-check your packing list and ensure everything you need is packed in your suitcase or carry-on
❑	Go to the bank to get cash and/or traveler's checks
❑	Leave a copy of your travel itinerary with a friend, relative, your secretary, boss, and/or co-workers (as appropriate)
❑	Lock your windows and doors
❑	Pay your household bills
❑	Record your "away" voice-mail message at work
❑	Take out the trash
❑	Set the burglar alarm
❑	Set your work e-mail account's auto responder with an "away" message
❑	Set your TiVo® or VCR to record your favorite shows while you're away
❑	Stop any deliveries to your home while you're away
❑	Turn off all unnecessary appliances and electronics
❑	Water your plants

SECTION III

© Douglas Litchfield

WHERE TO STAY WHILE IN
WASHINGTON, DC

When it comes to accommodations in the DC area, you'll find a vast selection, ranging from basic guestrooms offered by virtually every major hotel chain, to hotels like the Willard InterContinental, that are unique to the nation's capital. There are also many smaller boutique hotels, along with bed-and-breakfast establishments, that can meet your needs and budget. When you're ready to get some shut-eye after a long day of meetings, attending a convention, socializing, or sightseeing, you'll have literally hundreds of hotels in the DC area to choose from.

The average room rate at a three-star, business-friendly hotel is $200 to $250 per night. For a luxury suite in a five-star hotel (such as the Ritz-Carlton, the Four Seasons, the Mandarin Oriental, or the Willard), it's easy to spend $500 to $2,500 (or considerably more) per night for accommodations.

MONEY SAVER
If you're traveling on a budget, consider staying outside of the downtown DC area (or in nearby Maryland or Virginia) and then using public transportation to get into the city. You could save several hundred dollars per night. You can also save money by booking your hotel reservations using an online travel service, such as Hotwire.com or Hotels.com.

One thing to consider when choosing your hotel is its location. Where will you be conducting the majority of your business while visiting the DC area? If you'll be attending a trade show at the Washington Convention Center, you might want to consider the dozen or so hotels within walking distance. If, however, you'll be attending meetings closer to the Dupont Circle area or Georgetown, for example, you might opt to find accommodations in that area to avoid extra taxi or Metro rides.

CITY FACTOID
All guestrooms and most public areas within hotels in Washington, DC, are non-smoking.

Room rates within the DC area are based on a variety of factors, including:

- *The type of guestroom or suite requested.* Most basic hotel guestrooms consist of a single bedroom containing one king-size or two queen-size beds, a desk (work area), a TV, a dresser, a closet, and a bathroom. Larger suites might contain a separate sitting area, foyer, living room, kitchenette, terrace, one or more bathrooms, plus one or more separate bedrooms.

- *The view offered from the guestroom.* You'll typically pay more for a view overlooking a historic building, a tourist attraction, the Potomac River, or a monument. Guestrooms on higher floors with better views tend to cost more.
- *Whether the room is located on the concierge floor* (offered only at some hotels). Rooms on this floor cost more, but as a guest you're entitled to visit an exclusive VIP lounge where drinks, snacks, and sometimes full meals are served.
- *The overall quality of the hotel and the services and amenities offered.*
- *The time of year.* Expect to pay premium rates during peak travel times, such as holidays, and during the spring and summer months. March and April are the busiest tourism months in the DC area.
- *The overall current occupancy of the hotel and neighboring hotels.* The overall supply and demand for rooms in the city impact the cost of accommodations.

MONEY SAVER

If you use an online service, such as Hotels.com (www.hotels.com), Travelocity.com (www.travelocity.com), or Hotwire.com (www.hotwire.com), it's often possible to obtain accommodations in Washington, DC, at top-rated hotels for up to 30 to 60 percent off. When making your reservation, be sure to check the hotel's own web site for current rates, ask about discounts for AAA or AARP members, for example, then check the rates being offered on the popular online travel-related services. Keep in mind that each online travel service uses different criteria for categorizing a hotel as a three-, four-, or five-star property. Make sure you understand the criteria being used.

CHOOSE YOUR ACCOMMODATIONS BASED ON AMENITIES AND SERVICES OFFERED

Most upscale hotels in Washington, DC, proudly offer a wide range of amenities and services that are in demand by business travelers, such as high-speed internet access, a fitness center, a business center, concierge services, in-room flat-screen televisions (with cable TV programming), extremely comfortable beds, ample desk space for working, multiple phone lines, and 24-hour room service. Thus, what sets the most luxurious hotels apart are their commitment to customer service, their overall décor of the hotel, their location, and the collection of services and amenities they offer.

MONEY SAVER

Valet parking at any Washington, DC, hotel will cost an extra $20 to $35 *per night*. To save money, instead of renting a car, take advantage of public transportation, taxis, or limos. Few hotels in Washington, DC, offer convenient self-parking.

TIP

For a list of hotels located within walking distance of the Washington Convention Center, see Section VII, "Attending a Business Meeting or Convention."

Business Amenities and Services to Look For

When choosing where to stay in Washington, DC, consider the amenities and business services you want and need. The following checklist will help you evaluate your needs and find accommodations that'll make your stay as comfortable as possible. Many of the *Business Traveler* Top 15 Business-Friendly Hotels listed later in this section offer most or all of these services and amenities.

MONEY SAVER

At the same time you determine which services and amenities are being offered by the hotel you select, determine if you'll be charged extra to utilize them. For example, many hotels charge extra for high-speed (or Wi-Fi) internet access, overnight parking, and use of the hotel's fitness center. You could wind up spending $50 to $100 or more per night on basic amenities.

Within the nicer Washington, DC area hotels, you'll find the majority of the following popular amenities and services being offered. Expect to pay extra, however, for amenities like high-speed internet access, valet parking, pay-per-view in-room movies, long-distance telephone calls, and dry cleaning services, for instance.

SECTION III / WHERE TO STAY WHILE IN WASHINGTON, DC · 59

BUSINESS AMENITIES CHECKLIST	
❏	Ability to earn frequent flier miles for your stay
❏	Ample work space (including a desk) within the room
❏	Business center (equipped with computers, printers, fax machines, and copiers, in addition to the ability to ship packages via UPS, FedEx, DHL, etc.)
❏	Cell phone reception within the room
❏	Close proximity to the convention center, banquet hall, or meeting facility hosting your event
❏	Coffee machine (in room)
❏	Complimentary soaps, shampoo, and toiletries
❏	Concierge service (available 24 hours)
❏	Dry cleaning and laundry service
❏	Easy access to public transportation
❏	Express check-in and checkout
❏	Fax machine (in room)
❏	Hair dryer (in room)
❏	Health club and workout facility (open 24 hours)
❏	High-speed internet and Wi-Fi wireless internet (expect to pay between $9.95 and $19.95 per 24-hour period for internet access in most DC area hotel guestrooms)
❏	Iron and ironing board (in room)
❏	Meeting room availability
❏	Minibar/refrigerator (in room)
❏	Multiple electrical outlets in the room (with several located near the desk)
❏	Multiple in-room phone lines
❏	Newspaper delivery to your guestroom
❏	Night-time turndown maid service
❏	On-site restaurant(s)
❏	Cotton or terrycloth robes (in room)
❏	Room service (available 24 hours)
❏	Spa and salon
❏	Starbucks Coffee or coffee shop in the lobby (or nearby)
❏	Valet parking

The following is a list of amenities to look for that can help make your hotel stay more convenient and comfortable:

TIME SAVER

If the services and amenities you want or need aren't readily available at your hotel, see Section VIII, "Business Services," and Section IX, "Personal Services," within this guide for details on how and where to quickly find what you need. You could also contact your hotel's concierge.

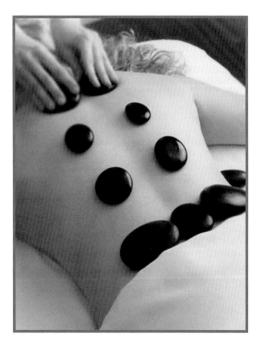

Many of the upscale hotels, like the Willard, offer world-class day spas on the premises. If you're a busy traveler, consider taking time to indulge yourself in a massage, a facial, or another treatment to help you relax or simply to pamper yourself. Day spas are utilized by both male and female clientele in need of a break from their otherwise hectic schedules.

THE *BUSINESS TRAVELER* TOP 15 BUSINESS-FRIENDLY HOTELS IN WASHINGTON, DC

Out of all the hotels in the area, listed here (in alphabetical order) are the *Entrepreneur Magazine's Business Traveler* Top 15 Business-Friendly Hotels in Washington, DC. The properties on this list were selected based on the services and amenities offered, overall value, location, and comfort.

While nightly accommodation rates vary greatly throughout the year, and many of these properties also offer luxury suites that cost hundreds or thousands of dollars per night, each of the following properties is ranked based on its average price range for standard guestrooms.

Understanding the Hotel Ratings

Each business-friendly hotel featured in this section is rated with between one and four stars based on comfort, amenities, service, business-friendly environment, and overall value. Here's a description of each rating:

- *One Star (☆)—Below Average.* Not up to the standards of other hotels in the Washington, DC area.
- *Two Stars (☆☆)—Average.* There's nothing luxurious offered, but the property is clean, functional, and adequate for business travelers.
- *Three Stars (☆☆☆)—Above Average.* You'll definitely enjoy your stay here as a business traveler looking for a comfortable, clean, friendly, quiet, and relaxing environment.
- *Four Stars (☆☆☆☆)—Superior.* This is the best that Washington, DC, has to offer to business travelers. You may pay a bit extra, but it's worth it. Expect to have a good night's sleep plus have access to a wide range of services and amenities designed to offer luxury, comfort, and convenience. Many of the four-star hotels in the DC area have a full-service day spa on property, along with a selection of upscale restaurants and lounges.

CITY FACTOID

If you counted up all of the hotel guestrooms in downtown Washington, DC, the total would be more than 27,000. One of the busiest times of year to visit this city is April, which is when the annual Cherry Blossom Festival is held. Be prepared to pay a premium for hotel accommodations between late March and mid-May during this peak travel period. December and January are the least busy for hotels in DC, unless it's an inaugural year.

An average nightly price for a standard guestroom at each featured hotel is also included in the following descriptions. (Expect to pay considerably more for multibedroom suites.) The average price range rating is as follows:

- *One dollar sign ($).* Less than $150 per night
- *Two dollar signs ($$).* Between $150 and $250 per night
- *Three dollar signs ($$$).* More than $250 per night

WARNING

Because of high occupancy rates, most DC area hotels strictly adhere to their posted check-in and checkout times. If you require early check-in (before 3 P.M.), or need to check out after 11 A.M. or noon on your day of departure, contact the hotel's front desk in advance to avoid extra charges and hassles. Upon request, all hotels will happily store your luggage after the posted checkout time until your actual departure later that day. Call the hotel's bell desk or concierge for details.

Listed here are our picks for the Top 15 Business-Friendly Hotels in Washington, DC. These are, however, just a sampling of the hundreds of hotels you'll find within the city and surrounding areas. No matter what your taste, chances are you'll be able to find accommodations to meet your needs and budget.

TIP
Few hotels offer in-room fax machines. If you travel often and need to send and receive faxes while on the go, consider registering for the eFax service (www.efax.com). For a flat monthly fee, you'll be given your own unique fax number and be able to send and receive faxes via the internet. Incoming faxes show up as e-mails and can be viewed on-screen or printed.

1. Capital Hilton

Address: 1001 16th Street NW, Washington, DC
Reservations phone number: (800) 445-8667
Main phone number: (202) 393-1000
Web site: www.hilton.com

Comfort	Amenities and Services	Customer Service	Business-Friendly Environment	Overall Value	Average Price Range
☆☆☆☆	☆☆☆☆	☆☆☆☆	☆☆☆☆½	☆☆☆☆	$$/$$$

DESCRIPTION
Centrally located in the heart of downtown DC, just two blocks from the White House, the Capital Hilton has been visited by numerous U.S. presidents, countless government officials, world leaders, artists, entertainers, and well-known businesspeople throughout modern history. The hotel is located about five miles from Reagan National Airport and two miles from Union Station.

The Capital Hilton offers 544 guestrooms, including 171 double-double rooms and 32 suites. All rooms feature high-speed internet access, multiple two-line telephones, a fully stocked minibar, 57-channel cable television, plus comfortable beds and decent-size bathrooms. The hotel itself features a full-service business center, several gift shops, multiple restaurants (and 24-hour in-room dining), plus the Capital City Club and Spa (a fully equipped fitness center and day spa). For spa information or to schedule a treatment, call (202) 639-4300 (www.capitalcityspa.com).

This hotel originally opened for business as the Statler Hotel in January 1943 and was one of the first luxury hotels to open in the DC area. In 1954 the property was purchased by Conrad Hilton. In 1977, the hotel's name was officially changed to the Capital Hilton. Throughout the hotel's history, eleven U.S. presidents since FDR have visited. Queen Elizabeth II, Prince Charles, and Winston Churchill have also been among the hotel's distinguished guests.

This is one of the more luxurious, nicely equipped Hilton hotels on the East Coast. It's an ideal option for business travelers looking for comfortable and convenient accommodations offered at a reasonable price.

TIP

Guests of this hotel who are members of the Hilton HHonors program can earn points for their stay here.

---

2. DC Guesthouse

Address: 1337 10th Street NW, Washington, DC
Reservations phone number: (202) 332-2502
Main phone number: (202) 332-2502
Web site: www.dcguesthouse.com

Comfort	Amenities and Services	Customer Service	Business-Friendly Environment	Overall Value	Average Price Range
☆☆☆☆	☆☆☆☆	☆☆☆☆	☆☆	☆☆☆☆	$$/$$$

DESCRIPTION

The DC Guesthouse is a small bed-and-breakfast conveniently located about two blocks from the Washington Convention Center (about a five-minute walk). From the outside, this six-bedroom B&B doesn't look like much, but once you step through the front door, you'll immediately notice the unusual, eclectic, and extremely luxurious décor, including the extensive art collection that's on display throughout the property.

The goal of the DC Guesthouse is to provide a luxurious, quiet, extremely clean, and very comfortable oasis, plus extremely friendly and attentive service, for its guests. Each guestroom is spacious, beautifully decorated, and nicely equipped with a satellite TV, DVD player, telephone, and wireless internet access. A fax machine, computer, printer, and scanner are available within the common area. The majority of the rooms also have a private bathroom, and some offer a working fireplace.

Guests are invited to enjoy the property's public areas, which include several comfortable living rooms and lounges, all featuring the eclectic décor and an impressive art collection. Informal meeting space for up to 15 people is also available.

In addition to the plush and extremely comfortable beds and the quiet, sanctuary-like environment offered at the DC Guesthouse, every morning guests are treated to a delicious home-cooked breakfast in the dining room. Plenty of free on-street parking in front of the B&B is available on 10th Street. The closest Metro station can be found at the convention center.

While this property is probably the furthest thing you could get from a traditional business-friendly chain hotel, any business traveler who is tired and stressed out after a long day's work will really appreciate the quiet serenity and top-notch service this establishment offers. As an alternative to a traditional hotel, the DC Guesthouse offers a more homey feel than most corporate hotels. For the overtraveled businessperson eager to experience something new when it comes to accommodations, a stay at the DC Guesthouse is well worth it.

3. Four Points Sheraton

Address: 1201 K Street NW, Washington, DC
Reservations phone number: (866) 716-8113
Main phone number: (202) 289-7600
Web site: www.starwoodhotels.com/fourpoints/property/overview/index.html?propertyID=1237

Comfort	Amenities and Services	Customer Service	Business-Friendly Environment	Overall Value	Average Price Range
☆☆☆½	☆☆☆½	☆☆☆½	☆☆☆½	☆☆☆½	$$/$$$

DESCRIPTION

This newly renovated Four Points Sheraton offers luxury, a convenient location (about .3 miles from the Washington Convention Center), plenty of business-friendly amenities, plus affordable rates. Located in downtown DC, the hotel is also situated close to the White House and other popular attractions. In addition to the multiple restaurants offered on-site, severals fine-dining restaurants are located within walking distance. The hotel also offers 24 hour in-room dining, a nicely equipped business center, concierge service, an indoor heated pool, 8,000 square feet of meeting and function space, plus a concierge level that's ideal for business travelers.

In addition to offering a free fitness center, this Four Points Sheraton features guestrooms with free high-speed internet access, the hotel chain's signature Comfort Bed, a nice-size desk, a 27-inch television, dual-line telephones, as well as a variety of other amenities in demand by business travelers.

Within the hotel, the Corduroy Restaurant and Lounge serves breakfast, lunch, and dinner, plus full bar service. The dress is "smart casual" and the menu features American cuisine. In addition to allowing guests who are members of Starwood's Preferred Guest program (www.spg.com) to earn points for their stay here, the hotel offers special deals to business travelers. For example, business travelers who stay two nights can receive a third night for free if they arrive on a Thursday, Friday, or Saturday.

This Four Points Sheraton offers clean, comfortable, spacious, and convenient accommodations at an affordable price. Guestrooms come in a variety of configurations, with a single king, a single queen, or two double-size beds. Guestrooms start around $250 per night.

4. Four Seasons

Address: 2800 Pennsylvania Avenue NW, Washington, DC
Reservations phone number: (800) 332-3442
Main phone number: (202) 342-0444
Web site: www.fourseasons.com/washington

Comfort	Amenities and Services	Customer Service	Business-Friendly Environment	Overall Value	Average Price Range
☆☆☆☆	☆☆☆½	☆☆☆☆	☆☆☆½	☆☆☆½	$$/$$$

DESCRIPTION

Located in historic Georgetown (a short drive from the downtown DC area), this Four Seasons hotel originally opened in 1979, but in 2005 it underwent a $40 million restoration and renovation. In January 2006, the hotel was acquired by Strategic Hotel and Resorts. This Four Seasons property offers 151 spacious guestrooms and suites in the East Wing, each elegantly styled by interior designer Pierre Yves Rochon. An additional 60 guestrooms and suites can be found in the hotel's West Wing.

The Four Seasons is one of the nicer upscale hotels in the DC area. It offers a timeless décor and sophistication with the modern amenities business travelers want and need.

All of the services and amenities you'd expect from a top-notch hotel are offered at the Four Seasons, including 24-hour concierge service, room service, a fully equipped fitness center, Wi-Fi internet access, a nicely equipped business center (offering secretarial services), on-site dry cleaning, several dining options, and twice-daily housekeeping services for the guestrooms. A full-service day spa offers a wide range of treatments, including its signature 80-minute Cherry Blossom Champagne Body Treatment.

Every guestroom and suite is designed to provide the ultimate in luxury and comfort. In the guestrooms and suites, you'll find a 32-inch flat-screen, high-definition television, several multiline telephones, an in-room safe, a DVD player, a CD player, a coffee machine, a private bar, down-filled duvets and pillows, a marble bathroom, plus a variety of other amenities. The décor is traditional, not ultramodern.

Upscale business travelers, government leaders, foreign diplomats, and Hollywood celebrities often stay at this luxurious hotel, which offers a sophistication that's expected from a Four Seasons property. In addition to the fine amenities, this hotel is also known for its superior service.

SECTION III / WHERE TO STAY WHILE IN WASHINGTON, DC · 67

The guestrooms and suites within the Four Seasons are luxurious and offer the finest amenities.

TIP

From the Four Seasons, getting to the downtown DC area takes about 10 minutes by car or taxi, or about 20 minutes by bus or Metrorail.

CITY FACTOID

Throughout this Four Seasons property, you'll see an exquisite 2,000-piece art collection on display.

5. Grand Hyatt Washington

Address: 1000 H Street NW, Washington, DC
Reservations phone number: (888) 591-1234
Main phone number: (202) 582-1234
Web site: http://grandwashington.hyatt.com/hyatt/hotels/index.jsp

Comfort	Amenities and Services	Customer Service	Business-Friendly Environment	Overall Value	Average Price Range
☆☆☆☆	☆☆☆☆	☆☆☆☆	☆☆☆☆	☆☆☆☆	$$/$$$

DESCRIPTION

Located about 1.5 blocks from the Washington Convention Center and a short walk from numerous restaurants and local attractions

The Grand Hyatt is located very close to the Washington Convention Center. It's large and offers plenty of amenities but has a somewhat impersonal, business-like atmosphere.

(including the Verizon Center), the Grand Hyatt Washington truly defines the business-friendly hotel concept by perfectly catering to the needs of business travelers and convention-goers. This large and upscale hotel offers 888 elegant and spacious guestrooms and suites, utilizing eight different room configurations. For business travelers, the Business Plan, Business Plan King, or Regency Club rooms are ideal.

Each guestroom offers an oversize desk and work area (with a Herman Miller chair), high-speed internet access, a 25-inch (or larger) television, an ultraplush bed with a thick down blanket and pillows, plus a wide range of other amenities designed to provide comfort. The clock radio near the bed also serves as a docking station and speakers for your iPod.

Within the main lobby area of this hotel is a lovely indoor lagoon. Many of the guestrooms facing inside offer a bird's-eye view of this area. The hotel features a full-service business center, an inhouse florist, two gift shops, valet and self-parking, multiple restaurants, a Starbucks Coffee in the main lobby, and more than 40,000 square feet of meeting and function space. A fitness center and a day spa are also available.

SECTION III / WHERE TO STAY WHILE IN WASHINGTON, DC ·· 69

The Grand Hyatt's massive lobby features an indoor lagoon. Many of the inside-facing guestrooms offer a view of this lovely area.

While the Grand Hyatt Washington lacks the historic charm of the Willard InterContinental, and the traditional décor of the Ritz-Carlton, for example, this property is an excellent choice for business travelers looking for mid- to high-end accommodations. Guests can earn Hyatt Gold Passport points. To join this frequent traveler program, visit http://goldpassport.hyatt.com.

TIP
This Hyatt offers the hotel chain's e-Concierge service, which allows you to interact with the hotel's concierge online to better preplan and coordinate your stay and arrange for a wide range of extra services before you check in.

6. Jurys Washington Hotel

Address: 1500 New Hampshire Avenue NW, Washington, DC
Reservations phone number: (866) JD-HOTELS
Main phone number: (202) 483-6000
Web site: www.jurysdoyle.com

The Jurys Washington Hotel is a midsize property located in the Dupont Circle area of downtown DC.

Comfort	Amenities and Services	Customer Service	Business-Friendly Environment	Overall Value	Average Price Range
☆☆☆½	☆☆☆½	☆☆☆½	☆☆☆½	☆☆☆½	$$/$$$

DESCRIPTION

Conveniently located in Dupont Circle (within the downtown DC area), Jurys Washington Hotel is situated close to a Metrorail station. The hotel offers 314 guestrooms, five one-bedroom suites, and a two-bedroom Presidential Suite. Each room is nicely equipped with a wide range of amenities, including high-speed internet access, a multiline telephone, an in-room safe, and minibar.

The hotel has a nicely equipped business center, several restaurants (including the Dupont Grille Restaurant, featured in Section V, "Where to Dine in Washington, DC"), 24-hour concierge service, and about 10,000 square feet of meeting and banquet space. Complete audiovisual services within the hotel are available through KVL Audio Visual Service (202-483-6000, ext. 590). Valet parking is also available.

The guestrooms in the Jurys Washington Hotel are nicely decorated and extremely comfortable. Plenty of work space is available for business travelers.

Offering a boutique hotel feel, Jurys Washington Hotel is an elegant and extremely comfortable, midsize, mid- to high-end hotel designed with business travelers in mind. Basic guestroom rates start at around $199 per night. The hotel offers room service (until 10 P.M.) as well as a small fitness center.

7. Madison, A Loews Hotel

Address: 1177 15th Street NW, Washington, DC
Reservations phone number: (866) 768-6658
Main phone number: (202) 862-1600
Web site: www.loewshotels.com/en/Hotels/The-Madison-Hotel/Overview.aspx#

Comfort	Amenities and Services	Customer Service	Business-Friendly Environment	Overall Value	Average Price Range
☆☆☆½	☆☆☆½	☆☆☆½	☆☆☆½	☆☆☆½	$$$

DESCRIPTION

Located in the heart of downtown DC, just blocks from the White House, Embassy Row, and the National Mall, plus a short drive from the Washington Convention Center, the Madison is an upscale, business-friendly hotel offering 353 newly renovated guestrooms and 42 suites. The hotel has a 24-hour fitness center (which includes a sauna and a steam room), a day spa, plus a full-service business center that is open 24 hours per day.

This mid- to high-end hotel offers plenty of modern amenities, plus all of the comfort and convenience you'd expect from a Loews Hotel. While some hotels focus on luxury, the focus of the Madison is definitely to offer guests comfort and convenience. Guestrooms feature high-speed internet access, multiline telephones, a large television, twice-daily housekeeping services, and well-equipped bathrooms. The concierge can assist business travelers with a wide range of services.

The hotel is surrounded by several fine-dining restaurants located within walking distance. Within the hotel you'll find the Palette Restaurant and Bar, and the Postscript, which serve a "power breakfast," followed by lunch and dinner. Guests who join the LoewsFirst guest recognition program (www.loews-first.com) can earn points for their stay. Premium guestrooms start at about $350 per night.

8. Mandarin Oriental

Address: 1330 Maryland Avenue SW, Washington, DC

Reservations phone number: (888) 888-1778

Main phone number: (202) 554-8588

Web site: www.mandarinoriental.com

Comfort	Amenities and Services	Customer Service	Business-Friendly Environment	Overall Value	Average Price Range
☆☆☆	☆☆☆	☆☆☆	☆☆☆	☆☆☆	$$$

The Mandarin Oriental is one of the most luxurious hotels in the downtown DC area.

DESCRIPTION

Located in downtown DC, overlooking the Jefferson Memorial, the Mandarin Oriental is an extremely upscale hotel that's situated a short walk from the National Mall and the Smithsonian Metro station. It's located about 10 minutes from Reagan National Airport and about 30 miles from Dulles International Airport.

The hotel offers 400 luxurious and spacious guestrooms and suites, each featuring high-speed internet access; three dual-line telephones; 24-hour room service; 24-hour valet and concierge services; twice-daily housekeeping; one or two extremely comfortable and plush beds; a large, flat screen, high-definition television; plus Asian-inspired design elements and furniture. Over each bed is a unique tapestry, a Western concept for dressing the walls using hand-woven Thai silk panels. This tapestry is complemented by stunning Asian artwork within the guestrooms and throughout the hotel's entire property.

All guestroom accommodations also feature luxurious Fili D'Oro linens and offer between 400 and 700 square feet of living space. The hotel's suites offer between 600 and 1,200 square feet of living space. All guestrooms and suites also contain a large, extremely elegant marble bathroom, complete with a walk-in shower and separate deep soaking tub.

The Mandarin Oriental contains plenty of banquet and meeting space, a fully equipped fitness center (with swimming pool), a luxurious day spa, plus a nicely equipped business center. Within

The guestrooms within the Mandarin Oriental are large, lavish, and bright. The marble bathrooms feature a deep soaking tub and separate walk-in shower.

the hotel, Café Mozu is an Asian-influenced café, while Cityzen offers a wonderful fine-dining experience (serving modern American cuisine with a French flair). On-site valet parking is available.

This hotel provides all of the luxury, top-quality service, and upscale amenities that a business traveler could desire. To enhance the experience offered to frequent business travelers, the Mandarin Oriental offers its membership-based Tai Pan club. Membership includes access to the hotel's exclusive Tai Pan club lounge, which has its own bar, lounge, dining area, terrace, business facilities, and library. Membership also includes access to the Tai Pan concierge and special privileges at the Spa at Mandarin Oriental, plus ensures premium guestroom accommodations. For membership information, call (202) 787-6777.

Open since March 2004, the Mandarin Oriental is one of Washington's most elegant and upscale hotel properties. It's ideal for business travelers. It's no wonder why this award-winning hotel is considered one of the very best in the world.

9. Park Hyatt Washington

Address: 24th and M Street NW, Washington, DC

Reservations phone number: (888) 591 1234

Main phone number: (202) 789-1234

Web site: http://parkwashington.hyatt.com/hyatt/hotels/

Comfort	Amenities and Services	Customer Service	Business-Friendly Environment	Overall Value	Average Price Range
☆☆☆☆	☆☆☆☆½	☆☆☆☆	☆☆☆☆½	☆☆☆☆	$$/$$$

DESCRIPTION

The Park Hyatt Washington is located near Washington Circle in the downtown DC area. It's located about 10 minutes away from the Washington Convention Center by car or Metro. Having recently been totally renovated and redesigned, this establishment now looks more like an upscale boutique hotel than a traditional Hyatt. The new hotel design and guestroom décor were conceived by award-winning interior designer Tony Chi. The results of this remodel are nothing short of impressive.

Each guestroom resembles a minisuite, complete with separate living room area, bedroom, and large bathroom. Averaging about 408 square feet of living space, the guestrooms offer custom-designed, sleek, and extremely comfortable furnishings and amenities, such as a large flat-panel, high-definition television,

Business travelers will appreciate the large and comfortable guestrooms and amenities offered by the newly renovated Park Hyatt.

high-speed internet access, several multiline telephones, and plenty of work space.

The beds are plush and feature top-quality Frette linens, while the bathrooms feature a marble walk-in shower and deep soaking tub. Within each shower (recessed in a marble-lined alcove within the wall) is a steam-resistant mirror and shelf—the perfect area for shaving while enjoying the soothing sensation of the oversize showerhead.

Guests of the Park Hyatt will enjoy the lavish amenities offered within the large bathrooms in each guestroom and suite. The walk-in, marble-lined shower with oversize showerhead provides for a very relaxing and cleansing experience.

In addition to the clean, comfortable, and spacious guestrooms, the hotel offers a business center, a fitness center, and a fine-dining restaurant, called Blue Duck Tavern. While some hotels feature an upscale afternoon tea, the Park Hyatt offers the Tea Cellar, an elegant café that serves more than 50 different types of tea from around the world throughout the day and evening. This is an ideal place to relax and unwind or host an impromptu business meeting.

Providing everything you'd expect from a top Hyatt hotel, plus many unique services and amenities typically found only in upscale boutique hotels, the Park Hyatt offers superior accommodations for business travelers. Guests can earn Hyatt Gold Passport points for their visit.

10. Renaissance Mayflower

Address: 1127 Connecticut Avenue NW, Washington, DC

Reservations phone number: (800) 228-7697

Main phone number: (202) 347-3000

Web site: http://marriott.com/hotels/travel/wassh-renaissance-mayflower-hotel/

Comfort	Amenities and Services	Customer Service	Business-Friendly Environment	Overall Value	Average Price Range
☆☆☆☆	☆☆☆½	☆☆☆☆	☆☆☆½	☆☆☆☆	$$/$$$

DESCRIPTION

The Renaissance Mayflower is the largest luxury hotel in the downtown DC area. The entire property recently underwent an $11 million renovation, allowing the hotel to offer the most modern amenities in demand by business travelers. In addition to containing more than 35,000 square feet of banquet and meeting space, this 10-floor hotel has 583 luxurious and spacious guestrooms plus 74 suites. Business travelers will appreciate the Concierge Level, which offers guestrooms with extra amenities plus access to the Concierge Lounge.

All guestrooms feature plenty of amenities, including high-speed internet access, multiline telephones, ample work space, large televisions, minibar, and cable TV. Concierge service, 24-hour room service, valet parking, and nicely equipped business and fitness centers are also available. The hotel is located within walking distance of the White House and is close to dozens of restaurants, shops, and attractions.

11. Renaissance Washington, DC Hotel

Address: 999 9th Street NW, Washington, DC
Reservations phone number: (888) 236-2427
Main phone number: (202) 898-9000
Web site: http://marriott.com/hotels/travel/wasrb-renaissance-washington-dc-hotel/

Comfort	Amenities and Services	Customer Service	Business-Friendly Environment	Overall Value	Average Price Range
☆☆☆½	☆☆☆½	☆☆☆½	☆☆☆½	☆☆☆½	$$/$$$

DESCRIPTION

For business travelers attending a trade show or convention at the Washington Convention Center, the most appealing feature of this hotel is its location—directly across the street from the Washington Convention Center and a Metrorail station. It's also within a short walk of dozens of upscale restaurants. This hotel offers midpriced accommodations and is designed primarily for business travelers.

The hotel contains 807 comfortable guestrooms plus 13 suites. Each room is equipped with the Renaissance hotel chain's signature Sleep Package bed, which includes a deluxe mattress and luxurious linens. The Concierge Level rooms are ideal for business travelers. In addition to extra amenities, guests have access to an exclusive

The Renaissance Washington, DC Hotel is located directly across the street from the Washington Convention Center. If you're attending a trade show or convention, this hotel offers the perfect location for overnight accommodations from a convenience standpoint.

Concierge Lounge, which serves continental breakfast, evening hors d'oeuvres, and all-day beverages. High-speed internet access is available throughout the hotel. On-site valet parking is available, but a large self-parking lot can be found directly across the street from the hotel's main entrance (adjacent to the convention center).

For breakfast, lunch, and dinner, guests can enjoy dining at Fifteen Squares, an upscale bistro. The hotel also offers a lobby bar, Liberty Market (which serves sandwiches), the President's Sports Bar, in-room dining, and a Starbucks Coffee located in the lobby. There are several restaurants nearby as well.

While this hotel doesn't offer the historic charm or incredible luxury of other upscale hotels in the DC area, it does provide clean, comfortable, and nicely equipped accommodations, as well as an ideal location.

12. Ritz-Carlton, Georgetown

Address: 3100 South Street NW, Washington, DC
Reservations phone number: (800) 241-3333
Main phone number: (202) 912-4100
Web site: www.ritzcarlton.com

Comfort	Amenities and Services	Customer Service	Business-Friendly Environment	Overall Value	Average Price Range
☆☆☆☆	☆☆☆☆	☆☆☆☆	☆☆☆☆	☆☆☆☆	$$$

DESCRIPTION

For the ultimate in upscale, private, secure, and business-friendly accommodations, the Ritz-Carlton's newest property in the DC area, called the Ritz-Carlton, Georgetown, offers a sophisticated and memorable experience for its guests. The hotel is located in a historic old factory, about five miles from the Ronald Reagan National Airport. These older design elements have been seamlessly blended with ultramodern amenities and stylish accents to create a truly unique but extremely lavish hotel.

The Ritz-Carlton, Georgetown is small, offering only 86 guestrooms and suites, which overlook the Potomac River, the Kennedy Center, and historic Georgetown. Each room features all of the luxurious amenities you'd expect from a Ritz-Carlton, from spacious living areas to marble bathrooms and plush feather duvets on the beds. High-speed internet access is available throughout the property.

Twice-daily housekeeping, 24-hour room service, a large flat-screen television, multiline telephones, an in-room safe, plus plenty of desk space make this property a true sanctuary for upscale business travelers. The hotel also offers an inhouse day spa, a business center, meeting and banquet facilities, and the top-notch concierge service that Ritz-Carlton hotels are known for. Because the hotel is situated in Georgetown, guests are surrounded by an extensive selection of restaurants, cafés, shops, and attractions. This is a choice property among top government officials, foreign diplomats, Hollywood celebrities, and business executives alike.

13. Ritz-Carlton, Washington, DC

Address: 1150 22nd Street NW, Washington, DC
Reservations phone number: (800) 241-3333
Main phone number: (202) 835-0500
Web site: www.ritzcarlton.com

Comfort	Amenities and Services	Customer Service	Business-Friendly Environment	Overall Value	Average Price Range
☆☆☆☆	☆☆☆☆	☆☆☆☆	☆☆☆☆	☆☆☆☆	$$$

DESCRIPTION

If you're looking for a very traditional and upscale business-friendly hotel, the Ritz-Carlton in the West End of the downtown DC area (near Washington Circle) may be for you. Offering superior service and top-notch accommodations, the hotel is located a short walk from the White House and many of DC's most popular attractions.

This luxurious Ritz-Carlton hotel shares space with a state-of-the-art, 100,000-square-foot Sports Club LA fitness complex and spa, to which hotel guests have full access.

This is also an excellent location to host a business meeting, since the hotel offers more than 16,000 square feet of extremely elegant banquet and meeting space.

This is one of two Ritz-Carlton properties in the DC area. This one features 300 deluxe guestrooms, 40 Ritz-Carlton Club rooms, 28 executive suites, two Presidential Suites, plus an ultraluxurious Ritz-Carlton suite. The club-level rooms are ideal for businesspeople who want access to the exclusive club lounge. Throughout the day, this lounge serves drinks along with five complimentary food presentations. It also offers a dedicated concierge staff.

All guestrooms and suites are spacious and luxurious and offer twice-daily housekeeping service, Frette linens, a plush goose-down blanket and pillows, an in-room safe, multiple dual-line telephones, high-speed internet access, a marble bathroom, plenty of work space, and a large flat-screen television.

One really nice perk for guests is that they receive unlimited access to the exclusive (members-only) Sports Club LA fitness center located on the Ritz-Carlton's property. This is a 100,000-square-foot facility, complete with basketball court, swimming pool, and state-of-the-art fitness equipment. Another nice bonus for business travelers is the superior concierge service offered at this hotel.

14. Watergate Hotel

Address: 2650 Virginia Avenue NW, Washington, DC
Reservations phone number: (800) 289-1555
Main phone number: (202) 965-2300
Web site: www.watergatehotel.com

Comfort	Amenities and Services	Customer Service	Business-Friendly Environment	Overall Value	Average Price Range
☆☆☆½	☆☆☆½	☆☆☆½	☆☆☆½	☆☆☆½	$$/$$$

DESCRIPTION

No listing of business-friendly hotels in the DC area would be complete without mentioning the historic Watergate Hotel, which is located close to Kennedy Center, along the Potomac River (to the west of the White House). Aside from being where the Watergate scandal took place when President Nixon was in office (back in 1972), the Watergate complex (which includes the hotel, apartments, and neighboring office buildings) continues to be a top choice among business travelers.

The Watergate Hotel offers 250 guestrooms, including 104 oversize guestrooms and 146 suites, each of which contains a nice collection of amenities that you'd expect from a midpriced, business-friendly hotel. The hotel was built in 1967, but it has since been refurbished and modernized. While there are certainly more luxurious hotels in the DC area, and many located closer to the convention center and other attractions frequented by business travelers, the Watergate Hotel offers clean and comfortable accommodations plus 10,000 square feet of banquet and meeting space.

CITY FACTOID
In 2004, the Watergate Hotel was purchased by a company that planned to transform the hotel into co-op apartments. However, as of early 2007, the hotel remained in business with no immediate plans to close.

15. Willard InterContinental

Address: 1401 Pennsylvania Avenue, Washington, DC
Reservations phone number: (800) 827-1747
Main phone number: (202) 628-9100
Web site: www.washington.interconti.com

The main lobby of the Willard has been refurbished to look very much like it did when the hotel first opened. The lobby area offers a preview of the lavish décor seen throughout the property.

SECTION III / WHERE TO STAY WHILE IN WASHINGTON, DC

The Willard InterContinental is one of the most historic hotels in the DC area. It has a very interesting history, which guests can immerse themselves in.

Comfort	Amenities and Services	Customer Service	Business-Friendly Environment	Overall Value	Average Price Range
☆☆☆☆	☆☆☆☆	☆☆☆☆	☆☆☆☆	☆☆☆☆	$$$

DESCRIPTION

Out of all of the hotels in the DC area, none boasts the rich history, timeless architecture, and beauty of the Willard InterContinental Hotel. This luxurious hotel is located across the street from the White House. Since it opened in 1901, it has hosted every U.S. president (since Zachary Taylor) as well as countless government and foreign dignitaries. Just as it did when President Lincoln spent a month living at this hotel, today the Willard continues to offer the ultimate in business-friendly accommodations.

A superior guestroom, priced starting at $299 per night, is the smallest room offered at the hotel, featuring about 425 square feet of living space. The hotel also offers 11 other guestroom configurations, with suites containing up to 2,300 square feet of lavish living space and multiple bedrooms. All of the rooms, regardless of their size, offer a clean, quiet, and comfortable

The guestrooms within the Willard are spacious and comfortable and feature many upscale, modern amenities.

Who couldn't relax in this luxurious, marble-lined, deep soaking tub found within the Presidential Suite of the Willard? It overlooks the Washington Monument.

environment with modern amenities. The desk/work area has multiple electrical outlets close by to accommodate the need for business travelers to recharge their laptop computer, cell phone, and iPod simultaneously.

Every guestroom features a large flat-screen television, plus high-speed internet access, DVD and CD player, and multiple dual-line telephones. Each room also offers a large desk area, a sitting area, and a large marble bathroom with deep soaking tub and separate shower. In-room fax machines and computer printers are available upon request. The business center, fitness center, and concierge service are also available 24 hours per day.

While this hotel has an extremely interesting history and is a historic landmark, it's been totally renovated to offer its original grandeur with every modern comfort and convenience imaginable.

CITY FACTOID

The Willard is where Julia Ward Howe originally wrote "The Battle Hymn of the Republic" and where Martin Luther King Jr. put the finishing touches on his "I Have a Dream" speech.

Within the grand lobby of the Willard is where President Ulysses S. Grant coined the term *lobbyist*. Inside the historic Round Robin Bar (located steps from the main lobby), you'll probably be surrounded by some of Washington's most elite business and government leaders enjoying an afternoon or evening drink. Some of the people who have visited this bar in the past include Woodrow Wilson, Walt Whitman, Calvin Coolidge, Mark Twain, Nathaniel Hawthorne, and Charles Dickens. The hotel's formal dining room, called the Willard Room, offers a true fine-dining experience for breakfast, lunch, and dinner.

TIP

Hotel guests and locals alike often come to the Willard's famous Peacock Alley to be seen and to enjoy afternoon tea (offered daily between 2:30 P.M. and 5 P.M.; $33.50 to $43.50 per person). This is the perfect place for an impromptu business meeting.

The Willard InterContinental offers not only the amenities in demand by business executives but superior and extremely friendly service. Guests will never feel like they're staying at a generic or impersonal business hotel. For any business traveler looking to truly experience Washington, DC, and get a taste for its history, a stay at the Willard InterContinental will be a memorable and enjoyable one. This hotel receives *our* highest recommendation.

TIP
See Section IX, "Personal Services," for complete information about the I Spa at the Willard (202-942-2700), which is one of Washington's most upscale and luxurious day spas, offering specialized massages and treatments for both male and female guests.

CITY FACTOID
The Willard InterContinental ranked number 76 on a list of the most iconic buildings in the United States. The list was published in February 2007 by the American Institute of Architects.

CITY FACTOID
The Willard InterContinental is one of many hotels that offer special events between late March and mid-April, when the annual Cherry Blossom Festival takes place throughout Washington, DC. For details about this festival, visit www.nationalcherryblossomfestival.org.

MAJOR HOTEL CHAINS IN THE WASHINGTON, DC AREA

In addition to the Top 15 Business-Friendly Hotels listed in this section, virtually every major hotel chain has at least one property (many have several) in the DC area. Often, these chain hotels allow you to earn points and/or frequent flier miles for your stay. Keep in mind, the Washington, DC, area also offers an abundance of smaller boutique hotels that provide a more unique or quaint experience.

The following is a list of the popular hotel chains with properties in and near DC. Many of these chains offer more affordable accommodations than the Top 15 Business-Friendly Hotels listed earlier in this section.

AREA ACCOMMODATIONS

Best Western	(800) HOTEL-NY	www.bestwestern.com
Carlyle Suites	(866) HOTEL-DC	www.carlylesuites.com
Clarion Hotels	(800) 258-4290	www.choicehotels.com
Comfort Inn	(877) 424-6423	www.choicehotels.com
Courtyard by Marriott	(800) 321-2211	www.marriott.com
Crowne Plaza	(800) 980-6429	www.crowneplaza.com
Days Inn	(866) 331-3414	www.daysinn.com
Econo Lodge	(800) 4-CHOICE	www.choicehotels.com
Embassy Suites	(800) EMBASSY	www.embassysuites.com
Four Points by Sheraton	(866) 837-4258	www.sheraton.com
Hampton Inn	(800) HAMPTON	www.washingtondc.hamptoninn.com
Hilton	(800) HILTONS	www.hilton.com
Holiday Inn	(888) HOLIDAY	www.holidayinn.com
Howard Johnson Express Inn	(800) 446-4656	www.hojo.com
Hyatt	(800) 233-1234	www.hyatt.com
La Quinta	(800) 567-7720	www.lq.com
Loews	(800) 23-LOEWS	www.loewshotels.com
Marriott	(800) 242-8685	www.marriott.com
Novotel	(800) 221-3185	www.novotel.com
Omni Hotels	(800) THE-OMNI	www.omnishorehamhotel.com
Ramada Inn	(800) 567-7720	www.ramada.com
Renaissance	(800) HOTELS-1	www.dcrenaissance.com
Residence Inn	(800) 331-3131	www.residenceinn.com
Ritz-Carlton	(800) 241-3333	www.ritzcarlton.com
Sheraton	(800) 223-6550	www.sheraton.com
Super 8	(800) 567-7720	www.super8.com
Westin	(800) WESTIN-1	www.westin.com
Wyndham	(800) 847-8232	www.wyndham.com

NEED ADDITIONAL HELP FINDING A HOTEL?

Do you need additional help finding occupancy at a hotel you can afford during your travel dates? In addition to the popular online travel-related services (such as www.hotels.com), point your web browser to the Washington, DC Convention and Tourism Corporation's web site (www.washington.org) or call (202) 789-7000. For the best selection of available hotels and guestrooms (at the lowest prices), don't wait until the last minute to make your reservations, especially during peak travel times.

TIP
Looking for bed-and-breakfast accommodations instead of a traditional business hotel? To learn about your options in the DC area, call (877) 893-3233 or visit www.bedandbreakfastdc.com. This service can also help you book reservations for a short-term stay in a fully furnished apartment within the DC area.

TAKE ADVANTAGE OF CONCIERGE SERVICES OFFERED AT YOUR HOTEL

Especially at upscale hotels, the concierge has been trained to accommodate or fulfill virtually any type of need or request you might have. In addition to suggesting restaurants and making your dining reservations, a concierge can help you obtain theater or sporting event tickets, even if they're sold out.

You can also consult a concierge for driving directions or to help you coordinate ground transportation, such as limo service, or help you track down and acquire a product or service you need, even if it's on a last-minute basis. For example, if you need to purchase or rent an outfit for a black-tie event, your hotel's concierge can suggest where to shop, then help you line up a tailor or seamstress so your purchase can be ready to wear in time for the event. The concierge can also help you recover luggage misplaced by an airline or run errands that you don't have time to do yourself.

The services offered by a hotel's concierge are typically free of charge. However, for the attention and personalized service you receive, you are expected to tip the concierge. If you anticipate having a handful of needs before leaving home, once you book your hotel reservation, contact the concierge in advance of your arrival and begin tapping the services offered in order to save time and make your trip planning easier.

TRAVEL NOTES

SECTION IV

© Stephen Fir

GETTING AROUND
TOWN

One of the great things about Washington, DC, is that virtually everything you could possibly want or need is located within the nation's capital or in surrounding areas. Thanks to multiple forms of efficient public transportation, including the Metro, getting around is easy. In fact, you'll often find it easier and significantly cheaper to utilize the Metro and other forms of public transportation (taxis and limousines, for example) than driving and having to park a rental car.

TAXIS

The benefit of utilizing taxis is that they're readily available, 24 hours per day, and they provide convenient door-to-door service.

Upon entering the taxi at the start of your trip, be prepared to tell the driver the exact address of your destination. When you're ready to exit the taxi, use the door facing the curb. Never exit on the side of oncoming traffic. Be sure to gather your personal belongings from both the passenger cabin and the trunk, and obtain a receipt from the driver upon paying the fare.

Taxi Rates

The thing to understand about taxis in the Washington, DC, area is that they charge based on a zone system, not a metered rate. If you stay within a designated zone in terms of your pickup and drop-off locations, the fare will be a flat rate of $6.50, regardless of distance or how long it takes. If your trip takes you from one zone to another, the flat rate for the ride goes up to $8.80. If your trip crosses into a third zone, the flat-rate is $11.00. Posted in the taxi will be a blue sticker that lists all flat-rate fares between multiple zones, plus surcharges.

The aforementioned rates apply for one passenger. There is an additional $1.50 surcharge for each additional passenger. Depending on the circumstances, additional surcharges may also apply. For example, there is a $2 fee to reserve a taxi by telephone. During rush hours (between 7 A.M. and 9:30 A.M., and between 4 P.M. and 6:30 P.M.), there's an additional $1 surcharge per trip. You'll also be charged extra for transporting luggage in the taxi's trunk (between $.50 and $2 per piece).

To predetermine what your taxi fare will be, see the following taxi zone map or point your web browser to http://citizenatlas.dc.gov/atlasapps/taxifare.aspx to access an online fare calculator. Be prepared to enter your starting and destination addresses.

For taxi transportation to and from the airports, a metered fare system applies. The rates are $3.25 for the first half mile (or part thereof) and $.90 for each additional half mile (or part thereof). Additional surcharges will also apply for additional passengers, luggage, and so on. See Section I, "Welcome to Washington, DC," for details about taxi transportation to and from nearby airports.

TAXI ZONE MAP

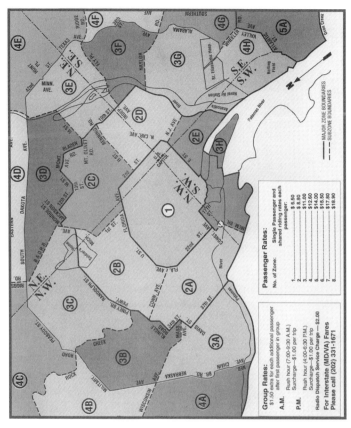

Courtesy of the District of Columbia Taxicab Commission.

TIP
Unlike New York City, not all of the licensed taxis operating in Washington, DC, are yellow and black. All, however, have the familiar taxi light on the roof of the vehicle. For additional information about taxis, visit the DC Taxicab Commission's web site at www.dctaxi.dc.gov.

While you'll often find taxis available in front of hotels, tourist attractions, and the convention center, for example, to preschedule a taxi, contact your hotel's concierge or call one of the independently owned and operated taxi companies serving in the Washington, DC, area. Be sure to call 20 to 40 minutes prior to when you'd like to leave.

The following is a sampling of the taxi companies:

- Action Cab Company—(202) 529-2666
- Allied Cab Company—(202) 636-8377
- Barwood DC Cab—(202) 526-7215
- Bay Cab Company—(202) 543-1919
- Capitol Cab—(202) 545-8900
- Central Cab Company—(202) 484-7100
- Diamond Cab Company—(202) 387-6200
- Diamond Cab of DC—(202) 387-4011
- Ritz Cab Company—(202) 832-4444
- Taxi Transportation—(202) 398-0500
- Yellow Cab Company—(202) 544-1212

TIP

For a complete list of taxi companies operating in the Washington, DC area, visit http://app.dctaxi.dc.gov/taxi list.asp.

RENTAL CARS

If you're traveling with multiple people, need to transport heavy or bulky items back and forth to the convention center, and/or want plenty of flexibility and convenience when you travel, renting a car can be worthwhile. While a rental car offers the ultimate in convenience, you'll also wind up paying for parking, gas, and possibly rental car insurance.

TIME SAVER

Always keep your vehicle rental agreement in the car with you. If you experience any problem with the vehicle, contact the rental car company immediately. Companies typically provide roadside service, towing, flat-tire repair, free vehicle replacement, or any other services required.

You can pick up and return your rental car at any of the Washington, DC area airports. There are also pickup and drop-off locations within the city itself and surrounding areas.

Through an online travel service (such as Hotwire.com, Travelocity.com, or Orbitz.com), you can often find competitive rates for car rentals. In some cases, however, your reservation made online cannot be changed or refunded. The rental fee charged by these online services does not include insurance, parking, or gas. All the popular rental car companies offer free unlimited mileage (except in some cases for high-end, premium cars.)

TIP
When making your reservation directly with a rental car company, make sure you reserve any additional services or add-ons you'll want, such as a navigation system, satellite radio capabilities, or a smoking versus nonsmoking vehicle.

If you want to be able to change your reservation, contact the rental car company directly. Keep in mind, many of the rental car companies provide discounts to corporate travelers, members of AAA or AARP, or members of certain airline frequent flier programs.

TIME SAVER
To obtain discounts and dramatically speed up the process of picking up or dropping off your rental car, when making your reservation, join the rental car company's frequent renters club (e.g., Hertz #1 Club or Avis Preferred Service). Membership is free, there's generally less paperwork to fill out when you arrive to pick up the car, and the vehicle will be waiting for you.

Like hotel guestroom rates, rental car rates fluctuate in Washington, DC based in part on current demand. During a slower travel time, finding a compact car for between $22 and $30 per day (plus insurance, tax, parking, and gas) is relatively easy. During peak travel times when demand is higher for cars, plan on spending upwards of $30 to $50 per day (plus insurance, tax, parking, and gas) for a compact rental car.

WARNING
When you pick up your vehicle, the rental car company will charge a $200 to $400 deposit to your credit or debit card. This is money that will be refunded when you return the vehicle undamaged, but that won't be available to you in the meantime for purchases, so plan your budget accordingly. Some rental car companies will rent vehicles

only to people with a major credit card in their name; they will not accept a debit card.

Once you have picked up the rental vehicle, if you want to extend the rental period, be sure to contact the rental car company *before* the car is due to be returned. The appropriate phone number to call is listed within your rental agreement. Failure to do this will likely result in additional fees, since vehicles returned late are often charged by the hour, not by the day. The rental agreement lists the date and time by which the vehicle must be returned, as well as the return location. Any delay over one hour will likely result in extra fees.

For an additional per-day fee (which can double the price of the rental), you can purchase a variety of insurance options from the rental car company to protect the vehicle, you, any passengers, your belongings, plus any victims of accidents. A loss damage waiver (LDW), for example, covers the cost to repair any damage to the rental vehicle, for any reason.

Some people automatically receive rental car coverage as part of their existing personal auto insurance policy, when they use a particular credit card, or through their business or employer. To save money, figure out what coverage you already have and purchase only the additional insurance you want or need, if any.

MONEY SAVER

Hertz offers a special discount program for small-business travelers. When making your reservation, mention discount code CDP#1188888.

Rental Car Companies Servicing Washington, DC

All of the popular rental car companies have a presence at each of the major Washington, DC area airports, plus pickup and drop-off locations within the city itself. Many of the hotels can also assist you with obtaining a rental car on-site or can arrange to have the rental vehicle delivered to your hotel. If your hotel doesn't have a ground transportation desk, contact the concierge.

To quickly compare prices between rental car companies and find competitive deals, visit www.rentalcars.com/City/Washington_DC/. The following are the major car rental companies with locations throughout the Washington, DC area.

RENTAL CAR COMPANIES IN WASHINGTON, DC		
Alamo	(800) 462-5266	www.alamo.com
Avis	(800) 331-1212	www.avis.com
Budget	(800) 527-0700	www.budget.com
Dollar	(800) 800-3665	www.dollar.com
Enterprise	(800) 261-7331	www.enterprise.com
Hertz	(800) 654-3131	www.hertz.com
National	(800) 227-7368	www.nationalcar.com
Thrifty	(800) THRIFTY	www.thrifty.com

TIP

Need driving directions? If you have a wireless Palm OS or Pocket PC Smartphone, you can purchase a Bluetooth GPS navigation system (for about $300) that will help you find your way to and from any destination within the United States. Small, stand-alone units that can be used with any vehicle (without any installation) are also available from companies such as TomTom (www.tomtom.com). These products can be extremely useful to business travelers driving in unfamiliar territories.

When you pick up your rental vehicle, it will contain a full tank of gas. Depending on your rental agreement, either you can return the car on empty (because you have prepurchased the gas) or you must return the car with a full tank of gas. Failure to meet your obligations could result in significant extra charges.

Do you need a rental car for just a few hours, not days? ZipCars (866-494-7227, www.zipcar.com) and Flexcars (202-296-1359, www.flexcar.com) offer hourly car rentals that include free parking within specific public lots throughout the DC area. Rates are under $10 per hour. Advance reservations are required.

TIP

In business, image is everything. While in DC, you can show important clients whom you want to impress that you mean business by driving around town in a flashy sports car. Capital Dream Cars (703-785-9357, www.capitaldreamcars.com) rents high-end vehicles, such as a Ferrari 360 Spider convertible, Maserati Spyder convertible, and a Bentley Continental GT. Needless to say, these rentals aren't cheap, but they're fun to drive and allow you to truly make a statement when you're sitting in the driver's seat. Plan on spending $800 to $1,800 per day to rent one of these cars.

CHAUFFEURED LIMOUSINES AND TOWN CARS

For the upscale business traveler, getting around Washington, DC in a chauffeured limousine or town car is a preferred and convenient way to travel. Chauffeured stretch limousines, standard limos, and town cars can be rented by the hour, half day, or full day. Rates vary among the different companies, but the average rate ranges from $75 per hour (for a basic limousine) to $125 per hour (for a superstretch limousine), plus tip and tolls. Some companies require a three-hour minimum.

Many of the hotels provide limo service upon request (for a fee), or you can book directly with any of the companies listed later in this section. You can also reserve limousine service online at www.limos.com.

All the limousine companies listed in this section offer airport pickup and drop-off service. Once you make your reservation, keep the limo company's phone number, reservation number, and pickup location handy. You want to be able to contact the company if your travel itinerary changes or if the limo is late.

Reasons to rent a limousine include:

- To pamper and impress an important client or customer
- Convenience and comfort
- To travel in luxury to or from the airport, convention center, a restaurant, or a business meeting
- To celebrate a special event
- To enjoy extra comfort when sightseeing

MONEY SAVER
Especially if you're reserving limousine service for an extended period of time, prices and services are often negotiable.

Limousine Companies Servicing Washington, DC

The following are just a few of the limousine companies operating in Washington, DC and surrounding areas.

LIMOUSINE COMPANIES IN WASHINGTON, DC		
Access Limousine Service	(703) 823-0005	www.access-limo.com
All Seasons Transportation	(202) 438-6180	www.allseasonslimos.com
BEW Transportation	(866) 939-8600	www.bewtransportation.com
Boston Coach	(703) 836-2601	www.bostoncoach.com
Capital City Limousine	(800) 441-6676	www.capitalcitylimo.com
CSI Shuttle and Transportation Services	(703) 584-2474	www.csi-dc.com
Fleet Transportation	(866) 933-2600	www.fleettransportation.com
International Limousine Service	(202) 388-6800	www.internationallimo.com
Majestic Limo Service	(703) 273-4222	www.majesticlimoservice.com
1600 Concierge	(877) 653-1625	www.1600concierge.com
1-800-BOOK-A-LIMO	(800) 266-5254	www.bookalimo.com
Reston Limousine Service	(703) 478-0500	www.restonlimo.com
Sunny's Limousine and Executive Sedan Service	(703) 845-8282	www.sunnylimo.com
Ward's Elite Limousines	(301) 574-4744	www.wardselitelimo.com

PUBLIC TRANSPORTATION—THE METRORAIL AND METROBUS

General information: (202) 637-7000
Lost and found: (202) 962-1195
Web site: www.wmata.com or www.metroopensdoors.com

The most inexpensive and convenient way to travel virtually anywhere within Washington, DC and the surrounding areas is the Washington Metropolitan Area Transit Authority, also known as the Metrorail and Metrobus public transportation system.

The subway system in Washington, DC (aka the Metrorail), has five routes (color-coded on the Metrorail system map). The Metro is an efficient, safe, clean, and economical way to travel throughout Washington, DC. Unlike the public transportation systems in other major cities, this one is easy to navigate, especially if you utilize the color-coded Metrorail system map.

Metrorail and Metrobus stations are conveniently located at Reagan National Airport, the Washington Convention Center (the Mount Vernon Square/7th Street stop on the yellow or green line),

The Metrorail system in DC provides a convenient, inexpensive, and safe way to travel around the city.

near many of the area's most popular tourist attractions, and throughout the city (and surrounding areas). Where the Metrorail system doesn't go, the Metrobus service is available throughout the city. For Metrorail or Metrobus stations, look for large "M" signs throughout the city, which will direct you to the closest station or stop.

To utilize the Metrorail system, you'll need to purchase a prepaid farecard, which is available from vending machines and from manned counters at all Metrorail stations. You can purchase a fare-

Where the Metrorail system doesn't go, the Metrobus system offers an inexpensive way to get around the city.

METRORAIL SYSTEM MAP

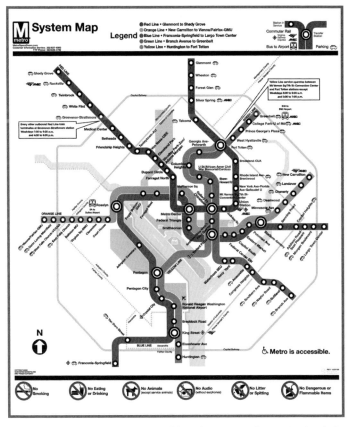

Courtesy of the Washington Metropolitan Area Transit Authority.

card using cash or a major credit or debit card. Fares are based on when and where you travel. Regular fares apply between 5 A.M. and 9:30 A.M. (weekdays), between 3 P.M. and 7 P.M. (weekdays), and between 2 A.M. and 3 A.M. on Fridays and Saturdays. At all other times, discounted fares apply. The best deal, however, is to purchase an unlimited one-day or multiday pass.

Metrorail Hours of Operation

Monday	5 A.M. to midnight
Tuesday	5 A.M. to midnight
Wednesday	5 A.M. to midnight
Thursday	5 A.M. to midnight
Friday	5 A.M. to 3 A.M.
Saturday	7 A.M. to 3 A.M.
Sunday	7 A.M. to midnight

METROBUS SYSTEM MAP

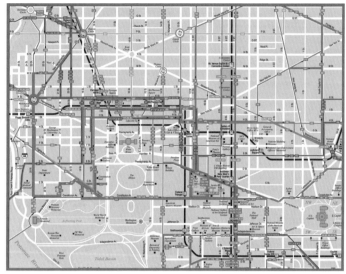

Courtesy of the Washington Metropolitan Area Transit Authority.

The hours of operation for the Metrobus system vary by route. You can download and print a bus schedule or download an interactive version of the entire schedule into your Smartphone, wireless PDA, or iPod by visiting www.wmata.com/timetables/timetables-state.cfm?State=DC or www.wmata.com/maps/maps.cfm.

Throughout the DC area, look for large pillars with an "M" displayed. These indicate where the entrances to underground Metrorail stations are located. Also throughout the city, you'll see blue signs that list popular attractions and arrows indicating where each is located.

METRO FARES

Metrorail per trip fare—$1.35 to $3.90
Metrorail unlimited one day pass—$6.50
Metrorail unlimited short-trip, 7-day pass—$22.00
Metrorail unlimited travel, 7-day pass—$32.50
Metrobus one trip—$1.25 or $3 for an express bus
Metrobus unlimited one day pass—$3
Metrobus unlimited weekly pass—$11

WARNING
Metrobus drivers do not carry cash. You must have exact change or use a SmarTrip card, pass, or token. SmarTrip Cards are rechargeable, prepaid cards used for both the Metrobus and Metrorail system.

TIP
A full-color map of the Metrorail system is offered within this guide. On the web (www.wmata.com/tripplanner_d/Trip Planner_Form_Solo.cfm) you can utilize an automated trip planner. Simply enter your starting point, destination, and time of travel, and you'll receive detailed directions for utilizing the train and/or bus system. The on-screen directions you'll receive are printable.

You can purchase your Metro tickets from these automated vending machines located in all Metro stations. Cash, credit cards, and debit cards are also accepted.

Tips for Using the Metro System

- Ask for detailed directions or study the Metro map so you know which trains to take and which stations to utilize in order to reach your destination quickly. You can also use the online automated trip planning guide (www.wmata.com/tripplanner_d/TripPlanner_Form_Solo.cfm).
- If you're traveling alone, stay in crowded, well-lit areas of the subway stations, and don't stand too close to the tracks. Avoid entering empty train cars, especially at night. Once aboard the train, consider riding in the front car of the train near the conductor for added safety.
- In every subway station, there is a bulletin board that displays a map, train schedules, and information about changes in service due to construction. Many subway stations also have a station agent available 24 hours per day to answer questions and provide directions.
- When you're riding on a subway, if all seats are taken, hold onto the available railing. Never lean against the subway car's doors.
- Avoid showing cash or your wallet in public. Keep in mind the subway and bus system is generally safe; however, pickpocketing and muggings can occur. Keep a firm grasp on your briefcase, purse, and wallet. Never leave your belongings unattended on a bus, on a subway, or within a subway station.
- Smoking, eating, and drinking are prohibited throughout the Metro system on both buses and trains.
- While aboard a train, if there's an emergency, you can use the emergency call box located at the end of each rail car to summon help.

WARNING
Because most of the Metrorail system is underground, cell phones do not typically work.

SHUTTLE AND CHARTER BUSES

If you're attending a large convention, your convention organizers may arrange for complimentary bus transportation between the convention center and the nearby hotels.

For a fee, shuttle bus and shared-van services are also available to and from the area's airports. See Section I, "Welcome to Washington, DC" for details. Information about tour buses and sightseeing trips in Washington, DC can be found in Section VI, "Entertainment in Washington, DC." You'll find a list of charter bus services (available for rent) within Section VIII, "Business Services."

DC CIRCULATOR BUS

For a daily fee of just $3 (or $1 per ride), riders of the bright red-and-silver DC Circulator Bus can enjoy transportation along three separate routes that cover the convention center and downtown Washington, DC area, the waterfront area, and the National Mall (weekends only). This bus offers a convenient and very inexpensive way of commuting between the convention center and your hotel, for example, without having to worry about parking or excessive walking.

For information, call (202) 962-1423. The DC Circulator Bus' web site (www.dccirculator.com) offers a detailed schedule and list of bus stops. Buses depart every five to ten minutes, between 7 A.M. and 9 P.M. The map outlines the three main routes that the DC Circulator buses follow.

DC CIRCULATOR MAP

Courtesy of the District Department of Transportation.

The Circulator Bus is a convenient and very inexpensive way to travel around the DC area, especially to areas not serviced by the Metrorail system.

WATER SHUTTLE

Traveling between Georgetown and Alexandria as well as between Alexandria and Mount Vernon is possible through the water taxi (boat) service offered by Potomac Riverboat Company (703-548-9000, www.rentalcars.com/City/Washington_DC/). The ride takes about 45 minutes, during which time you'll enjoy seeing some of the city's most famous sites. The one-way fare is $11 ($22 round-trip). Boats depart every two hours. During the winter months, only weekend service is available.

SCOOTER RENTALS

Several companies offer hourly, daily, or weekly scooter, Segway and bicycle rentals within the Washington, DC area. This is an alternative to renting a car. To rent a scooter, call ScootAround at (888) 441-7575. To rent a high-tech and fun-to-ride Segway, call (877) SEG-TOUR. Also, see Section VI, "Entertainment in Washington, DC," for more information about fun ways to tour around and see the city.

WALKING

When in Washington, DC, prepare to do some walking, whether you're attending a convention, exploring the city, or traveling between hotels to attend meetings. Be sure to wear comfortable shoes and appropriate clothing for the current weather conditions. The maps located in this guide will help you navigate your way around the city on foot.

SECTION V

© Joy Brow

WHERE TO DINE IN
WASHINGTON, DC

In this very historic and traditional city, some things seldom change. This can't be said, however, about Washington's restaurant and dining scene. During the past few years, dozens of world-renowned and celebrity chefs have opened up new upscale, ultratrendy, and business-friendly restaurants in the nation's capital, many of which can be found in the top hotels.

The DC area is home to hundreds of restaurants, offering everything from fast food to multicourse gourmet meals, many influenced by cultures, countries, and cooking styles from around the world.

While it would be impossible to profile all of the amazing dining experiences the Washington, DC area has to offer, this section offers information about our 15 Top Business-Friendly Restaurants, where you can enjoy a top-quality meal in an environment that's conducive to conversation and entertaining important customers, clients, coworkers, or friends.

TIP
For more personalized restaurant recommendations, contact your hotel's concierge, who can offer suggestions based on the type of cuisine you're looking for, your location, and your budget, plus assist you in making your dining reservations.

For a fast and inexpensive breakfast, lunch, or dinner, you probably won't have to walk more than one or two blocks from where you're staying to find a selection of dining options. Within the city, you'll also find virtually every franchised fast-food establishment in existence as well as an abundance of Starbucks Coffee locations to satisfy your craving for gourmet coffee and baked goods.

THE *BUSINESS TRAVELER* TOP 15 FINE-DINING RESTAURANTS IN WASHINGTON, DC

Out of the hundreds of fine-dining restaurants in DC, this guide describes a handful of options that were selected because they offer:

- A well-rounded menu, including steak, chicken, seafood, and a variety of other entrées.
- A business-friendly environment, featuring tables that can comfortably seat four, six, eight, ten, or more people. (Some of the restaurants offer private dining rooms.)
- Delicious, top-quality food that's expertly prepared by celebrity, award-winning, and/or world-renowned chefs.
- Superior service.
- An extensive wine list and full bar service.

Understanding Restaurant Ratings

The restaurants in this section are ranked between one (☆) and four (☆☆☆☆) stars in four categories: *food quality and variety, value, service*, and *business-friendly environment*. A final overall rating is also included, which takes all of these criteria into consideration.

Here's a description of each ranking:

- One Star (☆)—Below Average. Avoid, if possible.
- Two Stars (☆☆)—Average. There is plenty of room for improvement.
- Three Stars (☆☆☆)—Above Average. You'll definitely enjoy the dining experience.
- Four Stars (☆☆☆☆)—Superior. Best of the best! Well worth experiencing.

This section features our picks for the top 15 *Business Traveler* fine-dining restaurants in the DC area, listed in alphabetical order. At any of these restaurants, you're virtually guaranteed to enjoy a memorable meal. This is just a sampling of the many fine-dining restaurants throughout DC that offer a top-notch dining experience and business-friendly environment.

1. BLT Steak

Location: 1625 I Street NW, Washington, DC

Phone number: (202) 689-8999

Web site: www.bltsteak.com

Reservations required: Yes

Meals served: Dinner

Price range: $40 and up per person

Food Quality and Variety	Value	Service	Business-Friendly Environment	Overall Rating
☆☆☆½	☆☆☆½	☆☆☆½	☆☆☆½	☆☆☆½

DESCRIPTION

This famous modern American steakhouse that originated in New York City now has a home in Washington, DC. The restaurant was conceived by master chef Laurent Tourondel, who is no stranger to success. Several of his other restaurants have achieved incredible critical acclaim in New York City and Los Angeles. In this case, *BLT* doesn't stand for *bacon, lettuce,* and *tomato*. The *B* is for *bistro* and the *LT* are the restaurant creator's initials.

As you'd expect from an upscale steakhouse, this one offers the best beef available, along with a nice selection of tasty seafood dishes. You'll quickly discover that the menu is organized by category, and each entrée can be complemented with savory sauces. These optional sauces totally change the flavor of the meal. For example, you could indulge in a Kobe flatiron steak seasoned with the peppercorn sauce one night and return the next night to try the same dish with a horseradish, butter, or béarnaise sauce for a completely different experience. All beef is wet aged for a month, then broiled at 1,700° F. A wide range of side dishes and fine wines can be ordered to complement any meal.

Also, prepare your taste buds to experience one of the restaurant's signature desserts, like apple cobbler and green apple sorbet, or lemon meringue pie with lemon sorbet. The crêpe soufflé with passion fruit sauce is also extremely popular.

2. Blue Duck Tavern

Location: Park Hyatt Hotel, 24th & M Streets NW, Washington, DC

Phone number: (202) 419-6755

Web site: www.blueducktavern.com

Reservations required: Yes

Meals served: Breakfast, lunch, and dinner

Price range: $30 and up per person (dinner)

Food Quality and Variety	Value	Service	Business-Friendly Environment	Overall Rating
☆☆☆☆	☆☆☆☆	☆☆☆☆	☆☆☆☆	☆☆☆☆

DESCRIPTION

Having recently completed a massive renovation, the Park Hyatt is now home to the Blue Duck Tavern, a lovely, upscale restaurant with a dining room created by award-winning interior designer Tony Chi. Featuring an open kitchen and a menu created by award-winning executive chef Brian McBride, this restaurant attracts government leaders, locals, hotel guests, and upscale business travelers looking to experience an extremely enjoyable meal in a contemporary, yet sophisticated and stylish setting.

Lunch is served daily, between 11:30 A.M. and 2:30 P.M. Dinner is served daily, between 5:30 P.M. and 10:30 P.M. A weekend brunch is served from 11:30 A.M. to 2:30 P.M. Combining delicious food with top-notch service, this setting is perfect for a leisurely meal with friends, coworkers, or important clients.

The dining room has seating for 106 people. There's also a chef's table adjacent to the kitchen that seats 12 guests, plus a semi-private dining room for up to 10 guests. During the spring and summer months, outdoor dining on the terrace is available. Many of the entrées served at this restaurant are prepared in the wood-burning oven, which is the focal point of the kitchen.

Main entrées range in price from $14 to $26, and include wood-fired flatiron tavern steak, beer-braised beef casserole, 21-day aged New York strip steak, roasted half black feather chicken, roasted duck, prosciutto-wrapped monkfish, roasted Maine lobster, and jumbo crab cakes.

Be sure to leave room for the restaurant's mouthwatering desserts. All of the dessert offerings are made inhouse and include a chocolate pecan upside-down cake, hand-churned ice cream, and cream cheese buttermilk cake. An extensive wine list is available.

The Blue Duck Tavern offers top-notch service, excellent food, and a warm and inviting atmosphere. It's well worth experiencing firsthand.

3. Capital Grille

Location: 601 Pennsylvania Avenue NW, Washington, DC

Phone number: (202) 737-6200

Web site: www.thecapitalgrille.com

Reservations required: Yes

Meals served: Lunch and dinner

Price range: $50 and up per person (dinner)

Food Quality and Variety	Value	Service	Business-Friendly Environment	Overall Rating
☆☆☆☆	☆☆☆☆	☆☆☆☆	☆☆☆☆	☆☆☆☆

DESCRIPTION

Providing the ultimate in upscale steakhouse dining experiences, the Capital Grille offers a selection of fabulous steak and seafood entrées, all expertly cooked to perfection and served in a lavish and sophisticated dining room. This is the perfect place to gather for an important business lunch or dinner.

The chef's specialties include the filet Oscar (a 10-ounce filet mignon), the Kona-crusted dry-aged sirloin steak with caramelized shallot butter, and the porcini-rubbed Delmonico steak with eight-year aged balsamic vinegar. Broiled lobster, fresh grilled swordfish, and fresh seared salmon are a few of the seafood selections. To accompany any meal, the restaurant boasts a wine list containing more than 800 labels. The wait staff is trained to offer suggestions for perfect wine pairings.

Business casual attire is required. Hours: Monday through Saturday, 11:30 A.M. to 3 P.M. (lunch); Sunday through Thursday, 5 P.M. to 10 P.M. (dinner); and Friday and Saturday, 5 P.M. to 11 P.M. (dinner).

4. Cityzen

Location: The Mandarin Oriental Hotel, 1330 Maryland Avenue SW, Washington, DC

Phone number: (202) 787-6006

Web site: www.cityzenrestaurant.com

Reservations required: Yes

Meals served: Dinner

Price range: $50 and up per person

Food Quality and Variety	Value	Service	Business-Friendly Environment	Overall Rating
☆☆☆☆	☆☆☆☆	☆☆☆☆	☆☆☆☆	☆☆☆☆

DESCRIPTION

Located just off of the main lobby of the luxurious Mandarin Oriental hotel is the Cityzen restaurant and bar, which serves dinner on Tuesday through Thursday nights, between 6 P.M. and 9:30 P.M., and Friday and Saturday nights, between 5:30 P.M. and 9:30 P.M.

Featuring what executive chef Eric Ziebold refers to as "modern American cuisine with a French flair," the restaurant offers an impressive menu selection. There's a three-course menu available, for a *prix fixe* of $75 per person, plus a six-course chef's tasting menu available starting from $195 per person. Signature dishes include sweet butter-poached Maine lobster and pan roasted sirloin of prime midwestern beef.

To accompany your meal, the restaurant's sommelier offers a selection of 600 wines from around the world, with an emphasis on Bordeaux, Burgundy, and classic California cabernets. Many popular wines are available by the glass, as well as by the bottle.

Styled by award-winning interior designer Tony Chi, the main dining room offers seating for only 60 people. The atmosphere, however, is extremely elegant yet contemporary. There's also a private dining area that can hold 10 guests.

If you're a guest at the Mandarin Oriental, your stay isn't complete until you've dined at Cityzen. For nonguests, it's well worth the trip. Complimentary valet parking is available. "Sophisticated business casual" attire is required.

5. Dupont Grille

Location: Jurys Hotel, 1500 New Hampshire Avenue NW, Washington, DC

Phone number: (202) 939-9596

Web site: www.juryswashingtondc.com/washington_hotel_d.htm

Reservations required: Yes

Meals served: Breakfast, lunch, and dinner

Price range: $30 and up per person

Food Quality and Variety	Value	Service	Business-Friendly Environment	Overall Rating
☆☆☆☆	☆☆☆☆	☆☆☆☆	☆☆☆	☆☆☆☆

DESCRIPTION

Located on the lobby level of the Jurys Washington Hotel, the Dupont Grille offers delicious, midpriced cuisine that's expertly prepared by award-winning executive chef Russel Cunningham. The main dining room is elegant yet casual. It is surrounded by large glass windows that overlook Dupont Circle. Most of the dining room contains booth seating (which accommodates four people); however, stand-alone tables can be configured to accommodate larger groups.

To begin your dining experience, a nice selection of appetizers are available, such as the restaurant's signature butternut squash soup and the tempura fried lobster tail. For lunch, a variety of different panini sandwiches are offered, along with salads, streak *frites*, grilled chicken, grilled salmon, and lobster macaroni and cheese.

For dinner, main entrées include sesame-crusted tofu, porterhouse pork chops, filet mignon, grilled chicken, New York strip steak, salmon filet, venison chop, jumbo tiger shrimp, and a variety

Located in Jurys Hotel, the Dupont Grille offers top-notch service, an extremely comfortable dining room, plus delicious food and drink options.

of other tasty dishes. During the spring and summer months, outdoor dining on the patio is available.

If you're looking for excellent food in a friendly and business casual environment, the Dupont Grille is an ideal option. Full bar service is available. Lunch hours are Monday through Saturday 11:30 A.M. to 2:30 P.M.; dinner hours are Monday through Thursday 5 P.M. to 10:30 P.M., Friday and Saturday 5 P.M. to 11 P.M.; Sunday 5 P.M. to 10 P.M.; Sunday brunch is 11 A.M. to 3 P.M.

6. Il Mulino New York

Location: 1110 Vermont Avenue NW, Washington, DC

Phone number: (202) 293-1001

Web site: www.ilmulino.com

Reservations required: Yes

Meals served: Lunch and dinner

Price range: $30 and up per person (dinner)

Food Quality and Variety	Value	Service	Business-Friendly Environment	Overall Rating
☆☆☆☆	☆☆☆☆	☆☆☆☆	☆☆☆☆½	☆☆☆☆½

DESCRIPTION

As of February 2007, one of the most popular, upscale Italian restaurants in New York now has a home in the DC area. For more than 20 years, guests have enjoyed the fine Italian cuisine served at Il Mulino in Manhattan. Now, the same menu, high level of service, and top quality cuisine can be enjoyed during your trip to DC.

The menu features traditional Italian entrées infused with flavors from the Abruzzi region of Italy. Entrées include veal dishes expertly prepared in several different ways. Chicken and beef dishes round out the menu. If you crave a business-friendly environment and a great place to enjoy fine Italian cooking, Il Mulino is exactly what you're looking for.

Hours: Monday through Friday, 11:30 A.M. to 4:30 P.M. (lunch); Monday through Wednesday, 5 P.M. to 10:30 P.M. (dinner); and Thursday through Saturday, 5 P.M. to 11 P.M. (dinner).

7. McCormick & Schmick's Seafood Restaurant

Location: 1652 K Street NW (at 17th Street), Washington, DC

Phone number: (202) 861-2233

Location: 901 F Street NW, Washington, DC

Phone number:(202) 639-9330

Web site: www.mccormickandschmicks.com

McCormick & Schmick's is a very popular chain of seafood restaurants.

Reservations required: Yes

Meals served: Lunch and dinner

Price range: $40 and up per person (dinner)

Food Quality and Variety	Value	Service	Business-Friendly Environment	Overall Rating
☆☆☆☆	☆☆☆☆	☆☆☆☆	☆☆☆☆	☆☆☆☆

TIP

McCormick & Schmick's also has locations in nearby Arlington, Virginia (2010 Crystal Drive, Crystal City, 703-413-6400), Bethesda, Maryland (7401 Woodmont Avenue, 301-961-2626), Reston, Virginia (11920 Democracy Drive, 703-481-6600), and Tysons Corner, Virginia (Westpark Drive at Leesburg Pike, 703-848-8000).

DESCRIPTION

McCormick & Schmick's has more than 50 locations nationwide, and the DC locations of are known for their vast selection of fresh seafood dishes, which typically includes more than 30 seafood varieties offered daily. The restaurant's menu changes each day, based on fresh seafood deliveries. Alaskan halibut, northwest salmon, Hawaiian mahi-mahi, Oregon petrale sole, and oysters from the United States and Canada are among the house specialties at this upscale restaurant.

The service at McCormick & Schmick's is as exemplary as the food's preparation and presentation. This is a wonderful place to enjoy an elegant business lunch or dinner. Business casual attire is required. The restaurant also features a full bar. Hours vary by season.

8. Occidental

Location: 1475 Pennsylvania Avenue NW, Washington, DC

Phone number: (202) 783-1475

Web site: www.occidentaldc.com

Reservations required: Yes

Meals served: Lunch and dinner

Price range: $50 and up per person (dinner)

Food Quality and Variety	Value	Service	Business-Friendly Environment	Overall Rating
☆☆☆☆	☆☆☆☆	☆☆☆☆	☆☆☆☆	☆☆☆☆

DESCRIPTION

If you were to compile a list of the DC area's most well-known and established upscale restaurants, the Occidental would probably be at or near the very top of your list. Located around the corner from the White House, this restaurant has been serving statesmen, businessmen, tourists, and Washington's elite since 1906.

Executive chef Rodney Scruggs has created an award-winning lunch and dinner menu, featuring upscale American cuisine, including his rendition of dishes that have been served at this restaurant for almost a century. In January 2007, the Occidental reopened after undergoing a massive renovation and redesign. As you dine, be sure to check out the many photographs on the walls that showcase some of the restaurant's famous clientele. This restaurant is known for attracting celebrities and high-profile guests.

Throughout the year, the lunch and dinner menus change with the seasons. In addition to the regular dinner menu, a pretheater menu is available in the evening. During the spring and summer months, the restaurant's patio is open for outdoor dining. Complimentary valet parking is available.

The Occidental is the perfect place to enjoy a fabulous lunch or dinner with friends, coworkers, or important clients. The atmosphere is sophisticated and business-friendly. Hours: Monday through Thursday, between 11:30 A.M. and 3 P.M. (lunch) and between 5 P.M. and 10 P.M. (dinner); Friday, between 11:30 A.M. and 3 P.M. (lunch) and between 5 P.M. and 10:30 P.M. (dinner); and

Saturday, between 5 P.M. and 10:30 P.M. (dinner only). Closed Sunday. Private dining rooms are available.

9. The Oval Room

Location: 800 Connecticut Avenue NW, Washington, DC
Phone number: (202) 463-8700
Web site: www.ovalroom.com
Reservations required: Yes
Meals served: Lunch and dinner
Price range: $50 and up per person (dinner)

Food Quality and Variety	Value	Service	Business-Friendly Environment	Overall Rating
☆☆☆½	☆☆☆½	☆☆☆½	☆☆☆½	☆☆☆½

DESCRIPTION

Located in downtown DC, the Oval Room offers an elegant but relatively small, dimly lit main dining room and separate bar area. Lunch is served Monday through Friday, between 11:30 A.M. and 3 P.M., followed by dinner, which is served between 5:30 P.M. and 10 P.M. (5:30 P.M. to 10:30 P.M. on Friday and Saturday).

In addition to the five-course tasting menu ($70 per person) that is available during dinner hours, individual entrées include roasted cod, slow-baked salmon, venison, butter-poached lobster, and caramelized beef tenderloin. The entrée portions are

For lunch or dinner, the Oval Room offers a pleasant dining experience in a business-friendly atmosphere.

somewhat small, but by the time you're done with appetizers, your main entrée, and dessert, you'll feel pleasantly full having enjoyed a well-prepared and delicious meal.

10. Palm Restaurant

Location: 1225 19th Street NW, Washington, DC

Phone number: (202) 293-9091

Web site: www.thepalm.com

Reservations required: Yes

Meals served: Lunch and dinner

Price range: $50 and up per person (dinner)

Food Quality and Variety	Value	Service	Business-Friendly Environment	Overall Rating
☆☆☆☆	☆☆☆☆	☆☆☆☆	☆☆☆☆	☆☆☆☆

DESCRIPTION

For more than 80 years, the Palm Restaurant has set the standard for fine dining with locations in more than 20 U.S. cities. The Palm Restaurant serves huge cuts of prime beef, jumbo lobsters broiled to perfection, and a wide range of other tasty entrées. Veal, pasta dishes, salads, and lamb chops round out the extensive menu, which can be paired with a vast selection of fine wines.

This has been a favorite dining establishment among politicians and Washington's elite since 1972. In addition to the mouthwatering steaks and seafood dishes, the Palm is known for its signature martinis.

To accommodate small groups, private dining rooms are available. The main dining room is spacious and elegant. Hours of operation are from 11:45 A.M. to 10:30 P.M. (weekdays), 5:30 P.M. to 10:30 P.M. (Saturday), and 5:30 P.M. to 9:30 P.M. (Sunday).

11. Ruth's Chris Steakhouse

Location: 724 9th Street NW, Washington, DC
   (closest to the Convention Center)

Phone number: (202) 393-4488

Location: 1801 Connecticut Avenue NW, Washington, DC

Phone number: (202) 797-0033

Web site: www.ruthschris.com

Reservations required: Yes

Meals served: Dinner

Price range: $35 and up per person

Food Quality and Variety	Value	Service	Business-Friendly Environment	Overall Rating
☆☆☆☆	☆☆☆☆	☆☆☆☆	☆☆☆☆	☆☆☆☆

DESCRIPTION

Offering two convenient locations in the DC area (one within a few blocks of the Washington Convention Center and the Verizon Center), Ruth's Chris Steak House is well known for providing a superior fine-dining experience. For business travelers, private dining rooms are available.

In addition to its famous steak entrées (such as the filet mignon, rib eye, New York strip, and porterhouse), house specialties include ahi tuna steak, veal chop, stuffed chicken breast, fresh lobster, grilled portobello mushrooms, and cold-water lobster tail. An extensive wine list is also available. With any entrée, any of seven varieties of vegetables and/or jumbo shrimp, lobster tail, or other extras can be added. Be sure to leave room for dessert. The crème brûlée, bread pudding with whisky sauce, and chocolate sin cake are among the most popular options.

One thing that sets the steak entrées served at Ruth's Chris Steak House apart is how they are prepared. All beef is corn fed and cooked in specially designed ovens at 1,800°F.

For a mouthwatering steak in a business-friendly environment, consider dining at Ruth's Chris Steak House. There's a location just a few blocks from the Washington Convention Center and another near the Verizon Center.

Hours of operation are Monday through Thursday, 5 P.M. to 10 P.M.; Friday and Saturday, 5 P.M. to 10:30 P.M.; and Sunday, 5 P.M. to 9 P.M. Business casual attire is required and valet parking is available.

12. 701 Restaurant

Location: 701 Pennsylvania Avenue NW, Washington, DC

Phone number: (202) 393-0701

Web site: www.701restaurant.com

Reservations required: Yes

Meals served: Dinner

Price range: $40 and up per person

Food Quality and Variety	Value	Service	Business-Friendly Environment	Overall Rating
☆☆☆☆	☆☆☆☆	☆☆☆☆	☆☆☆☆½	☆☆☆☆

DESCRIPTION

Located between Capitol Hill and the White House, this establishment offers primarily American cuisine. Entrées include American red snapper, herb spiced salmon, ahi tuna, roasted baby chicken, prime New York steak, veal chop, moulard breast of duck, and kurobuta pork loin. A nice selection of appetizers, desserts, and fine wines is also available to round out any meal. One popular appetizer is the caviar sampler. A three-course pretheater menu is also available between 5:30 P.M. and 6:45 P.M. daily at a *prix fixe* of $25.95 per person.

701 Restaurant offers a semiformal, business-friendly atmosphere. Hours: Monday through Friday, between 11:30 A.M. and 3 P.M. (lunch); Monday through Thursday, between 5:30 P.M. and 10:30 P.M. (dinner); Friday and Saturday, between 5:30 P.M. and 11:30 P.M. (dinner); and Sunday, between 5 P.M. and 9:30 P.M. (dinner). Mo's Bar, which is housed within 701, is open until midnight Monday through Thursday, until 1 A.M. on Friday and Saturday, and until 11 P.M. on Sunday.

13. Smith & Wollensky

Location: 1112 19th Street NW, Washington, DC

Phone number: (202) 466-1100

Web site: www.smithandwollensky.com

Reservations required: Yes

Meals served: Lunch and dinner

Price range: $40 and up per person

Food Quality and Variety	Value	Service	Business-Friendly Environment	Overall Rating
☆☆☆☆	☆☆☆☆	☆☆☆☆	☆☆☆½	☆☆☆☆

DESCRIPTION

This popular Smith & Wollensky steakhouse features the same superior dining experience guests have come to expect from other locations of this upscale, nationwide restaurant chain. Featuring a traditional steakhouse menu (which also serves lobster and other fresh seafood entrées), Smith & Wollensky serves lunch and dinner in its elegant and sophisticated dining room. Private dining rooms are also available.

Steak entrées are made with USDA prime beef, dry aged on the premises. Popular steaks include sirloin, prime rib, filet mignon, and filet au poivre. Lamb chops and veal chops are among the other house specialties. In terms of seafood, you'll find specialties like South African, Tristan Island, and Australian lobster tail, wild salmon, halibut, sushi-grade tuna, and Indonesian shrimp all featured on the menu. Hours of operation are 11:30 A.M. to 12 A.M. daily (open until 1 A.M. on Saturday and 11 P.M. on Sunday).

14. The Willard Room

Location: Willard InterContinental Hotel, 1401 Pennsylvania Avenue NW, Washington, DC

Phone number: (202) 637-7440

Web site: www.washington.interconti.com

Reservations required: Yes

Meals served: Breakfast, lunch, and dinner

Price range: $50 and up per person (dinner)

Food Quality and Variety	Value	Service	Business-Friendly Environment	Overall Rating
☆☆☆☆	☆☆☆☆	☆☆☆☆	☆☆☆☆	☆☆☆☆

DESCRIPTION

Located on the main lobby level of the Willard InterContinental Hotel is the famous Willard Room restaurant, which offers an extremely elegant, traditional, and luxurious setting, combined with superior service and award-winning cuisine. Formal attire is required.

Specializing in American and European cuisine, the Willard Room is the perfect setting for a formal business lunch or dinner.

For dinner, appetizers include wild Burgundy escargot ravioli, house-smoked organic salmon, sautéed frog legs meuniere, and fresh oysters. A nice selection of soups and salads is featured on the menu. For the main course, some of the house specialties include Mediterranean sea bass, Maine lobster, Colorado loin of lamb, stuffed veal breast, roasted loin of venison, and filet mignon. To complete the meal, a full dessert menu is available.

In addition to individual entrées, the Willard Room also offers its popular tasting menu. The five-course meal is priced at $69 per person, and the seven-course meal is priced at $95 per person, excluding wine pairings. Every Sunday, between 11 A.M. and 3 P.M., a Taste of America Sunday Brunch is served ($75 per person, including American sparkling wine).

After dinner, consider having drinks at the hotel's famous Round Robin Bar, which is open daily, between noon and 11 P.M.

15. Zola

Location: 800 F Street NW, Washington, DC

Phone number: (202) 654-0999

Web site: www.zoladc.com

Reservations required: Yes

Meals served: Lunch and dinner

Price range: $40 and up per person (dinner)

Food Quality and Variety	Value	Service	Business-Friendly Environment	Overall Rating
☆☆☆	☆☆☆	☆☆☆½	☆☆☆½	☆☆☆½

DESCRIPTION

Featuring a contemporary and sophisticated main dining room, Zola offers what the chef calls "straightforward American cuisine" in a business-friendly environment. The restaurant is located next door to the International Spy Museum and is just one block from the Verizon Center.

Appetizers, like tuna tartar, grilled flat bread, and soup, range in price from $7 to $14, while main entrées are priced between $17 and $27. Entrées include roasted ahi tuna, broiled salmon filet, lobster roll, grilled veal, pan-roasted scallops, and clover honey-glazed brick chicken.

Between 5 P.M. and 7 P.M., Zola offers a delicious pre-event menu, which includes three courses for $30 per person. To accompany your meal, an extensive wine list is available, with many selections offered by the glass. Built into the main dining room's

ORDERING FINE WINE WITH DINNER

One challenge many business travelers face is choosing an appropriate wine selection to go nicely with the entrées or desserts that are being ordered. Not only do you want to impress the people you're dining with (such as important clients), but you want to order a quality wine that's within your budget.

Andy Myers is the sommelier at the Mandarin Oriental Hotel in Washington, DC. In addition to managing the hotel's massive wine collection, one of his responsibilities is to help guests dining at the hotel's restaurants choose the best wine to accompany their meals.

"Ideally, the restaurant has a sommelier. If they do, then ask for that person, give them a basic budget for the evening, a feeling for how much your guests are likely to drink, and a rough idea of what kind of wines you like—fruity, earthy, full-bodied, light, etc. That'll solve most of your problems, as a good sommelier likes to have a clear, basic profile of the table, budget, and drinking habits. Using this information, we love it when you trust us to make the experience great," said Myers.

If the restaurant you're dining at doesn't have a sommelier, Myers stated, "Assume that most people put away about half a bottle of wine during dinner. This will help when figuring out how much to order. Next, as you'll never please everyone at the table, go for wines that work with lots of flavors. I recommend Sauvignon Blancs, Dry Rieslings, and Chenin Blancs for whites and Pinot Noirs and Rhône Varietals (Syrah, Grenache, Mourvèdre) for reds."

Diners at upscale restaurants should know that even if a sommelier is not available, most restaurants train their waitstaff on how to assist guests in choosing appropriate wines. "Review the wine list to gather some ideas, and then ask your server or a manager what they think," added Myers.

It's important to understand that there are no hard, fast rules when it comes to pairing wines. "Very basically speaking, with beef, go with big, chewy, tannic Cabernets. Go to California if you like fruit, and go to Bordeaux if you want really dry. When ordering chicken, go with whatever wine you want, such as a white Burgundy, Chateauneuf-du-Pape blanc or Oregon Pinot Noir. Everything goes with chicken, as it has little flavor of its own to get

> ## ORDERING FINE WINE
> ## WITH DINNER, continued
>
> in the way. Pairing wine with fish and seafood dishes it a bit tougher. For white wines, go with quirky Italian whites, such as Vermentino, Vernaccia, Falanghina, or Orvieto," explained Myers.
>
> Since you might not want to admit to the people you're dining with that you know little about wine, Myers recommends pulling your server or the restaurant's sommelier aside to have an open and honest conversation about your wine needs, taste, and budget. "Ask for their help and utilize their recommendations to ensure the best dining experience possible."

lovely décor are windows that offer a view of the kitchen, so you can see your meal being expertly prepared. Once your food is served, you'll appreciate the artistic presentation and top-notch service.

Hours: Monday through Friday, between 11:30 A.M. and midnight; Saturday, between 5 P.M. and midnight; and Sunday, between 5 P.M. and 10 P.M. Private dining is available.

For a fine-dining experience that includes "straightforward American cuisine," visit Zola, which is located at 800 F Street NW.

TIP

If you're looking for an elegant and memorable way to enjoy a gourmet dinner, plus tour some of Washington, DC's most famous historical sites and memorials, consider taking an evening dinner cruise. Several companies offer dinner cruises along the Potomac River, including Spirit Cruises (202-554-8000, www.spiritcitycruises.com) and Odyssey Cruises (866-306-2469, www.odysseycruises.com). Parties of one to several hundred people can be accommodated.

THEME AND SPECIALTY RESTAURANTS

The following is a sampling of theme restaurants and midpriced dining experiences that offer something unique for lunch or dinner.

Ben's Chili Bowl

Address: 1213 U Street NW, Washington, DC

Phone number: (202) 667-0909

Web site: www.benschilibowl.com

DESCRIPTION

Offering its own unique homemade chili recipe for almost 50 years, this fast-food establishment serves chili dogs, chili burgers, and other award-winning chili entrées. Open for breakfast, lunch, and dinner (6 A.M. until 2 A.M. weekdays; Saturday 6 A.M. to 4 A.M.; Sunday 11 A.M. to 8 A.M.).

ESPN Zone

Address: 555 12th Street NW, Washington, DC

Phone number: (202) 783-3776

Web site: www.espnzone.com/washingtondc/

DESCRIPTION

Operated by ESPN (the Walt Disney Company), this chain offers a casual sports bar and restaurant environment in the heart of downtown DC. Featuring all-American cuisine, this restaurant is definitely a haven for local and visiting sports fans. In addition to large-screen televisions showing sporting events, the restaurant features many interactive video games. Open for lunch and dinner. Hours: Sunday through Thursday, 11:30 A.M. to 11 P.M.; and Friday and Saturday 11:30 A.M. to midnight. During busy periods, this place can get a bit loud and crowded. Plan on spending under $20 per person (plus alcohol).

Hard Rock Café

Address: 999 E Street NW, Washington, DC

Phone number: (202) 737-7625

Web site: www.hardrock.com

DESCRIPTION

On display here is an incredible collection of original music memorabilia. While enjoying the midpriced American cuisine, you can't help but look around at the priceless pieces of memorabilia from the Beatles, Led Zeppelin, Billy Joel, Elvis Presley, Madonna, John Lennon, Jimi Hendrix, and countless other musical greats. Recent additions to the collection include Bill Clinton's saxophone, Sammy Hagar's guitar, and authentic Gwen Stefani, Buddy Holly, and Freddie Mercury stage wear. You can always count on a loud and festive atmosphere. There's also a large gift and souvenir shop. The menu features burgers, salads, steaks, chicken, and seafood dishes, plus sandwiches and a wide range of other American favorites, like Texas chili and barbeque baby back ribs. Open for lunch and dinner.

Hooters

Address: 825-29 Seventh Street NW, Washington, DC

Phone number: (202) 628-6583

Web site: www.hooters.com

DESCRIPTION

This restaurant and bar caters primarily to a male clientele, with its cadre of world-famous (and scantily clad) female servers. The menu offers everything from fish and chips, soups, burgers, and steamed clams to sandwiches and salads. Hooters is also famous for its chicken wings and other appetizers, but most guys don't really come here just for the food. It's open for lunch and dinner.

Legal Sea Foods

Address: 704 Seventh Street NW, Washington, DC

Phone number: (202) 347-0007

Web site: www.legalseafoods.com

DESCRIPTION

This national chain of midpriced restaurants offers top-quality seafood plus other American cuisine in a business casual environment. You'll also find Legal Sea Foods locations at 2020 K Street NW in Washington, DC, at the Reagan National Airport, and in several of the DC area's shopping malls. It's a top choice among seafood lovers. Private dining is available at several of the DC locations.

Mystery Dinner Playhouse

Address: 300 Army Drive, Arlington, VA
Phone number: (888) 471-4802
Web site: www.mysterydinner.com

DESCRIPTION

This interactive dinner-theater experience offers a multicourse meal combined with an entertaining show. The dinner-and-show combo is priced at $42.95 per person. A choice of four main entrées is available. Enjoy a full night's worth of dining and entertainment. Reservations are required. The experience begins at 7:30 P.M. every Friday and Saturday. Private performances for groups of 40 people or more are available. The dining room holds 200 guests.

Potbelly Sandwich Works

Address: eight locations in the downtown DC area, including
    726 Seventh Street NW
Phone number: (202) 478-0070
Web site: www.potbelly.com

DESCRIPTION

If you're looking for a fast, inexpensive, yet quality sandwich place to dine for lunch, Potbelly Sandwich Works is a great choice. The restaurant offers custom-made sandwiches, soups, plus shakes, malts, and smoothies. All sandwiches cost just $3.99. Pot Belly also has delicious catering options for business meetings and trade show exhibitors. Open daily from 11 A.M. to 9 P.M. (10 P.M. on Fridays and Saturdays).

Tea Cellar

Address: Park Hyatt Hotel, 24th and M streets NW, Washington, DC
Phone number: (202) 419-6755
Web site: http://parkwashington.hyatt.com/hyatt/hotels/
    entertainment/lounges/index.jsp

DESCRIPTION

One of the newest trends in business entertaining is to forego the traditional midday or after-hours drink at the bar and instead meet business associates for tea. While many upscale hotels in the

The Hard Rock Café offers an extensive menu, plus a casual dining atmosphere.

The Legal Sea Food chain of restaurants offers the ideal setting for a semi-casual business lunch or dinner

Sports fans will enjoy the casual setting of this popular sports-oriented bar and restaurant.

DC area, like the Ritz-Carlton and the Willard InterContinental, offer midday tea, the Tea Cellar features a casual yet sophisticated atmosphere, a collection of more than 50 fine teas from around the world, and a place for business travelers to meet throughout the day and evening. Prices range from $6 to $300 per small pot. Coordinating meetings over afternoon tea has become popular with businessmen as well as businesswomen.

The Melting Pot

Address: 1220 19th Street NW, Washington, DC

Phone number: (202) 857-0777

Web site: www.meltingpot.com

DESCRIPTION

A fondue restaurant with six locations in the DC, Virginia, and Maryland areas, the Melting Pot is a fast-growing national chain of midpriced restaurants that offers an unusual yet sophisticated dining experience. The menu's focus is on a wide range of fondue dishes. Intimate seating in plush booths is provided, but small-group dining is also available. Choose the four-course dining option ($82 to $92 per couple) to truly get the full fondue experience, from appetizer to dessert.

ORDERING ROOM SERVICE

Most DC hotels have at least one or two restaurants on the premises, which are often well worth experiencing for a power breakfast, lunch, or dinner. However, if after a long day you just want to relax in your hotel room and dine in, consider ordering from your hotel's room service menu. The meals are typically prepared by the chefs from the hotel's inhouse restaurants and delivered to your guestroom in 30 to 45 minutes. Many business travelers opt for room service as opposed to dining out.

When ordering room service, be prepared to pay regular menu prices, plus an extra delivery charge *and* service charge (which can each be as high as 20 percent of the total bill), in addition to local sales tax and a 15 to 20 percent tip for the server. While in-room dining is convenient, utilizing room service can almost double the price of your meal (as opposed to eating at the hotel's restaurant within its regular dining room).

An alternative to ordering from your hotel's room service menu (which will be available in your guestroom, typically in a binder or folder on the desk) is to use a food-delivery service in DC that allows you to order from one of many local restaurants and have your food delivered to your hotel room.

TOP HOTEL CONCIERGES SHARE THEIR RESTAURANT TIPS

An excellent resource for discovering the best restaurants or getting the inside scoop on what to do and when to do it while in DC is your hotel's concierge. When it comes to top business-friendly restaurant picks, here's what three concierges from some of the most prestigious DC-area hotels had to say.

Daniel Klibanoff, head concierge at the Mandarin Oriental Hotel stated, "Some of the best business-friendly restaurants in the DC area are Café Mozu, the Palm, the Cactus Room, Occidental, and the Capital Grille. I also want to mention that our fine-dining restaurant, Cityzen, is a wonderful place to host that VIP business dinner."

According to Michael McCleary, assistant chief concierge at the Willard InterContinental, his top restaurant picks are the Willard Room, the Capital Grille, Tosca Ristorante, Taberna del Alabardero, and The Prime Rib.

Javier Loureiro, head concierge at the Four Seasons, added, "In addition to Seasons, the fine-dining restaurant at the Four Seasons, my top recommendations for a business-friendly fine-dining experience are Charlie Palmer, Marcel's, Citronelle, Equinox, and Taberna del Albardero."

MONEY SAVER
Typically, the hotel will automatically add a 15 to 20 percent tip for the server to your room service bill. This will be itemized separately. There will, however, be an additional line on the bill to add an extra tip. Determine if a tip has already been included before adding another one.

Three delivery services in the DC area—A La Cart Express (202-232-8646/www.alacart.com), Delivery.com (www.delivery.com), and Foodler.com (www.foodler.com)—allow you to view menus from dozens (in some cases hundreds) of restaurants online, then place your order online or by telephone, and have the food delivered for a small fee. Major credit cards are accepted by these services. Placing your order takes just minutes. Hiring one of these services allows you to experience some of the gourmet fare offered by the DC area's top restaurants without having to leave your hotel room.

Some of the reasons business travelers might prefer room service include:

- To save time
- As a matter of convenience
- To get additional work done in their guestroom while waiting for the food to be delivered
- To be able to relax and enjoy watching TV or a movie while dining in the comfort of their guestroom
- To have a quiet and relaxing dining experience, without having to travel to a restaurant or make reservations
- To enjoy a fine-dining experience without having to dress up for the occasion (pajamas or a bathrobe are appropriate attire for private in-room dining)
- To host a small business meeting in their guestroom with top-quality food, so they can have access to important work documents, their computer, and a telephone, for example
- To avoid dining alone in public

TRAVEL NOTES

SECTION VI

© Jason Mae

ENTERTAINMENT IN
WASHINGTON, DC

Aside from conducting the business you're traveling to Washington, DC for, hopefully you'll have time to enjoy some of what the nation's capital has to offer, such as the museums, memorials, historical and tourist attractions, shopping, world-class day spas, and fine-dining restaurants.

When visiting the DC area, it's impossible to not take absolute pride in the United States of America, especially if you have an opportunity to visit some of the patriotic sites, such as the White House, the Capitol, and the various presidential and war memorials.

This section offers an overview of just some of the ways you can enjoy your free time while visiting this exciting city. If you'll need to entertain and impress important clients, business associates, or friends while in town, you'll find a wide selection of memorable ways to do this—from one-of-a-kind tours to fabulous dining experiences.

TIP

For an up-to-date listing of special events happening in the DC area during the dates of your visit, check out a current issue of *Where* magazine (distributed free at many hotels), call (800) 422-8644, or visit the www.washington.org web site and click on "Events." The Washington, DC Event Guide web site (http://washington.dc.event-guide.com) also offers an excellent summary of events broken down by month and includes professional sporting event listings.

WASHINGTON, DC TOURS

Washington, DC offers many tourist attractions, national monuments, historical sites, and museums that are well worth visiting. No matter what your interests, time constraints, or budget, there are tours available that'll entertain and educate you. Whether you have just a few hours or several full days to experience the sights and attractions, participating in an organized tour is an excellent and cost-effective way to see the DC area. Don't forget to bring along your camera!

The following is information about some of the more popular tours offered in Washington, DC. To learn about other tour opportunities, consult with your hotel's concierge. Tour prices, departure times, and duration vary by tour operator, day of the week, and season. Many of the companies listed here also offer private tours for individuals or small groups.

- *Bike the Sites*—www.bikethesites.com, (202) 842-BIKE. Offers bicycle tours of the DC area. It's a fun way to see the sights while getting a workout. This tour is ideal for athletic people.

- *Boomerang Party Bus*—www.risetheboomerang.com, (202) 725-6226. This tour offers a great way to blow off some steam after a long day of meetings or attending a trade show. The Boomerang Party Bus takes passengers on a whirlwind tour of DC's hottest nightspots. It's a great way to meet people and experience local dance clubs and bars. The cost of beverages and food is not included in the tour price. Price: $25 per person.
- *Capital City Bike Tours*—www.citysegwaytours.com, (877) SEG-TOUR. This is one of several companies that offer bicycle, scooter, and Segway tours of the nation's capital.
- *Capital Segway Tours*—www.capitalsegway.com, (202) 682-1980, 1350 I Street NW, Washington, DC. Not only is riding a Segway fun, but it offers a convenient way to see many of DC's most popular (outdoor) tourist attractions and memorials. If your time is limited and you're looking for a unique tour, this one will allow you to see a lot while enjoying the thrill of riding a Segway. The 2.5-hour tour costs $65 per person. Each tour is limited to a small group. The Segway Personal Transporter (PT) is a state-of-the-art, self-balancing, two-wheeled personal transportation device that's designed to go anywhere you go. Driving one requires no special skills and virtually anyone can use one.
- *Dandy Dinner Boat*—www.dandydinnerboat.com, (703) 683-6076. Enjoy a fine-dining experience as you embark on

The Old Town Trolley is an inexpensive and convenient way to get to all of the popular tourist attractions, monuments, and historical sites in DC.

a daytime or evening cruise along the Potomac River. You'll see some of the DC area's most famous monuments. The three-hour cruise costs about $70 per person (including a multicourse lunch or dinner).

- *DC Ducks (seasonal)*—www.historictours.com, (202) 832-9800. During the spring and summer months, the DC Ducks tours offer a land-and-sea adventure as you ride on genuine WWII DUKW amphibious vehicles. This fun and informative 90-minute tour will take you through the city as well as along the Potomac River.
- *Martz Gray Line*—www.grayline.com, (800) 862-1400. Enjoy seeing the sights as you ride in a comfortable, climate-controlled bus and receive a fully narrated tour. The company also operates a L'il Red Trolley tour. More than 25 different tours are available, each with a different focus. Many of the tours last between three hours and a full day.
- *Old Town Trolley Tours*—www.historictours.com, (202) 832-9800. Ride a trolley that takes you to many of the DC area's most popular attractions, monuments, and historical sites. This is a two-hour tour. A new tour departs every 30 minutes, starting at 9 A.M. You can disembark from the tour at any of 19 locations and pick up a later trolley, so you can experience many of the attractions and sights at your own pace.
- *On Location Tours*—www.screentours.com, (212) 209-3370. Instead of showing off all of the monuments and historical sites, this fun-filled tour focuses on famous sites from popular TV shows and movies. This three-hour tour (priced at $32) takes you to about 30 different locations, like the mall where the movies *No Way Out* and *True Lies* were filmed; the house used in *The Exorcist*; and the bar used in *St. Elmo's Fire.* You'll also see shooting locations from *Wedding Crashers, West Wing, The X-Files, Independence Day, Forrest Gump,* and many other shows and movies. All of the tours are led by talented and knowledgeable actors. The tour operates on Friday, Saturday, and Sunday only.
- *Private Limousine Tours.* Virtually all of the limousine companies operating in the DC area offer personalized and narrated tours of the city in comfortable town cars or limousines. This is an efficient and elegant way to see the city. You'll also have the freedom to make whatever stops you wish at the various attractions, stores, and sights that are of

interest to you. See Section IV, "Getting Around Town," for a list of limousine companies, or contact your hotel's concierge. Private limousine tours are offered by the hour, half day, or full day. Prices vary because of the highly personalized nature of these tours.

- *Scandal Tours*—www.gnpcomedy.com/ScandalTours.html, (202) 783-7212. Countless political scandals have taken place in Washington, DC throughout our country's history. From this unusual tour, you can learn more about some of the most outrageous political scandals to grace the front pages of newspapers everywhere, plus visit the locations where the shameful events actually took place. This is a witty and irreverent guided tour hosted by performers from the comedy troupe Gross National Product. The tour runs seasonally, between April Fools' Day and Labor Day, every Saturday at 1 P.M. Private group tours are available throughout the year. Tickets are $30 per adult. This is a fun and memorable way to see DC.
- *Segs in the City*—www.segsinthecity.net, (800) SEGS-393. This is one of several companies that offer narrated Segway tours of the DC area.
- *Spirit Cruises*—www.spiritcruises.com, (202) 554-8000. Lunch and dinner cruises are offered which also feature live cabaret entertainment as you sail along the Potomac River. Tours operate seasonally.
- *Tourmobile Sightseeing*—www.tourmobile.com, (202) 554-5100. These narrated tours allow you to ride in comfortable

Tourmobile Sightseeing offers convenient and cost-effective guided tours of the DC area.

shuttle buses, disembark at about 20 tourist attractions, museums, and monuments, and then reboard to continue the tour at your leisure. Tours originate from the National Mall area. This is an economical and convenient way to get around the city and see the sights at your own pace. Prices start around $20 per person for a full-day pass.

- *Washington Photo Safari*—www.washingtonphotosafari.com, (202) 537-0937. If you enjoy photography and want to return home with a personalized and impressive photo album to commemorate your trip, this tour, which is hosted by E. David Luria (an award-winning professional photographer), is for you. You'll visit many of the most popular DC-area sites, where you'll receive instruction on

---

EXCLUSIVE TOURS FOR UPSCALE BUSINESS TRAVELERS

Many business travelers are on a tight schedule, but during what little free time they have, they want to experience tours, attractions, or other aspects of Washington, DC in the most exciting and time-efficient ways possible. Other business travelers are seeking out innovative and memorable ways to impress clients and customers while in the nation's capital. No matter what your motivation, one company has put together a menu of highly personalized, innovative, and truly memorable tour experiences that most everyday tourists never get to experience.

To learn about the many different tours available, from private limousine, helicopter, and yacht tours, to innovative and unusual walking tours, contact Viator (866-648-5873, www.viator.com).

By working closely with a wide range of highly reputable, competitively priced, independent tour operators and service providers, Viator is able to help business travelers choose from more than 112 different tour packages offered in Washington, DC and handles all scheduling and booking details on their behalf.

Contact a Viator representative to discuss your interests, schedule, and budget, and then learn about the various tour packages available in Washington, DC. The company offers a low-price guarantee for all tours booked through the service, and it allows participants to earn frequent flier miles (on American Airlines, Delta, or United) for their purchases. Viator specializes in booking tours for individuals or groups of any size.

how to best photograph the monument or attraction. Several different half-day and full-day versions of this highly informative and entertaining tour are available. It's an ideal way for anyone with a passion for picture taking—whether it's with a cheap disposable camera, a high-end 35 mm camera, or a state-of-the-art digital camera—to see and experience the DC area. No photography experience is necessary. This tour is much more interactive than simply riding on a tour bus or trolley and listening to a narrator. E. David Luria is also available for hire to shoot corporate events.

THEATER AND STAGE PERFORMANCES

The DC area is home to many lovely theaters that host an ever-changing and diverse selection of productions, ranging from touring Broadway musicals and shows to ballet and concerts.

A current listing of shows and events can be found in *The Washington Post* newspaper (www.washingtonpost.com) or in the current issue of *Where* magazine, which is distributed free of charge at most hotels. An events listing can be read online at www.wheremagazine.com/where_books/wheredc.shtml.

The following are some of the popular theater and concert venues in the DC area.

AREA THEATERS

Arena Stage	(202) 554-9066
www.arenastage.org	1101 6th Street SW, Washington, DC
DAR Constitution Hall	(202) 628-4780
www.dar.org	1776 D Street NW, Washington, DC
Ford's Theatre	(202) 347-4833
www.fordstheatre.org	511 10th Street NW, Washington, DC
Kennedy Center (aka the John F. Kennedy Center for the Performing Arts	(202) 467-4600
www.kennedy-center.org	2700 F Street, NW, Washington, DC
Lincoln Theatre	(202) 328-6000
www.lovethelincoln.com	1215 U Street NW, Washington, DC
Mystery Dinner Playhouse	(804) 649-2583
www.mysterydinner.com	300 Army Navy Drive, Arlington, VA
National Theatre	(202) 628-6161/(800) 447-7400
www.nationaltheatre.org	1321 Pennsylvania Avenue, Washington, DC
Shakespeare Theatre Company	(202) 547-1122
www.shakespearetheatre.org	450 7th Street NW, Washington, DC

AREA THEATERS

Studio Theatre	(202) 232-7267
www.studiotheatre.org	1501 14th Street NW, Washington, DC
Warner Theatre	(202) 626-8250
www.warnertheatre.com	513 13th Street NW, Washington, DC
The Washington Ballet	(202) 362-3606
www.washingtonballet.org	3515 Wisconsin Avenue NW, Washington, DC
Washington National Opera	(202) 295-2420
www.dc-opera.org	2600 Virginia Avenue NW, Washington, DC

MONEY SAVER

TICKETplace (202) TIC-KETS, www.ticketplace.org, 407 7th Street NW, Washington, DC, is Washington, DC's only discount ticket center, offering day-of-show, half-price tickets for shows and concerts throughout the DC area. Visit the ticket center in person, between 11 A.M. and 6 P.M. Tuesday through Friday; between 10 A.M. and 5 P.M. Saturday, to see what tickets are available that day.

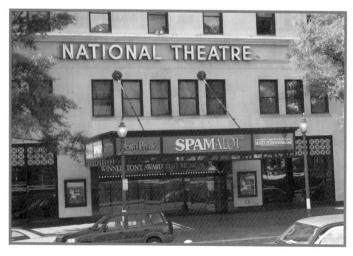

The National Theatre is among the venues where live shows, musicals, and concerts are presented throughout the year.

Shows, concerts, and other events are held at the Warner Theatre throughout the year.

Ford's Theatre has a rich history—it's where President Lincoln was shot—and continues to be a popular destination among theatre goers.

TIP

Want to see a stand-up comedy show? Check out who's performing at DC Improve (202) 296-7008, www.dcimprov.com, 1140 Connecticut Avenue NW, Washington, DC). There's also Capitol Steps (703) 683-8330, www.capitolsteps.com, a musical political satire troupe composed of congressional staffers who moonlight as comedians. Performances are held Friday and Saturday nights at the Ronald Reagan Building Amphitheater (210 North Washington Street, Alexandria, Virginia).

PROFESSIONAL SPORTING EVENTS

The Verizon Center

Address: 601 F Street NW, Washington, DC
Main phone number: (202) 628-3200
To purchase tickets by phone: (202) 397-SEAT
Web site: www.verizoncenter.com
Events calendar web site: www.verizoncenter.com/events
 or call (202) 661-5000

The Verizon Center is the DC area's largest indoor arena, which is host to more than 200 sporting events, shows, and concerts each year. It's home to the Washington Wizards (NBA), the Washington Capitals (NHL), the Washington Mystics (WNBA), and the Georgetown Hoyas (men's basketball team).

TIP

To purchase season tickets for the DC sports teams, call these numbers: Washington Wizards (202) 661-5050; Washington Mystics (202) 266-2277; Washington Capitals (202) 266-CAPS.

Other shows and events held here include the *Ringling Brothers and Barnum and Bailey Circus*, freestyle motocross,

The Verizon Center is located in downtown DC. It is the largest sports and concert arena in the city.

Champions on Ice, and WWE Presents RAW. Many top-name recording artists perform live in concert throughout the year.

The main box office for this 20,000-seat arena is located at 601 F Street NW. It also serves as a Ticketmaster location for all area events. Box office hours are Monday through Saturday, between 10 A.M. and 5:30 P.M., as well as during all events. The box office is closed on Sunday, unless an event is being held at the arena. Tickets for any Verizon Center event can also be purchased by calling Ticketmaster at (202) 397-SEAT.

CITY FACTOID
In 2009, the Verizon Center will host the NCAA Division I Men's Hockey Championships (Frozen Four) for the first time, in addition to the first and second rounds of the 2008 NCAA Division I Men's Basketball tournament for the third time.

This $220 million complex opened in 1997. The arena's 114 executive and luxury suites (which hold 12 to 18 guests each) are ideal for hosting corporate events and private parties during events and concerts.

In terms of dining, the arena offers the private Acela Club Restaurant (exclusively for club seat and suite holders), as well as the Johnnie Walker Coaches Club (exclusively for Gold VIP season ticket holders) and Dewar's 12 Clubhouse (which is open to the public, starting one hour before events). Throughout the arena, you'll find a wide selection of concession stands serving all types of fast food. Many sit-down restaurants are located within walking distance of the Verizon Center.

TIP
Using the Metrorail, which is the easiest and least expensive way to get to and from the arena, get off at the Gallery Place-Chinatown stop. It's serviced by the red, yellow, and green lines.

Parking near the arena is relatively easy. The Verizon Center has its own parking garage located on 6th Street NW, which is open for most events. The parking fee during events is $20 per vehicle. The garage opens one hour before the designated game or show time and closes one hour after the game or event. Additional nearby parking garages are also available, plus you'll find more than 10,000 parking spaces located within several blocks of the arena for on-street metered parking.

TIP

For information about DC United Soccer (Major League Soccer), call (202) 587-5459 or visit www.dcunited.com. This MLS team calls RFK Stadium (2400 East Capitol Street SE, Washington, DC) home.

FedEx Field

Address: 1600 FedEx Way, Landover, MD
Main phone number: (301) 276-6738
Web site: www.redskins.com
General seat ticket purchases: (301) 276-6050
Premium seat ticket purchases: (301) 276-6800

Located about eight miles from downtown DC, this sports complex holds 30,000 to 50,000 spectators and is home to the

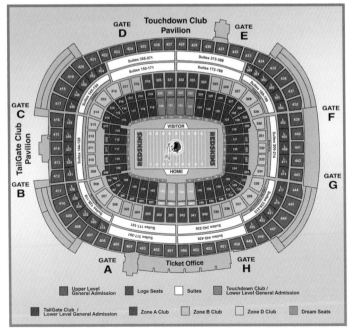

The FedEx Field seating chart for Washington Redskins games.

Washington Redskins NFL team. To reach the stadium by car from the DC area, take East Capitol Street (Central Avenue) to Harry S. Truman North. Turn right on Lottsford Road, and then follow it to Arena Drive. Parking is free.

MONEY SAVER
To purchase last-minute tickets for a sold-out game, visit StubHub at www.stubhub.com/washington-redskins-tickets/redskins-ticketcenter or call (866) STUB-HUB. This service allows season ticket holders to sell their unused tickets for specific games.

By Metrorail, take the orange line to the Landover station, then take a shuttle bus directly to FedEx Field. The alternative is to take the blue line to the Morgan Boulevard station (which is less than a one-mile walk from the stadium).

To access an interactive seating chart for football games (to find the location of your seats), visit www.redskins.com/fedex field/seating.jsp.

CITY FACTOID
Washington, DC will soon have a new Major League Baseball stadium, which will be home to the Washington Nationals (http://washington.nationals.mlb.com). The 22,000-seat stadium, scheduled to be completed by April 2008, will be located in southeast Washington, along the Anacostia River, bounded by South Capitol Street to the west, M Street to the north, First Street to the east, and Potomac Avenue to the south. By the time it's completed, construction of the stadium is expected to cost up to $611 million.

HOW TO SEE SOLD-OUT SHOWS, CONCERTS, AND SPORTING EVENTS

The fastest, safest, and easiest way to get your hands on tickets to any sold-out show, concert, or sporting event is to work with your hotel's concierge, who will have a pre-existing relationship with a reputable and licensed ticket broker. Be prepared, however, to pay a hefty premium for the tickets. Tickets purchased through a broker often go for double, triple, or even quadruple the original price, depending on demand. Some ticket brokers will purchase tickets from private sellers unable to utilize them.

Another, less reliable option is to purchase tickets from scalpers (often found outside of theaters or venues) or from private sellers using an online service, such as eBay.com. When utilizing one of these two methods, however, you never know if the tickets you're buying are authentic until you try to enter the theater or venue.

The following is a partial listing of independent ticket brokers you can contact yourself:

- Great Seats—(202) 347-7328
- Instant Seats—(202) 882-6573
- Razorgator—(800) 542-4466
- Ticket City—(202) 544-0919
- Ticketmaster—(202) 824-0786
- Tickets.com—(202) 518-1270
- Ticketsnow—(888) 896-9034
- Top Center Ticket Service—(202) 628-5555
- Unlimited Ticket Service—(202) 508-1488

GOLF COURSES

Throughout Washington, DC, Maryland, and Virginia, you'll find more than 65 golf courses, plus several driving ranges, many of which are open to the public (weather permitting, of course). The following is a list of just a few of the golf courses in the DC area.

AREA GOLF COURSES

Dulles Golf Center	(703) 929-3707
21593 Jesse Court, Dulles, VA	www.dullesgolf.com
East Potomac Park Golf Course	(202) 554-7660
972 Ohio Drive SW, Washington, DC	www.capitalcitygolf.net
Greendale Golf Course	(703) 971-3788
6700 Telegraph Road, Alexandria, VA	www.fairfaxcounty.gov/parks/golf/Greendale
Hilltop Golf Club	(703) 719-6504
7900 Telegraph Road, Alexandria, VA	www.hilltopgolfclub.com
Langston Golf Course	(202) 397-8638
28th and Benning Road NE, Washington, DC	www.capitalcitygolf.net
Pinecrest Golf Course	(703) 941-1061
6600 Little River Turnpike, Alexandria, VA	www.fairfaxcounty.gov/parks/golf/pinecrest
Rock Creek Golf Course	(202) 882-7332
1600 Rittenhouse Street NW, Washington, DC	www.capitalcitygolf.net

TIP

For a complete listing of golf courses in Washington, DC plus a printable map pinpointing exactly where each is located, visit: www.washingtonpost.com/wp-srv/health/specials/golf/golfmap/dcgolf05.pdf. For a listing of golf courses in nearby Virginia, visit www.fxva.com/fxva/recreation.html#golf or www.fairfaxcounty.gov/parks/golf/ (or call 877-776-3272 to reserve a tee time). For details about Maryland golf courses, visit http://mncppc.org/index.cfm?id=golf and www.montgomerycountygolf.com.

TIP

Since many of the golf courses in the area are located outside of Washington, DC, you'll probably need to arrange for transportation to get to and from the greens and your hotel. Consider reserving a town car or limo. Contact your hotel's concierge, the golf course, or one of the limousine companies listed in Section IV, "Getting Around Town."

THE *BUSINESS TRAVELER* TOP 15 TOURIST ATTRACTIONS IN WASHINGTON, DC

While there are literally hundreds of tourist attractions, museums, galleries, historical sites, memorials, monuments, and interesting places to see within the DC area, the following are 15 top picks for business travelers who want a taste of the nation's capital, but who have limited time. Admission to many of these attractions is free.

1. Arlington National Cemetery

Location: Arlington, VA

Phone number: (703) 607-8000

Web site: www.arlingtoncemetery.org

DESCRIPTION

This is the most honored cemetery in the nation and is where more than 285,000 soldiers and war heroes have been laid to rest. It's also the final resting place of several presidents and other top government leaders, and it is where the Tomb of the Unknowns is located. The cemetery is open daily from 8 A.M.

until 5 P.M. (or 7 P.M. between April and September). Free admission. The best way to see Arlington National Cemetery is by taking a guided tour.

CITY FACTOID
The Arlington National Cemetery comprises 200 acres. More than 300,000 people are buried here, including veterans from all of our nation's wars. The Tomb of the Unknowns is the most visited area of the cemetery.

---

2. Bureau of Engraving and Printing

Location: 4th and C Streets, SW, Washington, DC
Phone number: (202) 874-2330
Web site: www.moneyfactory.gov

DESCRIPTION

Ever wonder how money is created? Well, a visit to the Bureau of Engraving and Printing offers the opportunity to see literally millions of dollars in U.S. currency being created right before your eyes. Tours are offered on weekdays only and depart every 15 minutes. Hours of operation vary by season. Tickets are offered on a first-come basis and typically go extremely quickly, starting at 8 A.M. The walking tour lasts about 50 minutes. By Metrorail, the closest station is Smithsonian Station. Take the Independence Avenue exit (12th and Independence, SW) on the blue and orange line trains. Unfortunately, no free samples are offered after the tour. The good news is the tour is free of charge.

3. International Spy Museum

Location: 800 F Street NW, Washington, DC
Phone number: (202) 393-7798
Web site: www.spymuseum.org

DESCRIPTION

This self-guided tour (which takes between 1.5 and 2 hours to complete) allows you to see the world's largest collection of international espionage-related artifacts. If you're intrigued with spy novels and James Bond films, you'll really enjoy this museum. It chronicles the adventures of real-life spies. The gift shop offers a large assortment of spy-themed merchandise. Admission is $16 per person. Hours of operation vary by season.

The International Spy Museum is a state-of-the-art, fully interactive museum for adults that chronicles the world of real-life espionage on a global scale. This is a fun, unusual, and extremely interesting museum to visit.

4. Lincoln Memorial

Location: Independence Avenue and 23rd Street NW, Washington, DC
Phone number: (202) 426-6841
Web site: www.nps.gov/linc

DESCRIPTION

This extremely popular monument overlooks the Reflecting Pool, the Washington Monument, and the U.S. Capitol. Upon stepping

The Lincoln Memorial is one of the most popular attractions in the DC area.

Inside the Lincoln Memorial is the famous 19-foot-tall statue of President Lincoln.

inside this memorial, you'll see the famous, 19-foot-tall statue of President Lincoln. The Lincoln Memorial was built to be a symbol of democracy in our nation. Admission is free. Hours: 8 A.M. until midnight, daily.

5. National Archives

Location: Constitution Avenue (between 7th and 9th streets), Washington, DC
Phone number: (202) 357-5000
Web site: www.archives.gov

DESCRIPTION

This building, which is open to the public between 10 A.M. and 5:30 P.M. daily, houses the original Declaration of Independence, Constitution, Bill of Rights, and about three billion additional records. Admission is free.

6. National Gallery of Art

Location: Sixth Street and Constitution Avenue NW, Washington, DC
Phone number: (202) 737-4215
Web site: www.nga.gov

The National Archives offers a variety of different exhibits, and it houses some of the most important documents from our nation's history, including the Constitution and the Declaration of Independence, which are on display. Visitors can spend anywhere from 15 minutes to several full days exploring the exhibits here.

DESCRIPTION

This museum and gallery houses a massive and extremely impressive collection of European and American art, including paintings and sculptures. In addition to the permanent exhibits, many visiting exhibits from around the world can be seen here. Admission is free. Hours: Monday through Saturday, between 10 A.M. and 5 P.M.; and Sundays, between 11 A.M. and 6 P.M. This is a self-guided walking tour.

7. National Mall

Location: Between Constitution and Independence avenues SW, Washington, DC
Phone number: (202) 426-6841
Web site: www.nps.gov/nama/

DESCRIPTION

Not to be confused with the wonderful shopping experiences the DC area offers, the National Mall is a national park that spans about two miles between the U.S. Capitol and the Lincoln Memorial. Within the park, you'll find trees that are more than 200

Located along the perimeter of the National Mall are many different Smithsonian museums as well as several memorials. It's a beautiful, parklike atmosphere where visitors can walk around.

years old. Surrounding the park you'll find several of the Smithsonian museums, the National Archives, and several other popular memorials and tourist attractions. If the weather is nice, this is a beautiful place to walk around. Admission is free.

8. National Zoological Park (aka the National Zoo)

Location: 3001 Connecticut Avenue NW, Washington, DC
Phone number: (202) 633-4800 (recorded information line)
Web site: http://nationalzoo.si.edu

DESCRIPTION

You might think that zoos are for kids, but the National Zoological Park is a fun, educational, and inspiring attraction for people of all ages. This 163-acre park is home to more than 2,000 animals, including the world-famous giant pandas. This zoo is operated by the Smithsonian. It's open daily between 6 A.M. and 6 P.M. (or 8 P.M., depending on the season). Admission is free. By Metrorail, take the red line to Woodley Park–Zoo–Adams Morgan station or the Cleveland Park station. The zoo itself is located a short walk between these two stops.

9. The Pentagon

Location: I-395 South exit at Boundary Channel Drive, Arlington, VA
Phone number: (703) 697-1776
Web site: www.pentagon.afis.osd.mil

DESCRIPTION

According to the government, "Due to heightened security, the Pentagon is no longer offering public or walking tours. Currently, only groups associated with churches, schools, and military and government institutions are allowed to schedule tours. In addition, friends and family of Pentagon employees are allowed to tour the facilities, but the tour must be sponsored by military personnel. For more information, contact the Pentagon Tour Office at (703) 697-1776." The massive building can be seen from outside at anytime.

10. Smithsonian Institution Museums

Location: 17 locations throughout Washington, DC
Phone number: (202) 633-1000
Web site: www.si.edu

DESCRIPTION

In 1826, British scientist James Smithson created a last will and testament that named his nephew as his sole heir. In the event that his nephew died without any heirs of his own, the will stipulated that Smithson's estate be donated to the United States of America, under the name Smithsonian Institution. In 1846, the Smithsonian Institution was formed by President James Polk. Today, the Smithsonian encompasses 17 museums in the Washington, DC area, all of which are open to the public (with free admission). Some of these museums and galleries include the African Art Museum, Air and Space Museum, American Art Museum, American History Museum (which is closed for renovation until Summer 2008), American Indian Museum, the National Zoo, the Natural History Museum, the Portrait Gallery, Postal Museum, and Renwick Gallery. Most of the museums are open daily, between 10 A.M. and 5:30 P.M. It's easy to spend many days exploring all of these museums. If time is limited, start your visit at the Smithsonian Information Center (also known as the Castle), which is located at 1000 Jefferson Drive SW. For a complete list of exhibits for each of the museums, visit www.si.edu/visit/whatsnew. Within each museum, you'll find cafés, snack shops, and gift shops. The easiest and most cost-effective way to reach each of the museums is via the Metrorail or DC Circulator Bus (www.dccirculator.com). Plan on doing a lot of walking as you explore these massive museums. Ten of the museums in the DC area are located in close proximity, from 3rd to 14th Streets, between Constitution Avenue and Independence Avenue.

The U.S. Capitol is open for guided tours and is one of the most recognizable buildings in the DC area.

11. U.S. Capitol

Location: 1st Street, SW and Independence Avenue, Washington, DC
Phone number: (202) 225-6827
Web site: www.aoc.gov

DESCRIPTION

Guided tours are offered on a limited basis, between 9 A.M. and 4:30 P.M., Monday through Saturday. Tickets are distributed, free of charge, on a first-come basis. Visit the ticket kiosk located on the corner of First Street and Maryland Avenue SW. The tour lasts about one hour. Excellent photo opportunities are available outside of the U.S. Capitol building.

12. United States Holocaust Memorial Museum

Location: 100 Raoul Wallenberg Place, SW, Washington, DC
Phone number: (202) 488-0400
Web site: www.ushmm.org

DESCRIPTION

Through artifacts, films, photos, and oral histories, visitors to this very special museum will learn about the Holocaust and World War II. This internationally acclaimed museum offers a very emotional, vivid, and heartbreaking look at the events surrounding the Holocaust. Hours: 10 A.M. to 5:30 P.M. daily. Admission is free; however, tickets can be reserved in advance for a small fee through www.tickets.com (call 800-400-9373).

The Vietnam Veterans Memorial features the names of the soldiers killed in action during the Vietnam War. Two additional life-size statues, including this one, pay tribute to those who fought and died in this war.

13. Vietnam Veterans Memorial

Location: Between Constitution Avenue and Henry Beacon Drive NW, Washington, DC
Phone number: (202) 634-1568
Web site: www.nps.gov/vive/

DESCRIPTION

This memorial honors the names of the 58,209 Americans that went missing or were killed in the Vietnam conflict. The black granite memorial wall and two nearby statues are open 24 hours a day. Admission is free.

14. Washington Monument

Location: The National Mall, Washington, DC
Phone number: (202) 426-6841
Web site: www.nps.gov/wamo

DESCRIPTION

This 555-foot-tall monument, which is shaped like an Egyptian obelisk, can be seen from miles around and is one of the most recognizable sites in the DC area. It weighs 80,000 tons. Free same-day tickets for this attraction are available, starting at 8:30 A.M.

The 555-foot-tall Washington Monument can be seen from around the DC area.

daily, from the 15th Street kiosk. The monument is open daily, between 9 A.M. and 5 P.M. For advance ticket reservations, call (800) 967-2283 (a small fee applies).

15. The White House

Location: 1600 Pennsylvania Avenue NW, Washington, DC
Phone number: (202) 208-1631
Web site: www.nps.gov/whho

DESCRIPTION

According to the government, "Tours of the White House have been expanded from school, youth, military and veterans' groups to include any groups of ten. Groups of ten should submit a request through their member of Congress at least one month and up to six months in advance. The tours are self-guided and will run from 7:30 A.M. to 11:30 A.M., Tuesday through Saturday. For more information, call the White House Visitors Center at (202) 456-7041 or visit www.whitehouse.gov." The White House Visitor Center is located at 1450 Pennsylvania Avenue NW, and is open daily between 7:30 A.M. and 4 P.M. Excellent photo opportunities are available from outside the White House grounds.

TIP

In April 2007, Bodies: The Exhibition opened at 1011 Wilson Boulevard in Arlington, Virginia. This innovative exhibit showcases real human bodies in an extremely unusual, interesting, and thought-provoking way. For details, visit www.bodiestickets.com.

The White House is home to the president of the United States and is one of the most famous buildings in the world. Tours are available, but on a limited basis, and they must be scheduled well in advance.

TIP

The Washington National Cathedral (3101 Wisconsin Avenue NW, Washington, DC, 202-426-6841, www.nationalcathedral.org) is another extremely popular attraction. Daily worship services and guided tours are offered. This Gothic cathedral features beautiful stained-glass windows, priceless sculptures and artwork, and is an architectural masterpiece unto itself.

THE HOTEL CONCIERGES OFFER THEIR TOP PICKS FOR TOURISTS

If your leisure time in DC is limited, but you want to experience at least some of the museums, attractions, memorials, and entertainment opportunities available, and you need help deciding how to allocate your time, your hotel's concierge can offer some advice on what's worth seeing, based on your interests and schedule.

Daniel Klibanoff, concierge at the Mandarin Oriental stated, "I love the monuments. They are a large part of what sets this city apart from everywhere else. Primarily, you should see the Jefferson Memorial and its view of the Tidal Basin. It has one of the only unobstructed views of the White House. The Lincoln Memorial has an amazing view of the World War I memorial, Washington Monument, and Capitol building. I also love the National Archives, with the Declaration of Independence, Bill of Rights, and the Constitution. The Smithsonian Air and Space Museum and Smithsonian Natural History Museum are the most popular museums in town. If you are an art fan, the National Gallery of Art offers a What to See in an Hour tour."

To see and experience the most in DC within a limited time, Javier Loureiro, Chief Concierge at the Four Seasons added, "I would recommend you hire a private guide and arrange for transportation to take you to the major sights. The guides that we use are all private. Some only work for us at the Four Seasons. All are historians and published authors who can bring a wealth of knowledge and insight to a tour that is not otherwise possible. The National Mall area, including all of the surrounding monuments, memorials, and public buildings, can be seen in half a day. Our guides will give guests a tour in five hours that would otherwise take a week's worth of travel around town."

Michael McCleary, the assistant chief concierge at the Willard InterContinental stated that he advises to guests who are under tight time constraints to narrow their focus to a specific area of interest, such as the monuments or art museums. "One possibility is to take a general tour of the city that lasts about three hours. This would provide a general overview. One of my areas of focus would be on the major monuments and memorials, such as the Lincoln, Jefferson, FDR, Vietnam, Korean, and World War II memorials, and then a visit to one museum, such as the Smithsonian Air and Space Museum or the International Spy Museum. I'd also make time to quickly visit the National Archives and arrange to walk by the White House."

SHOPPING OPPORTUNITIES FOR BUSY BUSINESS TRAVELERS

The Washington, DC area is home to many one-of-a-kind stores plus dozens of department stores and several upscale malls. No matter what you're looking for, you'll be able to find it; the shopping offered in the DC area caters to all tastes and budgets.

The following is a summary of the best shopping experiences that a true shopoholic won't want to miss:

America!

Address: 7904 Hill Park Court, Lorton, VA

Phone number: (800) 927-8277

Web site: www.americastore.com

DESCRIPTION

This is one of the larger souvenir shops that offer a large selection of United States of America, patriotic, Air Force One, White House, military, and Washington, DC, merchandise, clothing, and gifts. A smaller version of this shop can be found at Dulles Airport.

Brooks Brothers

Address: 1201 Connecticut Avenue NW, Washington, DC

Phone number: (202) 659-4650

Web site: www.brooksbrothers.com

DESCRIPTION

If you need to purchase a casual or formal business outfit while in the DC area, plus have it tailored and ready to wear quickly, one of your best options is to shop at Brooks Brothers. It's open Monday through Saturday, between 9:30 A.M. and 7 P.M., and Sunday, between noon and 5 P.M.

Burberry

Address: 1155 Connecticut Avenue NW, Washington, DC

Phone number: (202) 463-3000

Web site: www.burberry.com

DESCRIPTION

This upscale clothing store offers fashionable yet traditional business suits and other attire for men and women. On-site tailoring is available.

Fashion Center at Pentagon City

Address: Intersection of South Hayes Street and Army Navy Drive, Arlington, VA

Phone number: (703) 415-2400

DESCRIPTION

This shopping mall offers dozens of retail shops, several department stores (including Nordstrom and Macy's), and a handful of restaurants.

Mazza Gallerie

Address: 5300 Wisconsin Avenue NW, Washington, DC

Phone number: (202) 966-6114

Web site: www.mazzagallerie.com

DESCRIPTION

This upscale mall features Neiman Marcus, Saks Fifth Avenue for Men, and Filene's Basement as its anchor stores. Hours of operation are Monday through Friday, from 10 A.M. to 8 P.M.; Saturday, from 10 to 7 P.M.; and Sunday, from noon to 6 P.M.

The Shops at Georgetown Park

Address: 3222 M Street NW, Washington, DC

Phone number: (202) 298-5577

Web site: www.shopsatgeorgetownpark.com

DESCRIPTION

This midpriced, four-level shopping mall is located in the heart of Georgetown and offers more than 100 stores, including a variety of clothing shops for men and women. In addition to a food court, you'll also find a variety of midpriced dining options here, such as Fire and Ice and Benihana. Mall hours are Monday through Saturday, 10 A.M. to 9 P.M., and Sunday, noon to 6 P.M.

TIP

If you're looking for the latest designer business and casual men's fashions, be sure to visit the Saks Fifth Avenue Men's Store for a large selection. It's located at the Mazza Gallerie (202-363-2059).

Smithsonian Store

Address: Various locations throughout Washington, DC

Phone number: (202) 275-1231

Web site: www.smithsonian.org

DESCRIPTION

Each of the Smithsonian museums in the DC area contains one or more gift shops that offer unique and often collectible merchandise and gifts.

Tysons Corner Center

Address: 1961 Chain Bridge Road, McLean, VA

Phone number: (703) 847-7300

Web site: www.shoptysons.com

DESCRIPTION

This is the DC area's largest shopping destination with more than 300 stores and restaurants. Here you'll find everything from Nordstrom, Bloomingdale's, Lord and Taylor, and L. L. Bean, to Banana Republic, Ann Taylor, Coach, Kenneth Cole, and Talbot's. There's also an Apple Store for your Mac computing needs. For fine-dining experiences, the Capital Grille is among the restaurants at this upscale mall. Store hours are Monday through Saturday, from 10 A.M. to 9:30 P.M., and Sunday, from 11 A.M. to 6 P.M. The Tysons Galleria Mall is also located nearby at 2001 International Drive, in McLean, Virginia (703-827-7700). It contains more than 100 shops and restaurants, including Neiman Marcus, Macy's, and Saks Fifth Avenue.

Union Station

Address: 50 Massachusetts Avenue, NE, Washington, DC

Phone number: (202) 289-1908

Web site: www.unionstationdc.com

DESCRIPTION

This mall features more than 130 shops on three levels, plus a variety of midpriced and fine-dining establishments. The easiest way to reach this shopping center (located within the train station) is to take the Metrorail's red line to Union Station.

TIP
Need Washington, DC, souvenirs and gifts to bring home for friends and family? The White House Gift Shop (202-662-7280, www.whitehousegiftshop.com), located at 529 14th Street NW (in the National Press Building),

Union Station serves as DC's Amtrak station and a Metro station, and it's also a lovely indoor shopping mall that features 130 shops and restaurants.

offers a wide range of gifts and souvenirs. Hours: Monday through Friday, 10 A.M. to 6 P.M., and Saturday, 10 A.M. to 5 P.M.

MEDIA LISTINGS FOR WASHINGTON, DC

To stay up-to-date on the latest news events and local happenings, become familiar with the local media in the DC area.

Major Newspapers and Regional Magazines

The following resources are available at newsstands throughout the city.

- *Washington Post* (www.washingtonpost.com). Daily newspaper. This is one of the most respected daily newspapers in America. It covers news, current events, politics, entertainment, sports, and all of the topics you'd expect from a major daily newspaper with a circulation over five million.
- *Washington Times* (www.washingtontimes.com). Daily newspaper. The Times is another highly regarded newspaper covering news, current events, politics, and a wide range of other topics.
- *Washington City Paper* (www.washingtoncitypaper.com). Weekly lifestyle and news-oriented newspaper.

- *Washington Life* (www.washingtonlife.com). Full-color lifestyle and news-oriented monthly magazine.
- *Washingtonian* (www.washingtonian.com). Full-color lifestyle and news-oriented monthly magazine.
- *Wall Street Journal* (www.wsj.com). A national daily newspaper covering Wall Street and finance. Published Monday through Friday.
- *USA Today* (www.usatoday.com). A nationwide, full-color newspaper covering news, travel, money, sports, lifestyles, national weather, and technology. Published Monday through Friday.

TIP

Channel numbers will vary based on the cable programming service offered at your hotel. Many hotels offer a full lineup of cable TV channels, including CNN, Showtime, HBO, the Weather Channel, and ESPN.

Local TV Stations

- WJLA Channel 7 (ABC affiliate)
- WUSA Channel 9 (CBS affiliate)
- WDCW Channel 50 (CW affiliate)
- WTTG Channel 5 (Fox affiliate)
- WRC Channel 4 (NBC affiliate)
- WETA Channel 26 (PBS affiliate)

TIP

For DC-area television listings, visit the *TV Guide* web site at www.tvguide.com/Listings/default.aspx.

Radio Stations

In addition to dozens of local news/talk, sports, and music AM and FM radio stations in Washington, DC, many stations from nearby Maryland and Virginia cities can also be heard in the DC area. Satellite radio (XM and Sirius) offer hundreds of stations that can be heard coast to coast. The following are some of the popular local AM and FM radio stations:

- Adult contemporary music—WASH 97.1 FM
- Hip-hop music—WKYS 93.9 FM

- News radio—WTOP 1500 AM
- News/talk radio—WMAL 630 AM
- News/talk radio—WOL 1450 AM
- Public radio—WAMU 88.5 FM
- Rock music—WWDC 101.1 FM
- Sports radio—WWRC 1260 AM
- Top 40 music—WIHT 99.5 FM
- Urban contemporary music—WHUR 96.3 FM

TIP
For a more complete radio station listing, visit: www.ontheradio.net/metro/Washington_DC.aspx.

SECTION VII

© Jim Lop

ATTENDING A BUSINESS MEETING OR CONVENTION

Every year, Washington, DC hosts many trade shows, conventions, conferences, symposiums, expos, and other large gatherings of business professionals from countless industries and from around the world. While small meetings are typically held at the various Washington, DC-area hotels (many of which offer function, banquet, and meeting rooms), and within rentable meeting space at some of the city's top tourist attractions and historical sites, the majority of the large conventions and trade shows are held at the Washington Convention Center.

THE WASHINGTON CONVENTION CENTER

Address: 801 Mount Vernon Place NW, Washington, DC, 20001
Main phone number: (202) 249-3000
Events hotline: (202) 249-3400
Web site: www.dcconvention.com

The original Washington Convention Center was built in 1874, about two blocks from the site of the current convention center, which is a state-of-the-art convention, banquet, and meeting facility that opened in 2003. The convention center features 2.3 million square feet of space (including 700,000 square feet of exhibit space with ceilings at least 30 feet high). The convention center covers six city blocks and is the largest building in downtown DC.

CITY FACTOID
From end to end, the Washington Convention Center is the length of two Washington Monuments and as big as six football fields.

The Washington Convention Center.

TIP
For a comprehensive list of events scheduled to be held at the convention center, visit www.dcconvention.com/events/default.asp.

The Washington Convention Center also houses a 52,000-square-foot ballroom (one of the largest on the entire East Coast), along with 125,000 square feet of flexible meeting space (which can be divided up into 66 separate meeting rooms). From a technological standpoint, the convention center offers both wired and wireless high-speed internet connectivity throughout the entire complex. More than $4 million worth of artwork, including suspended sculptures, oil paintings, and photographs, is on display throughout the convention center.

TIP
Situated within the Washington Convention Center is an Enterprise rental car location where cars can be picked up or dropped off. Call (202) 289-4707 to reserve a vehicle.

Directions to the Convention Center

The Washington Convention Center is conveniently located in downtown Washington, DC and is easily accessible by car, taxi, limousine, Metrorail, Metrobus, and the DC Circulator Bus. The convention center is approximately six miles from Regan National Airport, 27 miles from Dulles International Airport, and 30 miles from BWI Airport.

DRIVING DIRECTIONS FROM REAGAN NATIONAL AIRPORT

Take the George Washington (GW) Parkway North to I-395 and Washington, DC. Follow the signs to the 14th Street Bridge. Cross the bridge to Independence Avenue. Turn right onto Independence Avenue and proceed for two blocks, until you reach 7th Street. Turn left on 7th Street and proceed 12 blocks to Mount Vernon Place. Turn left onto Mount Vernon Place and the convention center will be on your right.

TIP

To take the Metrorail from Reagan National Airport directly to the convention center, proceed to the Metro station located outside of the main terminal at the airport and take the yellow line train (marked "Mt. Vernon Square/Convention Center"). Exit the train at the Mt. Vernon Square Convention Center stop. When you exit the Metro station, the convention center will be in front of you. Allow approximately 20 minutes for the trip.

DRIVING DIRECTIONS FROM DULLES INTERNATIONAL AIRPORT

Take I-66 East to Washington, DC. Exit at Route 50/Constitution Avenue. Proceed on Constitution Avenue until you reach 7th Street. Turn left on 7th Street and proceed nine blocks. Turn left on Mount Vernon Place. The convention center will be on your right.

TIP

To take the Metrorail from Dulles International Airport, pick up the Washington Flyer Shuttle Bus outside of baggage claim at the airport. Take this shuttle to the West Falls Church Metro station. At the Metrorail station, take the orange line train marked "New Carrollton." Exit the train at the L'Enfant Metro station and transfer to the yellow line train (on the upper level). The train will be marked "Mt. Vernon Square/Convention Center." Exit the yellow line train at the Mt. Vernon Square/Convention Center stop. The convention center will be located directly in front of you. Allow between 30 and 45 minutes for the trip.

DRIVING DIRECTIONS FROM BWI AIRPORT

Upon exiting the airport, take I-195 West to MD-295 South, via Exit 2B (toward Washington, DC). Continue west on US-50, which becomes New York Avenue. Continue on New York Avenue, which becomes Mt. Vernon Place. The convention center will be on your right.

TIP

To take the MARC (Maryland Commuter Train) and the Metrorail from the airport to the convention center, pick up the free BWI Rail station shuttle bus at the airport, which will take you to the BWI Rail station. Take the

MARC train from BWI Rail station to Washington's Union Square station. This station is located about 10 blocks east of the convention center. You can walk, take a taxi, or take the Metrorail to the convention center. Via Metrorail, take the red line train, marked "Shady Grove," from the Union station Metro stop to the Gallery Place station. Transfer at Gallery Place Station to the yellow line, marked "Mt. Vernon Square/Convention Center." Exit the yellow line train at the Mt. Vernon Square/Convention Center stop. The convention center will be located directly in front of you. Allow approximately one hour for this trip.

Nearby Public Parking Lots

Within a three-block radius of the convention center, there are more than 2,000 parking spaces available (including over 100 metered parking spaces on public streets). Hours of operation and parking fees vary greatly. Plan on spending between $20 and $30 per day to park your vehicle in a garage or lot, unless you find a metered parking space along a public street.

As you approach the convention center by car, look for signs for the following parking lots:

- On Massachusetts Avenue: PMI Parking (two locations) and Colonial Parking
- On New York Avenue: Park America, City Center Parking, Georgetown Parking, and Marc Parc
- Mount Vernon Square: Interpark (at the Renaissance Hotel)

Navigating around the Convention Center

Most trade shows, conventions, and meetings held at the Washington Convention Center do not utilize the entire facility. Refer to the program or trade show guide created for your specific event to more easily navigate around the appropriate areas of the convention center, keeping in mind that it's common for multiple, unrelated events, trade shows, and conventions to be held at the facility simultaneously.

WARNING
This convention center is large, so be prepared to do a significant amount of walking when you attend a trade show or convention here. Be sure to wear comfortable shoes.

The following are overall floor plans and maps of the entire Washington Convention Center complex.

MAP OF THE CONVENTION CENTER (LOWER LEVEL)

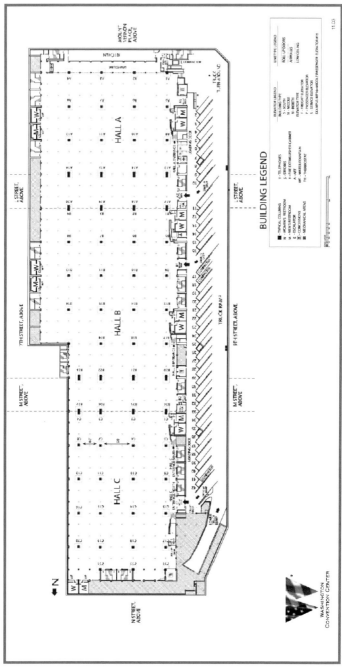

Map courtesy of the Washington Convention Center Authority.

SECTION VII / ATTENDING A BUSINESS MEETING OR CONVENTION ·· 169

MAP OF THE CONVENTION CENTER (CONCOURSE LEVEL)

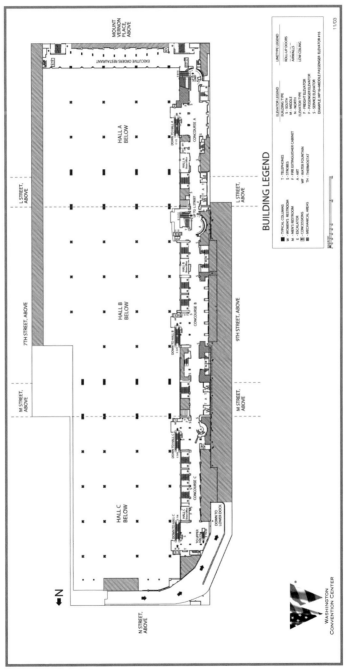

Map courtesy of the Washington Convention Center Authority.

170 · SECTION VII / ATTENDING A BUSINESS MEETING OR CONVENTION

MAP OF THE CONVENTION CENTER (STREET LEVEL)

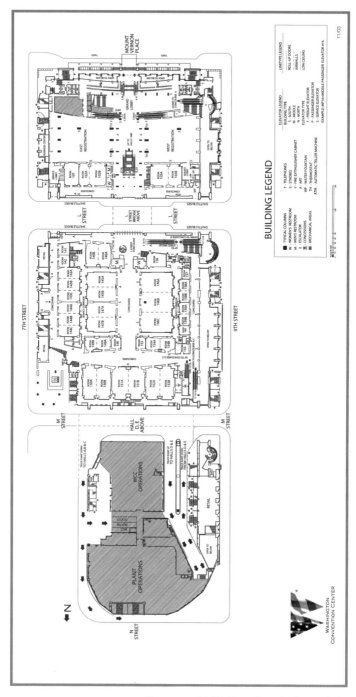

Map courtesy of the Washington Convention Center Authority.

MAP OF THE CONVENTION CENTER (LEVEL TWO)

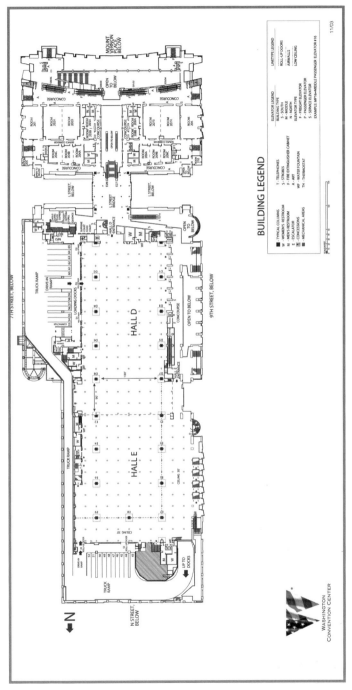

Map courtesy of the Washington Convention Center Authority.

172 ·· SECTION VII / ATTENDING A BUSINESS MEETING OR CONVENTION

MAP OF THE CONVENTION CENTER (LEVEL THREE)

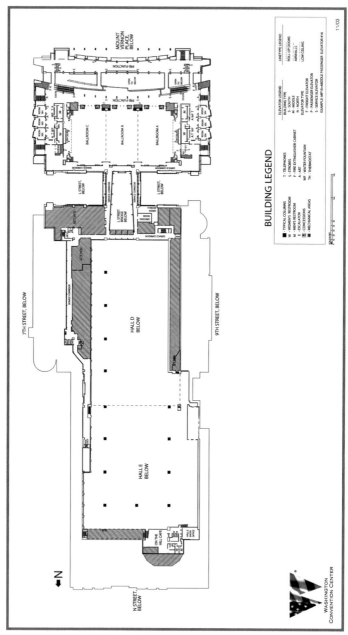

Map courtesy of the Washington Convention Center Authority.

Dining Options at and Near the Convention Center

The Washington Convention Center offers a variety of fast-food and casual dining options on-property, including Starbucks Coffee, Wolfgang Puck, Quizno's, Tosca Restaurant, Phillips Seafood, and

Nam Viet. In addition to these offerings, within walking distance from the convention center, you'll find more than 100 dining options—everything from inexpensive fast food (like Subway, which is located across the street) to gourmet fine-dining experiences.

For additional restaurant recommendations, see Section V, "Where to Dine in Washington, DC," or contact your hotel's concierge.

The following is a sampling of nearby restaurants, listed in alphabetical order. The majority of these restaurants are open for lunch and dinner. A few serve breakfast as well.

The price ranges for the following restaurants are categorized as follows:

$ = Under $20 per person
$$ = $20 to $30 per person
$$$ = Over $30 per person

CONVENTION CENTER DINING OPTIONS

A.V. Ristorante Italiano	607 New York Avenue
Food type: Italian	(202) 737-3133
Price range: $$/$$$	
Bistro d'OC	518 10th Avenue NW
Food type: French	(202) 393-5444
Price range: $$/$$$	
Breakwells Coffee & Tea	900 M Street NW
Food type: American	(202) 289-4601
Price range: $	
Butterfield 9	600 14th Street NW
Food type: American	(202) 289-8810
Price range: $$$	
California Tortilla	728 7th Street NW
Food type: Mexican	(202) 638-2233
Price range: $	
Capital Grille	601 Pennsylvania Avenue NW
Food type: Steakhouse	(202) 737-6200
Price range: $$$	
Capital Q	707 H Street NW
Food type: Texas style BBQ	(202) 347-8396
Price range: $	
Caucus Room	401 9th Street NW
Food type: Steakhouse	(202) 393-1300
Price range: $$/$$$	
Charlie Palmer's Steakhouse	101 Constitution Avenue NW
Food type: Steakhouse	(202) 547-8100
Price range: $$/$$$	

CONVENTION CENTER DINING OPTIONS

DC Coast	1401 K Street NW
Food type: Seafood	(202) 216-5988
Price range: $$/$$$	
ESPN Zone	555 12th Street NW
Food type: Sports Bar/Grill	(202) 783-3776
Price range: $$	
Hard Rock Café	999 E Street NW
Food type: American	(202) 737-7625
Price range: $$	
Kanlaya	740 6th Street NW
Food type: Thai	(202) 393-0088
Price range: $/$$	
Legal Sea Foods	704 7th Street NW
Food type: Seafood	(202) 347-0007
Price range: $$/$$$	
McCormick & Schmick's	1625 K Street NW
Food type: Seafood	(202) 861-2233
Price range: $$$	
Ruth's Chris Steakhouse	724 9th Street NW
Food type: Steakhouse	(202) 393-4488
Price range: $$$	
701 Restaurant	701 Pennsylvania Avenue
Food type: American	(202) 393-0701
Price range: $$/$$$	
Sushi AOI	1100 New York Avenue NW
Food type: Sushi/Japanese	(202) 408-7770
Price range: $/$$	
Vegetate	1414 9th Street NW
Food type: Vegetarian/Vegan	(202) 232-4585
Price range: $/$$	
Waffle Shop	522 10th Street NW
Food type: Breakfast (served all day)	(202) 638-3430
Price range: $	

Nearby Hotel Accommodations (within Walking Distance)

Listed in alphabetical order, the following ten hotels are located within a half mile from the convention center (within easy walking distance). Because of their close proximity to the convention center, when large events and trade shows are being held, these hotels tend to book up the fastest, so make your reservations early.

Reservations for any of these hotels can be booked by contacting the hotel directly or by visiting the www.washington.org web site. Discounted rates for these hotels may also be available from the travel-related web sites listed in Section I, "Welcome to Washington, DC," or from Hotels.com (www.hotels.com).

TIP
Additional hotel options, including the *Business Traveler* Top 15 Business-Friendly Hotels" list, can be found in Section III, "Where to Stay While in Washington, DC."

HOTELS WITHIN WALKING DISTANCE OF THE CONVENTION CENTER	
Comfort Inn Convention Center (202) 682-5300	1201 13th Street NW www.choicehotels.com
Embassy Suites Convention Center (202) 739-2001	900 10th Street NW http://embassysuites.hilton.com/en/es/ hotels/index.jhtml?ctyhocn=WASCCES
Four Points Downtown by Sheraton (202) 349-2205	1201 K Street NW www.starwoodhotels.com
Grand Hyatt Washington (202) 582-1234	1000 H Street NW www.hyatt.com
Hampton Inn DC Convention Center (202) 842-2500	901 6th Street NW www.hamptoninn.com
Henley Park Hotel (202) 638-6638	926 Massachusetts Avenue NW www.henleypark.com
Marriott at Metro Center (202) 737-2200	775 12th Street NW www.radisson.com
Morrison-Clark Inn (202) 898-1200	1015 L Street NW www.morrisonclark.com
Red Roof Inn Downtown DC (202) 289-5959	500 H Street NW www.redroof.com
Renaissance Washington, DC Hotel (202) 898-9000	999 9th Street NW www.washingtondchotels.com

Services and Amenities at Washington Convention Center

Whether you're attending a trade show or convention or exhibiting at one, you may want to utilize the following services and amenities located within the convention center.

- *Coat and luggage check.* Several coat and luggage check locations are available within the convention center complex. Follow signs for the appropriate location being utilized by the event you're attending. You'll have to pay a fee to store your coat and/or luggage.
- *Information desk.* Several information counters are available throughout the convention center.

- *FedEx Kinko's printing center.* There is a FedEx Kinko's Printing and Shipping Center located across the street from the convention center (800 K Street, 202-682-0349). Hours of operation are 6 A.M. to 11 P.M. daily. FedEx packages slated for overnight delivery must be dropped off no later than 6:30 P.M. (4 P.M. on Saturday). Packages slated for FedEx Ground service must be dropped off by 6 P.M. (Monday through Friday). This location offers a full complement of office, printing, and business services, including self-service and full-service black-and-white and color copying, along with printing, binding, and finishing services, plus computer rentals, sign and graphic printing, packing, and FedEx Express and FedEx Ground shipping services.
- *Business center.* A fully equipped business center is available to exhibitors and attendees within the convention center complex. Call (202) 249-3969. Hours of operation vary based on the current events being hosted at the convention center.
- *Restrooms.* There are 68 public restrooms located throughout the convention center complex.
- *Printer.* Miller Copying Service is a full-service printer located across the street from the Washington Convention Center (next to Subway and Happy Cleaners). There's also a FedEx Kinko's location nearby.

Tips for Attending a Convention or Trade Show

The following tips will help you maximize your time and efficiency when attending a trade show or convention:

- *Preregister for the event you'll be attending.* This will allow you to avoid long registration lines at the start of the event. Don't forget to bring your registration papers and/or ID badge to the event. Make your hotel accommodations early to get the best rates and ensure you're able to get the room configuration and hotel you desire.
- *Preschedule your meetings/appointments.* Use the Trade Show Meeting Planner (found in the Appendix of this guide). For each meeting, write down the scheduled time and date, the location (booth or meeting room number), the name of the person you're meeting, his or her company, and the purpose of the meeting. Allow ample time (at least five to ten minutes) between meetings to walk between

exhibit booths or meeting rooms. You can obtain an advance listing of trade show exhibitors by visiting the web site operated by the company coordinating or hosting your event.
- *Bring a durable backpack, shoulder bag, or wheeled suitcase* to store and carry around brochures, catalogs, swag, freebees, and trade show materials you collect.
- *Wear comfortable shoes* (be prepared for a lot of walking and standing around), plus a comfortable, business casual outfit that's appropriate for the event you'll be attending.
- *Bring a stack of business cards and/or company literature to distribute at the event.*
- *Bring a pad and pen to take notes during seminars and meetings.*
- *Utilize the coat check at the convention center to store heavy items* that you don't want to lug around on the convention show floor.

TIP
It's often easier to ship home the catalogs, brochures, press kits, freebees, and other materials you collect at a trade show than it is to pack them in your luggage. If these items cause your suitcase to weigh more than 50 pounds, you'll need to pay an overweight-bag charge to your airline when you check in at the airport.

Exhibitor Services at the Washington Convention Center

If you're exhibiting or hosting a meeting at the convention center, the following are services that will be useful. For additional information, call the Washington Convention Center's management office at (202) 249-3213. The majority of these trade show exhibitor services must be preordered.

- *Audio/video equipment, production, and lighting.* To coordinate all of your audio/visual equipment rental, set-up, and production needs, call Projection Presentation Technologies at (202) 249-3700.
- *Internet and telephone service.* To order internet and/or telephone service at your booth or within your meeting room, contact Smart City at (202) 249-3800.
- *Electrical and plumbing service.* Hi-Tech Electric is the convention center's exclusive electrical and plumbing contractor.

To coordinate these services for your trade show booth or meeting room, call (510) 293-6151.

- *Food and beverages (catering).* Whether you're in need of in-booth catering or plan to host a large sit-down meal within a meeting room or ballroom, you can coordinate catering with Centerplate/NBSE, which can be reached at (202) 249-3500 (www.ezplanit.com). A wide range of menu options are available.
- *Meeting room rental.* To inquire about private meeting room rentals, rates, and availability at the convention center, call (202) 249-3402.
- *Press release electronic distribution services*
  - PR Newswire. (888) 776-0942, www.prenewswire.com
  - Businesswire.com. (800) 221-2462, www.businesswire.com

TIP

For additional business services of interest to trade show exhibitors and attendees alike, see Section VIII, "Business Services."

SECTION VIII

© Feng Yu

BUSINESS
SERVICES

If you're hosting or attending business meetings; participating in a convention, trade show seminar, or workshop; or visiting Washington, DC to entertain important clients, you may need various business services during your trip. Many of the larger hotels offer nicely equipped business centers capable of handling the majority of your business-related needs, including:

- Black-and-white or color copies
- Cell phone rentals
- Computer and printer rentals
- Fax machines
- High-speed internet access
- Meeting room rentals (with catering)
- Messenger services
- Packing and shipping of packages (via FedEx, UPS, or DHL)
- Secretarial, typing, and translation services

You typically pay a premium to utilize the services offered through a hotel at these business centers; however, they do provide convenience. This section focuses on your needs beyond what the business centers within the hotels typically offer.

TIP

Your hotel's concierge or business center can help you track down and utilize a wide range of business-related services that are not offered inhouse. Also see Section VII, "Attending a Business Meeting or Convention."

Keep in mind, the companies and services listed here are for reference or referral purposes only, and are only a sampling of the many companies offering similar products and services within the nation's capital. Inclusion in this section does not constitute an endorsement. Additional referrals can be obtained from your hotel's concierge or the local Yellow Pages. All addresses are in Washington, DC, unless otherwise noted.

AUDIOVISUAL EQUIPMENT RENTALS

For your trade show or meeting audiovisual needs, contact your hotel, the Washington Convention Center, or any of the following companies.

WASHINGTON, DC AUDIOVISUAL EQUIPMENT RENTALS	
Access Audio Visuals, Inc.	(703) 535-5705
435 Calvert Avenue, Alexandria, VA	www.accessaav.com
American Audio/Video	(703) 573-6910
2862 Hartland Road, Falls Church, VA	www.aavevents.com

AUDIOVISUAL EQUIPMENT RENTALS IN WASHINGTON, DC

AudioLink Services	(202) 887-8060
1001 Connecticut Avenue NW	www.audiolinks.com
EPRAV	(800) 264-0440
4201 Wilson Boulevard, Arlington, VA	www.eprav.com
Immediate Connections, Inc.	(202) 387-7877
1623 Connecticut Avenue NW	
Meridian Hill Productions, LLC	(240) 271-3117
1650 Harvard Street NW	www.meridianhillpro.com

BALLOONS

The following companies can provide balloons for events, parties, or trade shows, or have balloons sent anywhere as a gift suitable for almost any occasion.

WASHINGTON, DC BALLOON SERVICE

A-1 Ballroom Balloons	202-737-3311
Air Express-Balloons	703-413-7171
American Balloon Company	(703) 751-3556
	www.allballoons.com
Balloon Bouquets Nationwide	202-785-1290
	http://balloonbouquets.com
Balloonsanywhere.com	(202) 785-1131
	www.balloonsanywhere.com
Magical & Memorable Balloons	(301) 490-8935
	www.magicalmemorableballoons.com

TIP

A unique and fun alternative to sending flowers or balloons as a gift is to send a fruit creation by Edible Arrangements (202-955-5660, 1740 M Street NW, Washington, DC). These lavish arrangements look like colorful floral bouquets, but they're made from edible fruits and vegetables. They can be delivered or shipped anywhere in the country. These bouquets also make a great centerpiece for catered events and parties.

BANKING AND FINANCIAL SERVICES

There are ATMs located in most of the hotels and airports and within the Washington Convention Center. You'll also find full-service banks and ATMs throughout Washington, DC. The hotel where you're staying probably also offers check-cashing services.

WARNING
The ATMs located in the hotels and airports often charge a hefty fee for withdrawals (up to $3 or more). You can save money by utilizing an ATM owned and operated by your own bank or one that's affiliated with your bank's ATM network.

BOXES AND SHIPPING SUPPLIES

Shipping boxes and related supplies are available at all FedEx Kinko's locations, as well as from the following companies.

WASHINGTON, DC BOX AND SHIPPING SUPPLY COMPANIES	
The Container Store 4500 Wisconsin Avenue NW	(202) 478-4000
Extra Space Storage	(800) 343-5818
Parcel Plus 3509 Connecticut Avenue NW	(202) 244-6669
Thrifty Paper Boxes, Inc. 2508 24th Street NW	(202) 529-7474
U-Haul 1750 Bladensburg Road NW	(202) 529-4676
U Haul 26 K Street NE	(202) 289-5480
U Haul 1501 S Capitol Street SW	(202) 554-2640
The UPS Store 1419 37th Street NW	(202) 687-7438

BUS CHARTERS

For small groups or large ones, when your transportation needs exceed the capacity of a stretch limousine, contact these companies to charter anything from a minivan to a full-size, luxury bus.

WASHINGTON, DC BUS CHARTER COMPANIES	
All About Town www.allabouttown.com	(301) 856-5556

WASHINGTON, DC BUS CHARTER COMPANIES

Boston Coach www.bostoncoach.com	(703) 836-2601
Callaway Transportation www.callawaytransportation.com	(410) 795-8300
Capital City Tours www.capitaltours.com	(301) 336-9400
Fleet Transportation www.fleettransportation.com	(866) 933-2600
National Transportation www.national-transportation.com	(202) 232-1000
1-800-Book-A-Limo www.bookalimo.com	(800) 226-5254
Transpro Services www.transprolimo.com	(301) 270-0406

CAR RENTALS

See Section IV, "Getting Around Town," for a listing of rental car companies in the DC area.

CATERERS

While all of the hotels, banquet halls, and meeting room facilities, as well as the Washington Convention Center, offer inhouse catering services, here are some alternatives. The following is a selection of the DC area's many independent catering companies, capable of handling functions of any size.

WASHINGTON, DC CATERING COMPANIES

Box Lunch Specialists	(202) 387-1072
Catering by Windows	(703) 519-3500
CenterPlate www.ezplanit.com	(202) 249-3000
Dish Caterers www.dishcaterers.com	(202) 863-1213
Federal City Caterers www.federalcity.com	(202) 408-9700
Occasions Caterers www.occasionscaterers.com	(202) 546-7400
3 Citron Caterers www.3citron.com	(202) 342-3400

CELL PHONE SERVICES AND ACCESSORIES

Authorized service agents for AT&T/Cingular, Sprint/Nextel, T-Mobile, and Verizon Wireless are located throughout Washington, DC. Cellular phone accessories (chargers, headsets, etc.) can also be purchased at Radio Shack stores and from hundreds of other consumer electronics dealers citywide.

WASHINGTON, DC CELL PHONE SERVICES	
AT&T Wireless/Cingular	(800) 888-7600 (AT&T),
www.cingular.com	(800) 331-0500 (Cingular)
Sprint/Nextel	(866) 438-1371
www.sprint.com	
T-Mobile	(800) 866-2453
www.t-mobile.com	
Verizon Wireless	(800) 922-0204
www.verizonwireless.com1	

MONEY SAVER

If you need a temporary cell phone while in DC, you can rent one for a high per-day fee (plus high airtime charges, up to $2 per minute), or you could purchase a prepaid cellular phone for under $50, along with prepaid airtime for as low as $.12 per minute. Companies like Tracefone (800-867-7183, www.tracefone.com), Virgin Mobile (888-322-1122, www.virginmobileusa.com), AT&T/Cingular, and T-Mobile all offer inexpensive but full-featured prepaid phones and service plans with no long-term contracts. This is an ideal option for international travelers visiting DC, anyone who needs a replacement phone, or anyone who quickly needs to establish temporary cell phone service.

COMPUTER RENTALS, REPAIRS, AND TECHNICAL SUPPORT

If your computer breaks and needs emergency repair, if your system crashes and you lose important data, you require technical support, or you need to rent a computer or peripherals while in the DC area, contact one of the following companies.

WASHINGTON, DC COMPUTER SERVICES	
A Mac Heaven	(202) 408-9559
N/A	Apple Mac computer repairs and support

WASHINGTON, DC COMPUTER SERVICES

Apple Store (Arlington, VA) www.apple.com/retail	(703) 418-1093 Mac sales, repairs, and support
Apple Store (Bethesda, MD) www.apple.com/retail	(301) 299-0723 Mac sales, repairs, and support
Apple Store (Bethesda, MD) www.apple.com/retail	(301) 951-6100 Mac sales, repairs, and support
Apple Store (Richmond, VA) www.apple.com/retail	(804) 360-3118 Mac sales, repairs, and support
Best Buy Geek Squad www.geeksquad.com	(800) 433-5778 24-hour repairs, upgrades, data recovery, and tech support
Computer Geeks www.geeksdc.com	(202) 686-9097 PC or Mac repairs and tech support
Cyber Laptops.com www.cyberlaptops.com	(202) 462-7195 Laptop computer repairs, data recovery, screen replacements, virus removal, hard drive replacement and memory upgrades
Dataprise www.dataprise.com	(888) 414-8111 Network support
ESS Data Recovery N/A	(800) 913-1591 Data recovery
Flat Rate Computer Solutions http://flatratecomputersolutions.com	(703) 453-9181 Computer repairs, data recovery, and networking support
Geeks On-Time www.geeksontime.com/ Washington_dc_computer_service.html	(800) 433-5766 Computer repairs, data recovery, and tech support
Laptop Rescue www.laptoprescue.com	(800) 574-7642 Laptop computer repairs and data recovery
MyTeks www.myteks.com	(866) 544-4132 Computer repair and data recovery
Techs in a Sec N/A	(866) 692-TECH PC or Mac repairs, data recovery, and networking support, and tech support

TIP

For major laptop computer repairs, for example, determine if your unit is still covered under the manufacturer's warranty. If so, you can typically ship it back to the manufacturer, have it repaired, and have it returned to you via overnight courier. The process takes just a few days, especially if you pay extra for expedited services. If the unit is not covered under warranty, the manufacturer will typically charge a fortune to conduct diagnostic and repair work.

CREDIT CARD COMPANIES

Listed below are the 24-hour emergency phone numbers for the major credit card companies. For customer service issues pertaining specifically to your account, call the phone number displayed on the back of your credit card or on your monthly statement. Use the phone numbers below to report a lost or stolen credit card, request an emergency replacement card, obtain an emergency cash advance, access account balances, or find an ATM near you.

WASHINGTON, DC CREDIT CARD COMPANIES

American Express www.americanexpress.com	(800) 528-4800, (800) 528-2122
Diner's Club www.dinersclub.com	(800) 234-6377
Discover www.discovercard.com	(800) 347-2683
MasterCard www.mastercard.com	(800) 622-7747
Visa www.usa.visa.com	(800) 847-2911

DRY CLEANING AND TAILORING

Virtually all DC area hotels offer on-site same-day or overnight dry cleaning and laundry services. There are also hundreds of dry cleaning companies and tailors located throughout the city, many of which offer rush service. For a referral, ask your hotel's concierge or call one of the following businesses. Your hotel's concierge can also arrange for your garments to be picked up and delivered back to your room.

WASHINGTON, DC LAUNDRY SERVICES

Barr Cleaners 910 17th Street NW, #104	(202) 785-1155
DC Cleaners 1901 Pennsylvania Avenue NW	(202) 530-0123
Dry Cleaners, Inc. 1300 Pennsylvania Avenue NW	(202) 289-8257
Elite Concierge 1730 K Street NW, #304	(202) 508-3894
Esteem Cleaners 2100 Pennsylvania Avenue NW	(202) 429-0591
Fara Dry Cleaners 320 21st Street NW	(202) 659-5099
Franklin Valet 1301 K Street NW	(202) 289-3870
Lee's Custom Tailoring 529 14th Street NW, #296	(202) 639-8590
Lee's Custom Tailoring & Cleaners 1105 15th Street NW	(202) 289-8121
Market Square Cleaners 801 Pennsylvania Avenue NW	(202) 628-5822
Melvin's Custom Tailoring 1317 F Street NW	(202) 727-2100
Oxon Hill Cleaners 1850 F Street NW	(202) 408-0839
Parks Cleaners & Shoe Repair 1212 New York Avenue NW	(202) 371-0777
Pentagon Cleaners The Pentagon Concourse	(703) 271-5280
Royal Cleaners 1990 K Street NW, #25	(202) 223-8544
Star Rapid Dry Cleaners 820 15th Street NW	(202) 898-2508
VIP Cleaners 600 19th Street NW	(202) 289-4070
Woodward Dry Cleaners 805 15th Street NW, #2	(202) 393-3111

EMBROIDERY AND SCREEN-PRINTING COMPANIES

For custom embroidered or screen-printed promotional items, such as T-shirts, jackets, or hats, contact one of these DC area companies. Most offer low minimum quantity orders and fast turn-around times.

WASHINGTON, DC EMBROIDERY AND SCREEN-PRINTING SERVICES	
ABC T-Shirt Company 1000 Wisconsin Avenue NW	(202) 333-0025
Classic Embroider, Screen Printing & Promotional Products 433-C East Diamond Avenue, Gaithersburg, MD	(301) 926-4550
Enchanted Embroidery 3222 M Street NW	(202) 333-3008
G-Land Embroidery & Apparel 1516 Wisconsin Avenue NW	(202) 333-3583
Petro's Embroidery 1338 5th Street NE	(202) 544-8484
Total Sports 201 Davis Drive, Unit D, Sterling, VA	(703) 444-3633

FEDEX KINKO'S LOCATIONS

Phone number: (800) 463-3339

Web site: www.fedex.com/us/officeprint/main

There is a full-service FedEx Kinko's location across the street from the Washington Convention Center. There are also more than 60 other full-service locations and hundreds of FedEx drop boxes throughout the DC area.

Each FedEx Kinko's location offers FedEx supplies and package drop-off service, plus copying, collating, printing, sign making, internet access, on-site computer rentals, and a wide range of other services. Rates are typically considerably less than at the business centers located in the hotels. There isn't a surcharge added to packages shipped using your FedEx account.

TIP

FedEx's rush delivery service (800-399-5999) offers same-day, door-to-door delivery of packages up to 70 pounds. This service is available 365 days per year to and from all 50 states. Other services include overnight delivery (between 8 A.M. and 10 A.M.), overnight delivery by 10:30 A.M., overnight delivery by 3 P.M., second-day, third-day, and ground delivery for letters and packages.

SELECT FEDEX KINKO'S LOCATIONS IN THE DC AREA	
800 K Street NW 6 A.M.–11 P.M., Monday–Saturday	(202) 682-0349 Latest package drop-off: 6:30 P.M. (4 P.M. on Saturdays)
1400 K Street 6 A.M.–11 P.M., Monday–Saturday	(202) 898-1712 Latest package drop-off: 6:30 P.M. (4 P.M. on Saturdays)
1350 New York Avenue NW Noon–8:30 P.M., Monday–Friday	(202) 628-3192 Latest package drop-off: 8:30 P.M.
1612 K Street NW Open 24 hours, Monday–Saturday	(202) 466-3777 Latest package drop-off: 6:30 P.M. (4 P.M. on Saturdays)
1029 17th Street NW 11 A.M.–8:45 P.M., Monday–Friday; 1 P.M.–5:45 P.M., Saturday	(202) 659-2833 Latest package drop-off: 8:45 P.M. (5:45 P.M. on Saturday)
325 7th Street Open 24 hours, Monday–Saturday	(202) 347-8730 Latest package drop-off: 6:30 P.M. (4 P.M. on Saturday)
2020 K Street Open 24 hours, Monday–Saturday	(202) 331-9572 Latest package drop-off: 7 P.M. (4 P.M. on Saturday)
3329 M Street NW 7 A.M.–midnight (Sunday); Open 24 hours, Monday–Thursday; midnight to 10 P.M. (Friday); 7 A.M.–10 P.M. (Saturday)	Latest package drop-off: 6:30 P.M. (4 P.M. Saturday)
2300 Clarendon Blvd., Arlington, VA Open 24 hours, Monday–Saturday	Latest package drop-off: 7:30 P.M. (2:45 P.M. on Saturday)

FLORISTS

Some of the larger and more upscale DC area hotels offer full-service florists inhouse. All the florists listed below can have flower arrangements, plants, balloons, and other gift items shipped anywhere. They can also provide flower arrangements for trade shows, banquets, and other functions. This is a sampling of the many florists located in the DC area.

SELECT WASHINGTON, DC FLORISTS	
Blumenhaus Flower Service www.blumenhaususa.com	(301) 469-5001
CitiFlowers www.citiflowers.us	(202) 842-3092
Encore Décor www.encoredecorinc.com	(301) 565-0020
FTD www.ftd.com	(800) SEND-FTD
Greenworks Florist www.greenworksflorist.com	(202) 265-3335
1-(800) FLOWERS www.1800flowers.com	(800) FLOWERS
Urban Jungle www.urbanjungleinc.com	(703) 241-8545

FOREIGN CURRENCY EXCHANGE SERVICES

Many full-service banks in Washington, DC (and surrounding areas), offer currency exchange services. You'll also find Travelex (www.travelex.com) currency exchange kiosks at all of the DC area

Travelex kiosks and offices are located in the DC area airports and at Union Station. Travel insurance can be purchased at these locations, which also offer foreign currency exchange services.

airports and within Union Station. You could also contact Thomas Cook Currency at (202) 783-3654 or American Express Travel Services at (202) 457-1300.

FULL-SERVICE BANKS

Throughout the city and surrounding areas, you'll find hundreds of full-service bank branches. The following are customer service phone numbers for popular banks with branches and ATMs located throughout the DC area. Call to determine where the closest branch to where you're staying is, or ask your hotel's concierge. While the following customer service centers are open 24 hours per day, the hours of operation of each local branch will vary.

WASHINGTON, DC BANKS

Bank of America www.bankofamerica.com	(800) 841-4000
Chevy Chase Bank www.chevychasebank.com	(800) 987-BANK
Citibank www.citibank.com	(202) 857-6980
PNC Bank www.pnc.com	(202) 835-5048
Presidential Savings Bank www.presidential.com	(800) 383-6266
Sun Trust Bank www.suntrust.com	(800) 786-8787
United Bank www.unitedbank-dcmetro.com	(800) 730-6169
Wachovia Bank www.wachovia.com	(800) 922-4684
Washington Mutual www.wamu.com	(800) 788-7000

TIP
To locate an ATM that's close to you and that's affiliated with your bank's ATM network, check the back of your ATM, debit, or credit card and look for the "Cirrus" or "PLUS" logo, then call the appropriate network: Cirrus (800-424-7787) or PLUS (800-843-7587).

GOLF COURSES
See Section VI, "Entertainment in Washington, DC."

JET CHARTER COMPANIES
If your travel plans cannot be accommodated by a major commercial airline, consider utilizing a charter jet. The cost is, of course, higher, but the added luxury and convenience may be worthwhile to you and your company.

WASHINGTON, DC JET CHARTER SERVICES

Air Royale www.airroyale.com	(800) 7-ROYALE
Blue Star Jets www.bluestarjets.com	(866) 471-2856
Executive Charter Service www.executivecharterservice.com	(888) 522-0883
I Fly Jet Set www.iflyjetset.com	(877) 301-9609
Imperial Jets www.imperialjets.com	(888) 599-5387
Jet Charter	(212) 856-5747
Luxury Air Jets www.luxuryairjets.com	(866) 420-5060
Skyline Jets www.skylinejets.com	(888) 898-5387

LAWYERS
For a lawyer referral in DC, call the District of Columbia Bar referral line at (202) 296-7845 or visit www.dcbar.org. Depending on your needs, you could also contact the Virginia State Bar (804-775-0808, www.vsb.org) or the Maryland State Bar Association (410-951-7760, www.msba.org).

LIMOUSINE AND TOWN CAR SERVICES
For listings, see Section IV, "Getting Around Town."

LOCKSMITHS
These companies offer 24-hour emergency service. Be sure the locksmith you hire is fully licensed and insured.

WASHINGTON, DC LOCKSMITH SERVICES

24-Hour Emergency Locksmith	(202) 883-4311
A-1 Emergency Locksmith	(202) 338-1010
Elite Locksmith	(866) 374-5414
Expert Lock-Smith	(202) 448-9425
KeyWay Lock Service	(202) 338-2254
Len's Lock Service	(301) 927-2446
Liberty Locksmith	(800) 359-3216
USA Lock	(202) 293-8911

MALLS AND SHOPPING

See Section VI, "Entertainment in Washinton, DC," and Section IX, "Personal Services."

MEETING AND BANQUET ROOM RENTALS

To rent a meeting room of any size at the hotel where you're staying, contact the concierge, sales office, or business center (see Section III, "Where to Stay while in Washington, DC" for a partial listing of area hotels). Meeting rooms can also be rented at the Washington Convention Center. The following is a partial listing of other companies that rent fully equipped meeting room space throughout the DC area. Many of the city's most popular historical sites and tourist attractions also offer meeting, function, and banquet room rentals.

Many available meeting rooms offer high-speed internet access; conference room, theater-style, or classroom seating; video conferencing; teleconferencing; television and DVD player; projectors; whiteboards; photocopying services; flipcharts with easel; and catering services. Meeting rooms can be rented by the hour, half day, or full day from many of these companies.

WASHINGTON, DC MEETING SPACE RENTAL COMPANIES

DC Executive Conference Center (202) 662-1419
440 1st Street NW   www.amanet.org/meetings
Facility type: meeting rooms

WASHINGTON, DC MEETING SPACE RENTAL COMPANIES

Georgetown University Conference Hotel   (202) 687-3242
3800 Reservoir Road NW   www.conferencecenters.com
Facility type: banquet and meeting rooms

Hyatt at Dulles Airport   (703) 713-1234
2300 Dulles Corner Blvd., Herndon, VA   www.dulles.hyatt.com
Facility type: banquet and meeting rooms

KStreet   (202) 962-3933
1301 K Street NW   www.kstreetdc.com
Facility type: banquet rooms

National 4-H Conference Center   (301) 961-2800
7100 Connecticut Avenue, Chevy Chase, MD   www.4hcenter.org
Facility type: banquet and meeting rooms

National Press Club   (202) 662-7522
529 14th Street NW   www.press.org
Facility type: banquet and meeting rooms

Ronald Reagan Building and International Trade Center   (202) 312-1310
1300 Pennsylvania Avenue NW   www.itcdc.com
Facility type: banquet and meeting rooms

Smithsonian American Art Museum   (202) 633-6333
8th and F Streets, NW   N/A
Facility type: banquet rooms

Torpedo Factory Art Center   (703) 838-0088
105 N. Union Street, Alexandria, VA   N/A
Facility type: banquet rooms

Union Station Special Events   (202) 289-8300
50 Massachusetts Avenue NE   www.unionstationevents.com
Facility type: banquet and meeting rooms

TIP
To learn about additional event sites, visit the Special Event Sites Marketing Alliance web site (www.sesma.org). Also, contact the Washington DC Convention Services Department at (202) 798-7094 or www.washington.org.

MESSENGER SERVICES

The following services can transport documents and packages within the DC area (including Maryland and Virginia). Same-day and immediate rush service are typically available. Some of these services operate 24 hours per day.

WASHINGTON, DC MESSENGER SERVICES	
A1 Express Delivery Service www.a1express.com/Washington_DC_courier.asp	(877) 219-7737
Excel Group www.excelgroup.com/courier.html	(703) 478-0140
Global Messenger www.globmessenger.com	(800) 891-5113
Quick Messenger Service	(202) 783-3600
Washington Courier www.washingtoncourier.com	(800) 827-4500

MODELING AGENCIES AND TEMPORARY TRADE SHOW PERSONNEL

The following companies provide professional models and temporary personnel for trade shows, meetings, parties and other events.

WASHINGTON, DC MODELING AND TRADE SHOW PERSONNEL AGENCIES	
The Artist Agency www.theartistagency.com	(202) 342-0933
Carlyn Davis Casting and Production Services www.carlyndavis.com	(703) 532-1900
Doran Model and Talent Agency	(202) 333-6367
National Event Staffing www.nationaleventstaffing.com	(866) 565-9939
On Point Marketing and Promotions www.onpoint-marketing.com	
Promo Models www.promomodels.com	
Washington, DC Convention and Tourism Corporation's Services www.washington.org	(202) 789-7032

OFFICE SUPPLY SUPERSTORES

These retail stores also offer copying and printing services, as well as same-day or next-day delivery of office supplies and products. You can, of course, also shop at the stores for all of your office supply needs.

Staples

Phone number: (800) 333-3330

Web site: www.staples.com

Offers 20 retail locations within a 12-mile radius of Washington, DC, including:

- 1250 H Street NW, Washington, DC—(202) 638-3907
- 1901 L Street, Washington, DC—(202) 293-4415
- 3301 Jefferson Davis Highway, Alexandria, VA—(703) 836-9485
- 910 North Glebe Road, Arlington, VA—(703) 528-8207

Office Depot

Phone number: (800) GO-DEPOT

Web site: www.officedepot.com

Offers 10 retail locations within an 11-mile radius of Washington, DC, including:

- 1515 N. Courthouse Road, Arlington, VA—(703) 387-0990
- 4455 Connecticut Avenue NW, Washington, DC—(202) 363-5758
- 5845 Leesburg Pike, Bailey's Crossroads, VA—(703) 379-0319

PHOTOGRAPHY SERVICES

WASHINGTON, DC PHOTOGRAPHY SERVICES

Capitol Memories by Memory Makers www.capitalmemories.com	(703) 671-9293
Event Digital Photography www.eventdigital.com	(301) 229-3305
Focused Images Photography www.focusedimages.com	(703) 435-3456
Mattox Photography www.mattoxphotography.com	(703) 587-0900
Reflections Photography www.reflections-photo.com	(202) 204-6700

SECRETARIAL AND TEMPORARY EMPLOYMENT SERVICES

Whether you need temporary personnel to help staff or facilitate a meeting, or require the use of a secretary, bookkeeper, or other specialist while in the DC area, any of these temporary employment agencies will be able to help you meet your short-term, last-minute staffing needs.

WASHINGTON, DC STAFFING SERVICES	
AppleOne	(877) 221-5171
Labor Finders	(800) 864-7749
Labor Ready	(877) 221-2080
Manpower	(888) 222-6495
Office Team	(800) 804-8367

SHIPPING AND FREIGHT SERVICES

Packages can be dropped off at the business center of any hotel; however, you will be charged an additional service fee. To find a courier or shipping company-owned drop box or to schedule a package pickup yourself, contact the company you want to use directly.

WASHINGTON, DC SHIPPING AND FREIGHT SERVICES	
DHL www.dhl.com	(800) CALL-DHL
FedEx www.fedex.com	(800) GO-FEDEX
UPS www.ups.com	(800) PICK-UPS

TICKET BROKERS

See Section VI, "Entertainment in Washington, DC," for information on ticket brokers.

TRADE SHOW AND PRIVATE SECURITY SERVICES

For your private security needs within a hotel, contact the hotel's management or concierge. For private security services within the Washington Convention Center, call (202) 249-3213 or visit www.dcconvention.com/exhibitors/default.asp. Additional private security firms include the following.

WASHINGTON, DC SECURITY SERVICES	
Guards to Go www.guardstogo.com	(800) 970-3437
IWG Protection Agency www.iwgprotection.com	(410) 837-5544
King's Security Service	(202) 299-9850
Lorence Detective and Protection Agency www.lorencedetective.com	(301) 753-1688
Off Duty Officers www.offdutyofficers.com	(888) 408-5900
Tactical Solutions, Inc. www.tacticalsolutionsgroup.net	(631) 924-5030
Unlimited Security	(202) 371-1561
Watchman Protective Services www.watchmanprotective.com	(866) 608-8000

TRADE SHOW EXHIBIT SALES, INSTALLATION, REPAIR, AND DISMANTLING

For trade show exhibit sales, installation, emergency repairs, or dismantling, contact any of the following companies. The trade show coordinator or hosting venue where your event is being held will also be able to offer referrals. For information relating to exhibiting at the Washington Convention Center, call (202) 249-3213, or visit www.dcconvention.com/exhibitors/default.asp.

WASHINGTON, DC TRADE SHOW SERVICES	
Atlantic Skyline www.atlskyline.com	(703) 802-6800
Image Works Studio www.imageworksstudio.com	(703) 968-6767
Impact Displays www.impact-displays.com	(888) 988-2131

WASHINGTON, DC TRADE SHOW SERVICES	
Maxatrax www.maxatrax.com	(301) 420-1700
Nimlok http://nimlok-washingtondc.com	(301) 856-7000
Sign Concepts www.signconcepts.net	(703) 642-5511
The History Factory www.historyfactory.com	(703) 631-0500

TRANSLATORS AND INTERPRETERS

To find a translator or interpreter to meet your specific needs, visit the National Capital Area Chapter of the American Translators Association at www.ncata.org/search/index.cfm for a referral, or contact one of the following companies.

WASHINGTON, DC TRANSLATION SERVICES	
ALS Conference Interpreting	(202) 887-8060
Als Translation	(301) 439-2243
Berlitz Interpretation Service	(202) 331-1887
Center for Applied Linguistics	(202) 362-0700
International Translation Center	(202) 296-1344
Multilingual Experts	(202) 393-0766
TransPerfect	(202) 347-2300

TRAVELER'S CHECKS

Traveler's checks are widely accepted and can be used at most locations just like cash. They typically come in a variety of different denominations, including $20, $50, $100, and $500. If you need to acquire traveler's checks or need to report lost or stolen traveler's checks, contact the following companies:

- American Express—(800) 807-6233
- MasterCard Traveler's Checks—(800) 223-9920
- Visa Traveler's Checks—(800) 732-1322

You can acquire traveler's checks at most banks. They are an excellent alternative to carrying large sums of cash when traveling, because if they're lost or stolen, they are replaceable. When you first acquire the checks, be sure to sign them in the appropriate location, and keep the receipt for the checks (listing the check numbers) in a separate location from the traveler's checks themselves.

MONEY SAVER
If you're a member of AAA, you can obtain traveler's checks with no processing fee at any AAA travel office. In other words, you pay only the face value of the traveler's check(s) you acquire.

U.S. POST OFFICE LOCATIONS

Phone number: (800) ASK-USPS

Web site: www.usps.com

The following are just some of the full-service post offices located in the downtown DC area. For additional locations, call (800) ASK-USPS.

WASHINGTON, DC SELECT FULL-SERVICE U.S. POST OFFICES	
1222 9th Street SE	9 A.M.–4:30 P.M., Monday-Friday
416 Florida Avenue NE	8:30 A.M.–1 P.M., 2 P.M.–5 P.M., Monday-Friday
800 K Street NW	8:30 A.M.–5 P.M., Monday-Friday
1400 K Street NW	8 A.M.–5:30 P.M., Monday-Friday (8 A.M.–2 P.M., Saturday)
2400 6th Street NW	8 A.M.–5 P.M., Monday-Friday
2 Massachusetts Avenue NE	7 A.M.–11:59 P.M., Monday-Friday (7 A.M.–8 P.M., Saturday and Sunday)
200 Constitution Avenue NW	8:30 A.M.–4:30 P.M., Monday-Friday
437 L'Enfant Plaza SW	8 A.M.–5 P.M., Monday-Friday
2201 C Street NW	7:30 A.M.–4 P.M., Monday-Friday
2512 Virginia Avenue NW	8:30 A.M.–5 P.M., Monday-Friday

VIDEO PRODUCTION SERVICES AND EQUIPMENT RENTAL

While these companies can often fill your last-minute audio and video production or equipment rental needs, ideally you should book these services in advance.

WASHINGTON, DC VIDEO PRODUCTION AND RENTAL COMPANIES	
American Audio Video www.aavevents.com	(703) 573-6910
Audio Visual Management	(636) 379-3889
Crew Works www.thecrewworks.com	(800) 294-2739
Event Strategies, Inc. www.eventstrategies.com	(703) 684-0025
Presentation Media www.presmedia.com	(301) 470-6300
Simax Event Productions www.simaxevents.com	(301) 601-8006
TJS Productions www.tjsproductions.com	(703) 823-7960

WESTERN UNION ELECTRONIC MONEY-TRANSFER SERVICES (WORLDWIDE)

Customer service: (800) 325-6000

Web site: www.westernunion.com

Money can be sent from the Western Union web site, but it must be picked up in person at a Western Union location. There are about 20 locations in the DC area. Call (800) 325-6000 for the location closest to you.

TRAVEL NOTES

SECTION IX

© Robert Pitman

PERSONAL
SERVICES

Whether you're looking for a tailor, fitness center, hairstylist, hospital, dentist, or massage therapist, these all-important personal products and services can be found throughout Washington, DC and the surrounding areas.

Keep in mind, the companies and services listed here are for reference or referral purposes only and are just a sampling of the many companies offering similar products and services within the nation's capital. Inclusion in this section does not constitute an endorsement. Additional referrals can be obtained from your hotel's concierge or the local Yellow Pages. All addresses are in Washington, DC unless otherwise noted.

AIRLINE DIRECTORY
See Section I, "Welcome to Washington, DC."

ALCOHOLICS ANONYMOUS
To find an Alcoholics Anonymous meeting in Washington, DC, visit www.aa-dc.org or call (202) 966-9115.

CHIROPRACTORS
For a referral to a chiropractor close to where you're staying, visit www.chirodirectory.com. When setting up an appointment, determine if your out-of-state medical insurance will cover the cost of the visit and treatment. The following chiropractors offer same-day appointments for emergencies.

WASHINGTON, DC CHIROPRACTIC SERVICES	
Absolute Chiropractic 650 Pennsylvania Avenue SE	(202) 548-6000
Back and Neck Institute 4301 Connecticut Avenue NW	(202) 966-2214
Back to Health Holistic Center 1234 19th Street NW	(202) 293-2225
Back to Health Holistic Center 210 7th Street SE	(202) 544-4478
DC Chiropractic 1522 K Street NW	(202) 682-9222
Downtown Chiropractic 918 16th Street NW	(202) 466-3803
Dupont Circle Chiropractic 1330 New Hampshire Avenue NW	(202) 877-6787
Friendship Heights Chiropractic 5100 Wisconsin Avenue NW	(202) 362-0900

DENTISTS

The following dentists offer same-day appointments for emergencies. There are hundreds of dentists in the DC area. For additional referrals, contact your hotel's concierge, or call 1-800-DENTIST or visit www.1800dentist.com. You can also visit www.dentists.com and select "Washington, DC."

WASHINGTON, DC DENTAL SERVICES	
Advanced Dental Associates 4912 Massachusetts Avenue NW	(202) 244-4477
American Dental Service 4303 Connecticut Avenue NW	(202) 362-1024
Avenue Dental Georgetown 2123 Wisconsin Avenue NW	(202) 333-9145
Dr. Joel W. Sendroff, DDS 5415 Connecticut Avenue NW	(202) 244-4149
Embassy Row Dental 2111 Phelps Place NW	(202) 265-0525
Washington Center for Dentistry 1925 K Street NW	(202) 223-6630

DEPARTMENT STORES

In addition to countless stores and boutiques located throughout the DC area (see Section VI, "Entertainment in Washington, DC"), some of the major department stores, which offer designer (casual, business formal, and business casual) apparel for men and women, include the following.

WASHINGTON, DC DEPARTMENT STORES	
Bloomingdale's Tysons Corner Center, 1961 Chain Bridge Road, McLean, VA	(703) 556-4600
Brooks Brothers 1201 Connecticut Avenue NW	(202) 659-4650
Lord & Taylor Tysons Corner Center, 1961 Chain Bridge Road, McLean, VA	(703) 506-1156
Macy's Pentagon City 1000 South Hayes Street, Arlington, VA	(703) 418-4488
Macy's Tysons Corner 1651 International Drive, McLean, VA	(703) 556-0000

WASHINGTON, DC DEPARTMENT STORES	
Neiman Marcus Mazza Gallerie Mall, 5300 Wisconsin Avenue NW	(202) 966-9700
Nordstrom Tysons Corner Center, 1961 Chain Bridge Road, McLean, VA	(703) 761-1121
Nordstrom Fashion Centre at Pentagon City, Arlington, VA	(703) 415-1121
Saks Fifth Avenue for Men Mazza Gallerie Mall, 5300 Wisconsin Avenue NW	(202) 363-2059

EYEWEAR STORES AND OPTOMETRISTS

For prescription eyeglasses and contact lenses, there are hundreds of optometrists and eyewear stores throughout the DC area. Many are open seven days a week for eye exams or can create or repair prescription eyewear within hours.

Blink Optical

Web site: www.blinkoptical.com

Offers three locations in the DC area, including:

- Downtown: 1776 Eye Street NW, (202) 776-0999
- Logan Circle: 1413 P Street NW, (202) 234-1051
- Georgetown: 3029 M Street NW, (202) 625-5351

For Eyes

Phone number: (800) 367-3937

Web site: www.foreyes.com

Offers five locations in the DC area, including:

- 1335 G Street NW, (202) 783-7171
- 1775 K Street NW, (202) 463-6364
- Landmark Mall, 5801 Duke Street, Alexandria, VA, (703) 642-0720
- Pentagon City Mall, 1100 South Hayes Street, Arlington, VA, (703) 415-5544
- Tenley Circle, 4301 Wisconsin Avenue NW, (202) 237-8500

LensCrafters

Web site: www.lenscrafters.com

Offers six locations in the DC area, including:

- 1100 South Hayes, Arlington, VA, (703) 416-1525
- 3500 East West Highway, Hyattsville, MD, (301) 559-1110
- 4238 Wilson Blvd., Arlington, VA, (703) 524-6060
- 5801 Duke Street, Alexandria, VA, (703) 256-5996
- 11160 Veirs Mill Road, Wheaton, MD, (301) 949-0170
- 801-A Capital Center Boulevard, Landover, MD, (301) 333-1877

Pearl Vision

Web site: www.pearlevision.com

Offers four locations in the DC area, including:

- 2914 Colebrook Drive, Temple Hills, MD, (301) 423-4242
- 6284 Arlington Boulevard, Falls Church, VA, (703) 237-2131
- 5801 Duke Street, Alexandria, VA, (703) 914-1130
- 5900 Greenbelt Road, Greenbelt, MD, (301) 441-3643

Wal-Mart Vision Centers

Offers four locations within 20 miles of Washington, DC, including:

- 8745 Branch Avenue, Clinton, MD, (301) 877-0502
- 3300 NW Crain Highway, Bowie, MD, (301) 805-8850
- 3549 Russett Green East, Laurel, MD, (301) 604-0180
- 11930 Acton Lane, Waldorf, MD, (301) 705-7070

1-800-CONTACTS

Phone number: (800) 266-8228

Web site: www.1800contacts.com

Order prescription contact lenses and have them delivered overnight to your hotel.

FITNESS CENTERS AND GYMS

There are more than 250 gyms and fitness centers in the Washington, DC area. Many welcome guests willing to purchase a day pass to use the facilities. If you are already a member of a club that is part of a nationwide chain, you can probably visit that gym's DC area location for free or for a reduced fee.

You'll discover that most upscale hotels have a fitness center on-site, however, some charge a fee for usage. Other hotels have a relationship with a nearby gym, allowing hotel guests to utilize the gym's facilities. Contact your hotel's concierge for details.

TIP
Many of these fitness centers and health clubs also feature full-service day spas and offer massages, facials, and a wide range of body treatments.

WASHINGTON, DC FITNESS CENTERS

Bally Total Fitness 2000 L Street NW	(800) 695-8111
Body College Pilates 4708 Wisconsin Avenue NW	(202) 237-0080
Capital City Club & Spa 1001 16th Street NW	(202) 639-4300
Crunch Fitness 1339 Green Court NW	(202) 216-9000
Curves 3220 17th Street NW	(202) 319-7007
Curves 1334 North Capitol Street NW	(202) 332-2241
Curves Colorado Avenue NW	(202) 722-5991
Fitness First Health Club 1828 L Street NW	(202) 659-1900
Four Seasons Fitness Club 2800 Pennsylvania Avenue NW	(202) 944-2022
Gold's Gym 1120 20th Street NW	(202) 223-4145
Gold's Gym 4310 Connecticut Avenue NW	(202) 237-1471
Gold's Gym 409 3rd Street SW	(202) 479-0186
H&H Spa 4654 Wisconsin Avenue NW	(202) 537-7260
Living Well 4321 Markham Street, Annandale, VA	(703) 914-1616
Mint Fitness Club 1724 California Street NW	(202) 328-6468

WASHINGTON, DC FITNESS CENTERS

Northwest Sport & Health Club 4001 Brandywine Street NW	(202) 244-6090
One on One Fitness 1616 Belmont Street NW	(202) 265-7944
Sports & Health Clubs Watergate	(202) 298-4460
Sports Club LA 1170 22nd Street NW	(202) 974-6600
Washington Hilton Sport Club 1919 Connecticut Avenue NW	(202) 483-3061
Washington Sports Club 1835 Connecticut Avenue NW	(202) 332-0100
Washington Sports Club 1990 K Street NW	(202) 466-6500
Washington Sports Club 214 D Street SE	(202) 547-2255
Washington Sports Club 783 7th Street NW	(202) 737-3555

FLORISTS AND BALLOON DELIVERY

See Section VIII, "Business Services."

HAIRSTYLISTS, HAIR SALONS, AND BARBERS

Some of the upscale hotels offer a full-service salon inhouse or can arrange to have a hairstylist come to your hotel room (contact your hotel's concierge for details). In the DC area, visiting a hairstylist or barber can cost anywhere from $20 to $300 (or more), depending on the salon and stylist.

To ensure you find exactly the services you're looking for, seek out a reliable referral from your hotel's concierge, since there are literally thousands of hairstylists, salons, barbers, and manicurists working in the DC area.

HOSPITALS

In case of a medical emergency, call 9-1-1 from any telephone. Following is a sampling of hospitals located in Washington, DC. For medical emergencies, go to the hospital's emergency room. Call any hospital's main number to obtain nonemergency referrals for local doctors or medical specialists.

TIP

The Poison Control Hotline (available 24 hours per day) can be reached at (800) 222-1222. The Rape Crisis Line (available 24 hours per day) can be reached at (202) 561-7000. If you encounter a crisis during your travels and need help, contact Travelers Aid Society International at (202) 546-1127 or visit www.travelersaid.org.

WASHINGTON, DC SELECT HOSPITALS	
Children's Hospital National Medical Center 111 Michigan Avenue NW	(202) 884-5000
George Washington University Hospital 900 23rd Street NW	(202) 715-4000
Georgetown University Medical Center 4000 Reservoir Road NW	(202) 444-3111
Howard University Hospital 2041 Georgia Avenue NW	(202) 865-6100

LIMOUSINE AND TOWN CAR SERVICES

See Section IV, "Getting Around Town."

MASSAGE THERAPISTS AND DAY SPAS

Many of the upscale hotels have a full-service day spa inhouse. To schedule an in-room massage or treatment at almost any hotel, contact the concierge. Throughout Washington, DC, you'll also find dozens of independent world-class day spas, some affiliated with fitness centers.

For help finding a spa that offers the facilities and treatments you're looking for, visit the SpaFinder web site at www.spafinder.com. The following is a sampling of the DC area's upscale day spas.

WASHINGTON, DC SPAS	
Anu Day Spa 617 Pennsylvania Avenue, SE	(202) 544-8268
Capital City Club & Spa 1001 16th Street NW	(202) 393-1000
Celadon Spa 1180 F Street NW	(202) 347-3333

SECTION IX / **PERSONAL SERVICES** · **211**

WASHINGTON, DC SPAS	
Elizabeth Arden Red Door Salon and Spa 5225 Wisconsin Avenue NW	(202) 362-9890
Fountains Day Spa 422 South Washington Street, Alexandria, VA	(703) 549-1990
Grooming Lounge (for men) 1745 L Street NW	(202) 466-8900
Hands-On Health Professional massage service that comes to your hotel	(202) 744-5032
Hela Spa 3209 M Street NW	(866) 870-7103
JC Spa 5249 Duke Street, Alexandria, VA	(703) 212-7301
Massages on the Run Professional massage service that comes to your hotel	(703) 612-6514, (800) 984-6687
Nusta Spa 1129 20th Street NW	(202) 530-7500
Serenity Day Spa 4000 Wisconsin Avenue NW	(202) 362-2560
SomaFit 2121 Wisconsin Avenue	(202) 965-2121
Spa at Mandarin Oriental 1330 Maryland Avenue SW	(202) 787-6100
Trinity Fitness and Spa 45965 Nokes Blvd., Sterling, VA	(703) 430-0494
Well Being Massage and Spa JW Marriott Hotel Health Club 1331 Pennsylvania Avenue	(202) 626-1968

NAIL SALONS

The following are just some of the many nail salons within the DC area.

WASHINGTON, DC NAIL SALONS	
A Nails by Cynthia 2602 Connecticut Avenue NW	(202) 232-8342
Anna of Georgetown 3222 M Street NW # 420	(202) 965-5708

PAMPER YOURSELF AND RELAX AT THE WILLARD I SPA

Whether you're a man or woman, if you're looking for the ultimate spa experience, your search will end once you step through the doors of the I Spa at the Willard (1401 Pennsylvania Avenue NW, 202-942-2700). While this world-class spa might not be the largest in the nation's capital, it offers an extensive menu of treatments, plus extremely personalized and highly professional and friendly service. Whether you experience a facial or one of the spa's ten different massage offerings, you'll be truly pampered.

For men, the facility offers the Barber Spa package ($380), a three-hour experience that includes four separate spa treatments—a gentlemen's facial, scalp massage, executive manicure, and hot stone massage. Combine this with the use of the spa's sauna and steam room, and you'll leave totally relaxed and rejuvenated. It's the perfect way to counteract the stresses associated with travel or having to attend seemingly endless meetings and trade shows. For the men's treatments, the spa uses products from the Art of Shaving.

If you can't fit several hours into your hectic schedule to relax and truly pamper yourself, the I Spa also offers a selection of express treatments, which include a 30-minute massage or 30-minute facial (available for men or women). In conjunction with these express treatments, a gourmet lunch can be provided within one of the spa's luxurious and tranquil lounges.

For men and women alike, the I Spa offers many one-hour or 90-minute signature treatments that you won't find elsewhere, such as The Willard Chardonnay Massage. This massage utilizes the Willard InterContinental's private-label chardonnay as one of the ingredients within the massage oil used. The hot stone massage is also incredibly relaxing and rejuvenating.

This full-service spa also offers a variety of bath treatments, ten types of facials, plus several unique skin care treatments. The spa facility itself offers a quiet, extremely clean and comfortable relaxation lounge, multiple private treatment rooms, plus nicely equipped locker room facilities. Robes, towels, and slippers are, of course, provided. The rates at The I Spa are surprisingly reasonable considering the extremely high level of service and overall quality of the treatments being offered.

By combing a superior spa facility with personalized and highly professional attention, and an extensive menu of extremely relaxing treatments designed to relieve stress and pamper guests, the I

PAMPER YOURSELF AND RELAX AT THE WILLARD I SPA, CONTINUED

Spa is definitely among the very best day spas in the DC area. It's well worth the trip to the Willard InterContinental Hotel to experience this world-class spa firsthand. You won't be disappointed! Hours of operation are Monday through Saturday, between 9 A.M. and 7 P.M., and Sundays, between 9 A.M. and 5 P.M. Appointments are required.

For men and women alike, the I Spa at the Willard is one of the most luxurious day spas in the DC area. In addition to massages, facials, and skin treatments, waxing, manicures, and pedicures are also available.

WASHINGTON, DC NAIL SALONS

Arlene's Unisex 2524 Pennsylvania Avenue SE	(202) 575-4777
At Your Fingertips 1917 I Street NW # 200	(202) 293-5293
Attia Art & Coiffure 5252 Wisconsin Avenue NW	(202) 966-6200
Beau Nails 3335 Georgia Avenue NW	(202) 882-2911
Bebe Nails 615 Pennsylvania Avenue SE	(202) 543-0260
Betty's Nail Salon 610 Irving Street NW	(202) 722-4042

WASHINGTON, DC NAIL SALONS

Broadmoor Beauty Salon 3601 Connecticut Avenue NW	(202) 244-2992
Capelli Designs 500 C Street SW	(202) 484-0900
Capitol Nail Salon 201 Massachusetts Avenue NE	(202) 543-5420
City Nails 1610 Wisconsin Avenue NW	(202) 333-1463
D C Nails 5213 Georgia Avenue NW	(202) 291-4774
Elegance 10 Nails 3941 Minnesota Avenue NE	(202) 388-5144
Elegance Nails 3619 Georgia Avenue NW	(202) 722-7865
Expressly Nails 1717 K Street NW # 1	(202) 223-1388
Extremities 1400 L Street NW	(202) 371-1177
Fingertip Nail Salon 3413 Wisconsin Avenue NW	(202) 363-5569
Georgetown Nail Salon 1800 Wisconsin Avenue NW	(202) 965-2715
Headliner Hair Nail & Skin 5008 Connecticut Avenue NW	(202) 966-9662
Image Beauty Salon 18th Street NW	(202) 234-4194
Larosa 604 11th Street NW	(202) 628-3512
Lee Nails 3222 M Street NW # 243	(202) 333-6307
Mai Nails 4017 S Capitol Street SW	(202) 562-2855
Modern Nails 1567 Maryland Avenue NE	(202) 398-6937
Nail Avenue 4483 Connecticut Avenue NW	(202) 966-6799
Shantam's Place 1775 K Street NW	(202) 452-8890
Star Nails 2558 Virginia Avenue NW	(202) 333-6993
Tammy Nails 309 Pennsylvania Avenue SE	(202) 543-2015

PERSONAL SHOPPING SERVICES

Many of the top designer clothing stores, boutiques, and department stores, along with jewelry stores located throughout Washington, DC (and surrounding areas), offer personal shopping services. For a busy business traveler, there are many reasons to hire a personal shopper. For example, he or she will often save you time and help you find exactly what you want or need in terms of clothing, gifts, or other items.

The job of a personal shopper is to understand your goals, needs, and budget. These professionals know all the stores in the area and what they carry, plus they have good relationships with vendors. When it comes to clothing, a skilled personal shopper will preselect items for you to try at stores and will do what's necessary to find your exact color, style preference, and size. If necessary, the shopper will also hire a tailor or seamstress on your behalf. A personal shopper can also work as your temporary personal assistant to run errands for you.

MONEY SAVER

Hire a personal shopper who does not work on a sales commission. This ensures you will receive the shopper's honest opinions when selecting clothing, gifts, or other purchases. Your hotel's concierge can either provide personal shopping services or refer you to someone who does.

WASHINGTON, DC PERSONAL SHOPPING SERVICES

Pam Shops 4 You	(202) 262-8976
www.pamshops4you.com	
Global Image Group	(888) 873-8017
www.globalimagegrp.com	

PHARMACIES

For prescription medication refills and over-the-counter remedies, many DC area pharmacies are open 24 hours per day. If you have an out-of-state doctor, be sure to carry a copy of your written prescription and your health insurance card with you. Otherwise, your doctor will have to make contact with the pharmacy directly to call in or verify your prescription.

SECTION IX / PERSONAL SERVICES

TIP

In addition to over 40 CVS Pharmacy locations, you'll also find full-service pharmacies within all Giant Food and Safeway supermarket locations in the DC area. For additional pharmacy listings, visit: www.thecityofwashingtondc.org/pharmacy/index.html.

WASHINGTON, DC PHARMACIES

Capitol Hill Care Pharmacy 650 Pennsylvania Avenue SE	(202) 548-0008
Cathedral Pharmacy 3000 Connecticut Avenue NW	(202) 265-1300
Center Pharmacy 4900 Massachusetts Avenue NW	(202) 363-9240
CVS Pharmacy www.cvs.com	(888) 607-4287
Offers more than 40 locations around the Washington, DC area, including:	
· 1275 Pennsylvania Avenue NW	(202) 638-4583
· 1403 Wisconsin Avenue NW	(202) 337-4848
· 1901 Pennsylvania Avenue NW	(202) 331-7077
· 1990 K Street NW	(202) 223-8735
· 2819 M Street NW	(202) 333-1592
· 3031 14th Street NW	(202) 332-4865
· 320 40th Street NE	(202) 396-1152
· 3240 Pennsylvania Avenue SE	(202) 584-5700
· 3601 12th Street NE	(202) 529-8559
· 4851 Massachusetts Avenue NW	(202) 363-9554
· 661 Pennsylvania Avenue SE	(202) 543-3305
· 680 Rhode Island Avenue NW	(202) 526-4828
· 801 7th Street NW	(202) 842-3567
Rite Aid Pharmacy 1034 15th Street NW	(202) 296-7737
Rite Aid Pharmacy 3301 New Mexico Avenue NW	(202) 966-4900
Rite Aid Pharmacy 801 H Street NW	(202) 675-2555
Rite Aid Pharmacy 1825 Connecticut Avenue NW	(202) 332-1718

RENTAL CARS

See Section IV, "Getting Around Town" for more information about ground transportation, rental cars, and the Metrorail system.

WASHINGTON, DC RENTAL CAR COMPANIES	
Alamo www.alamo.com	(800) 462-5266
Avis www.avis.com	(800) 331-1212
Budget www.budget.com	(800) 527-0700
Dollar www.dollar.com	(800) 800-3665
Enterprise www.enterprise.com	(800) 261-7331
Hertz www.hertz.com	(800) 654-3131
National www.nationalcar.com	(800) 227-7368
Thrifty www.thrifty.com	(800) THRIFTY

SHOE AND LUGGAGE REPAIR AND LUGGAGE SALES

There are dozens of shoe and luggage repair shops located throughout the DC area. Some offer immediate or while-you-wait service.

WASHINGTON, DC SHOE AND LUGGAGE REPAIR SERVICES	
Bon Voyage 50 Massachusetts Avenue NW	(202) 898-1598
Cobbler's Bench 1800 I Street NW	(202) 775-1952
Cobbler's Bench 1050 Connecticut Avenue NW	(202) 776-0515
Cobbler's Bench 40 Massachusetts Avenue NE	(202) 898-9009
Doudaklain Leather Goods & Luggage 1814 K Street NW	

WASHINGTON, DC SHOE AND LUGGAGE REPAIR SERVICES

Innovation Luggage 3068 M Street NW	(202) 333-6299
Lane's Luggage 1146 Connecticut Avenue NW	(202) 452-1146
Tumi Luggage 1246 Wisconsin Avenue NW	(202) 298-6670

TAILORS AND CLOTHING ALTERATIONS

All of the major department stores in the DC area, as well as the upscale clothing stores and boutiques, offer inhouse tailoring services for their customers. Same-day or next-day service is often available. Many of the upscale hotels also have inhouse tailoring and alteration services available to guests. Contact your hotel's concierge for details.

TUXEDO RENTALS

Formalwear for men and women can be purchased at many of the designer clothing shops, boutiques, and department stores in the DC area. The following are tuxedo rental locations, virtually all of which have tailors on the premises.

WASHINGTON, DC TUXEDO RENTAL COMPANIES1

After Hours Formalwear 2715 Wilson Boulevard, Arlington, VA	(703) 522-6455
All Star Formal Wear 1083 Wisconsin Avenue NW	(202) 338-5999
Christopher Kim's Men's Wear 2000 M Street NW	(202) 955-5467
Esteem Formal Wear 2100 Pennsylvania Avenue	(202) 429-0591
Georgetown Formal Wear 1251 Wisconsin Avenue	(202) 625-2247
Lustre Formal Wear 311 Pennsylvania Avenue SE	(202) 544-0002
M Stein & Co. 1900 M Street NW	(202) 659-1434
Royal Formal Wear 1206 G Street NW	(202) 727-7144
Scogna Formal Wear 1908 L Street NW	(202) 296-4555

WHEELCHAIR AND SCOOTER RENTALS

The following companies offer wheelchair and scooter rentals on a daily, weekly, or monthly basis. For details about other services available to physically challenged travelers, visit www.disabilityguide.org.

WASHINGTON, DC WHEELCHAIR AND SCOOTER RENTAL COMPANIES	
E-Car (scooter rental) 8673 Grovemont Circle, Gaithersburg, MD	(301) 527-6119
ILH 1301 Belmont Avenue NW	(240) 505-8655
Roberts Home Medical 20465 Goldenrod Lane, Germantown, MD	(301) 353-0300
Zask Medical 4600-C Pinecrest Office Park Drive, Alexandria, VA	(703) 35401266

TRAVEL NOTES

SECTION X

© Wolfgang Sha[...]

HELP FOR TRAVEL-RELATED PROBLEMS AND EMERGENCIES

Let's face it, no matter how much preplanning you do for a trip, sometimes things go wrong. As a business traveler, you always run the risk of losing your wallet, having your luggage lost or delayed by the airline, having to deal with unexpected travel delays, or running into a situation where you must change your travel itinerary at the last minute. This section will help you deal with some of the more common problems business travelers encounter.

MAKING LAST-MINUTE CHANGES TO YOUR TRAVEL ITINERARY

If you decide to save money and purchase a deeply discounted airfare from one of the popular travel-related web sites, such as Hotwire.com or Priceline.com, your airline ticket, rental car, and/or hotel accommodations must be prepaid and typically cannot be changed or refunded. In other words, unless you experience a medical emergency (and can get a letter from a doctor), you lose the money you paid if you don't take advantage of exactly what you purchased.

By paying a full coach, business, or first-class fare with one of the major airlines (by calling the airline's toll-free phone number, booking from the airline's own web site, or utilizing the services of a travel agent), you generally have the option to change your ticket for a fee. Depending on the airline, the change fee can be anywhere from $25 to $200, plus any change in price of the ticket based on the new travel itinerary you request. One of the most flexible airlines in terms of last-minute itinerary changes is JetBlue, available at (800) JET-BLUE or www.jetblue.com.

WARNING
If you plan to change your airline ticket, you must do it *before* the scheduled flight's departure. Otherwise, the value of your existing ticket will be lost.

In some situations if you want to change your flight, the airline allows you to fly standby. When flying standby, there generally isn't a change fee; however, you are not guaranteed a seat on the aircraft until the very last minute. If you're traveling with checked baggage, many airlines won't allow you to fly standby.

Purchasing travel insurance (for an additional fee) allows you to be refunded for your airline ticket, hotel accommodations, rental car, and so on, as long as the reason for the claim is covered by the insurance. While medical emergencies are covered, a change in your personal or business schedule generally is not covered.

WARNING
If you make a change to your travel itinerary, don't forget to call the hotel and/or rental car company to change or cancel your reservation as far in advance as possible to avoid being charged. Attempting to cancel a hotel reservation within 24 hours before your scheduled check-in often results in a fee, unless extenuating circumstances apply.

If you think you may need to change your travel itinerary, consider purchasing a full-fare airline ticket directly from the airline, but ask in advance what the policy is for last-minute changes. One of the most flexible options is to book your airline ticket using frequent flier miles. Many airlines allow these reward tickets to be changed without extra fees.

Many corporate travel agents are able to make changes to travel itineraries, even on a last-minute basis, and eliminate or greatly reduce the fees charged by the airline. Depending on the circumstances, the airline ticket agents at the airport, the airline gate attendants, or the airline customer service representatives (available by calling the airline's toll-free number) all have varying degrees of discretion when it comes to helping a passenger make changes to a nonchangeable travel itinerary.

If you need to make any change to your travel itinerary, the first step should be to contact the airline, travel agency, or online travel service through which the travel reservations were made.

TIP
The customer service desks operated by the airlines (located within the airline's terminal at the airport) are always staffed by airline representatives who are trained to help passengers experiencing travel-related problems. If your flight is canceled or you need to be rerouted, these tend to be the most helpful people to consult.

DEALING WITH TRAVEL AND WEATHER DELAYS

If you experience bad weather in Washington, DC, or you're traveling from or returning to a city experiencing bad weather, travel delays or even flight cancellations are always a possibility. By calling the airline, you can sometimes determine if your flight is delayed or canceled before leaving for the airport. If your flight is canceled or delayed because of bad weather, the airline is not responsible for putting you up in a hotel or paying for meals.

When your flight gets canceled, the airline must rebook you on the next available flight to your destination. If, however, a flight is canceled because of mechanical problems with the aircraft or for a reason caused by the airline itself, the airline is responsible for rebooking you on another flight (possibly with another airline), putting you up in a hotel, and/or paying for meals during the time your travel is delayed.

Depending on the situation, you may find yourself stuck at an airport waiting for the delayed flight to take off. If you're able to remain in the airport terminal (as opposed to on the aircraft), consider using the time to shop, eat, read, catch up on phone calls, or check your e-mail. (Most airports offer wireless internet access, so you can use your laptop to access your e-mail account via the web.)

For a fee, you can pay for a one-day pass to utilize an airline's VIP club or private lounge. In these lounges you likely can find comfortable couches, TVs, newspapers, magazines, telephones, business services, and full bar service, all in a quiet, living room-like atmosphere. The airline VIP lounges are also staffed by competent customer service representatives. These people can assist you with booking alternative flights, if necessary.

MONEY SAVER

It's common for the airlines to oversell seats on flights leaving Washington, DC, especially on a Friday. To ensure all ticketed passengers get to their destinations, the airlines sometimes ask for passengers to voluntarily give up their seat on an aircraft and take a later flight. In exchange for the inconvenience, an airline will sometimes offer a travel voucher good for one free round-trip airline ticket within the continental United States, along with a meal voucher and possibly a voucher for a free night of hotel accommodations. This is a great way to earn free travel if you have flexibility in your schedule. The award vouchers can be transferred to friends, co-workers, or relatives, but they must be used within one year of receipt. Listen at the gate for announcements asking for volunteers to give up their seats. If you're interested, approach the ticket counter and submit your name.

LOST LUGGAGE

According to *Air Travel Consumer Report*, which is published by the U.S. Department of Transportation, in April 2007, a total of 336,732 pieces of luggage were reported lost, delayed, or mishandled by the country's 20 largest airlines. One year earlier, this figure was 271,389. For airline passengers, the chances of experiencing some type of luggage-related problem is about 6.32 in 1,000.

If an airline does misplace or delay your luggage, immediately report the missing bags to your airline by visiting the baggage assistance desk located near baggage claim at any airport. You will need to present your claim stubs (provided at check in), plus you'll be asked to fill out a written report that describes your lost bags and their contents. You will then be given a special claim tracking number, as well as a toll-free phone number to track your claim.

Most lost luggage is found within a few hours and placed on the next flight to your destination city. It will then be delivered by a third-party messenger service to whatever address you supply. This delivery process can take up to 12 additional hours, so if you're in a hurry to reclaim your delayed luggage, agree to pick it up in-person at the airport when it arrives. You may find it necessary to keep calling the airline to get an accurate estimated time of arrival for your delayed bags.

When bags are delayed for more than 24 hours, you may be entitled to receive compensation to purchase toiletries or clothing, for example, that you need immediately at your destination. Be prepared to negotiate hard for this, as airlines tend to offer as little as possible. You will be required to supply receipts for purchases that have been pre-approved by the airline.

In the rare case when luggage is truly lost, the airline is responsible for reimbursing you for the depreciated value (not the replacement value) of the bag itself, along with its contents, up to a total value of $3,000 (for a bag lost on a domestic flight).

When filing an insurance claim with the airline for lost or damaged luggage, it could take eight to 12 weeks to receive a reimbursement check. If you have your own travel insurance or homeowner's insurance, consider filing a claim with these insurance providers as well.

To help minimize the chances of your luggage being delayed or lost by an airline, follow these six basic steps:

1. Remove all old airline tags from your luggage.
2. When checking your luggage with the airline, make sure correctly labeled tags are attached to each of your bags by

the ticket agent. The tag, which is printed on a large white sticker, should display the airport code of your destination city, along with your full name.
3. Arrive at the airport and check your luggage with the airline at least 60 to 120 minutes prior to your flight.
4. Attached one or two of your own luggage tags to each bag, listing at least your name and phone number. Listing your address is optional. Also include your contact information inside each bag.
5. Attach a colored ribbon around the bag's handle or use a neon-colored luggage tag to help differentiate your bag from others with a similar design. This will reduce the chance of another traveler accidentally picking up your luggage in the baggage claim area.
6. Never pack any valuables, including camera or computer equipment, jewelry, or important business papers in your checked luggage. Anything of value or that you'll need as soon as you get off the airplane should be packed in your carry-on and kept with you.

If an airline loses, delays or damages your luggage, here are some of special Lost Luggage Tracking and Claims phone numbers for the major airlines:

- American Airlines—(800) 535-5225
- Continental Airlines—(800) 335-2247
- Delta Airlines—(800) 325-8224
- JetBlue Airways—(866) 538-5438
- Southwest Airlines—(800) 533-1222
- United Airlines—(800) 221-6903

TIP
For domestic flights, the airline baggage liability is capped at $3,000 per person for checked baggage and $400 per person for carry-ons. To file a claim and recover your losses, you will need to produce receipts for lost or damaged items. For an additional fee, you can purchase "excess valuation" protection for your luggage when you check in at the airport. Keep in mind, there is a long list of items that an airline will not take responsibility for or be willing to replace. Most airlines require that you file a claim within 21 to 45 days.

If you have a meeting within the first few hours of your arrival, it's an excellent strategy to bring everything you need for that meeting with you in your carry-on. Thus, if your checked luggage is lost or delayed, it does not affect your ability to be attend the meeting.

WARNING
There are a variety of items—such as electronics, computers, antiques, jewelry, and business documents—that none of the airlines will take responsibility for. Never pack any of these items in your checked luggage.

For coverage above and beyond what the airline or your homeowner's insurance policy offers for lost, stolen, or delayed luggage, consider purchasing independent travel insurance. This insurance can be purchased with a major credit card from any travel agent or by contacting an insurance provider on the phone or online. Travel insurance must be purchased before your trip begins.

You can learn more about travel insurance and what it covers, or purchase an insurance policy, by contacting any of these companies:

- CSA Travel Protection—www.csatravelprotection.com or (800) 348-9505
- Insure My Trip.com—www.insuremytrip.com or (800) 487-4722
- Travel Guard International—www.travelguard.com or (800) 826-4919
- Travel Insurance Center—www.travelinsurancecenter.com or (866) 979-6753
- Travelex Insurance Services—www.travelex-insurance.com or (800) 228-9792

The cost of travel insurance varies, based on the amount of coverage, the duration of your trip, and the value of the travel and your belongings. Make sure you understand what coverage you're purchasing and be sure to file any claims immediately by calling the insurance company's toll-free phone number and following their directions. If your claim involves a theft, it is often necessary to obtain a police report relating to the incident, so contact the local police department. Expect to wait four to six weeks for your claim to be processed and to be reimbursed for your covered losses.

One way to minimize the risk that your important luggage will get lost or stolen is to utilize a "luggage forwarding service."

This type of service picks up your luggage from your home or office two to seven days prior to your departure, and arranges to have it delivered to your hotel (or any location) on the date of your arrival. All details are handled on your behalf, and you don't have to worry about airport security or the airline misplacing your bags.

Utilizing a luggage forwarding service isn't cheap, but this type of service can take some of the stress and hassle out of business travel. These services also handle oversize luggage items, such as golf clubs, skis, trade show displays, and wheelchairs. Some of companies that offer luggage forwarding services include:

- Luggage Club—www.theluggageclub.com or (877) 231-5131
- Luggage Concierge—www.luggageconcierge.com or (800) 288-9818
- Luggage Forward—www.luggageforward.com or (866) 416-7447
- Luggage Free—www.luggagefree.com or (800) 361-6871

Fees for these services are based on the size and weight of your luggage, desired delivery time, and the pick-up/drop-off fees charged by the service provider.

WARNING
All of the major airlines now strictly adhere to their luggage weight guidelines. If a bag weights more than 50 pounds (for domestic flights), expect to pay an overweight fee of between $25 and $75, depending on the airline. When you pack, be sure your luggage adheres to airline guidelines to avoid extra charges.

LOST OR STOLEN CREDIT CARD, DRIVER'S LICENSE, AND/OR PASSPORT

If your wallet is lost or stolen, immediately call your bank or financial institution; the phone number is listed on your statement and on the back of your ATM card(s).

TIP
If you suspect the theft of your credit cards or personal identification, call the local police department and file a police report immediately. Also, contact the three major

credit bureaus—Equifax (800-525-6285), Experian (888-397-3742), and TransUnion (800-860-7289)—to report possible identify theft. You should also call the Identity Theft Data Clearing House at (877) ID-THEFT.

Immediately call the toll-free phone numbers for all your credit cards and ATM and debit cards individually to report the situation. This can be done 24 hours a day. Following is the contact information for major credit card companies:

- American Express—www.americanexpress.com or (800) 528-4800, (800) 528-2122
- Diner's Club—www.dinersclub.com or (800) 234-6377
- Discover—www.discovercard.com or (800) 347-2683
- MasterCard—www.mastercard.com or (800) 622-7747
- Visa—www.usa.visa.com or (800) 847-2911

If your driver's license is lost or stolen, contact the department of motor vehicles in your home city to arrange for a replacement license.

For a lost or stolen passport, if you're an American citizen, contact the U.S. Department of State, Passport Services, at (202) 955-0430 or visit http://travel.state.gov/passport/lost/us/us_848.html. You need to complete and file a Statement Regarding Lost or Stolen Passport Form (Form DS-64). For additional information, call (877) 487-2778.

WARNING

Without a valid government-issued form of identification, you cannot travel on any airline. Some airlines also require that you present a credit or debit card as a secondary form of identification when checking in at the airport using an automated kiosk.

LOST, STOLEN, OR DAMAGED LAPTOP COMPUTER

If your laptop is stolen, file a report with the local police and your insurance company immediately. You can purchase or rent a new computer while in Washington, DC, or you can utilize the computers available at the business centers found in the various hotels.

For emergency laptop repair or data recovery, see the companies listed in Section VIII, "Business Services."

TIP

Before leaving your home or office, be sure to back up all your important computer data. Also, be sure to keep current records pertaining to your computer, including the sales receipt from when it was purchased, as well as its serial number, make, and model numbers. If you purchased the extended warranty for your computer, bring the necessary information with you so you can contact the manufacturer if an emergency repair or replacement is required.

BUYING A NEW OUTFIT FAST OR REMOVING A STAIN

If you accidentally stain or damage your outfit, or if you need to purchase a new business outfit fast, many of the upscale clothing boutiques in Washington, DC, plus all the major department stores, offer same-day tailoring. Section IX, "Personal Services," lists local tailors who offer while-you-wait or same-day service. Some tailors even come to your hotel room for on-the-spot fittings or alternations. If you need help finding a tailor or seamstress who will come to your hotel, contact your hotel's concierge.

Many of the popular hotels have inhouse, same-day laundering and dry cleaning services that will pick up garments from your guestroom, which is helpful when you need to have a stain removed. Section VIII, "Business Services," lists laundry and dry cleaning services.

TIP

To clean up or remove clothing stains yourself, consider packing a travel-size container of OxiClean, Tide to Go, or another popular stain remover. For tips on removing specific types of stains, visit the Tide web site (www.tide.com). Also consider traveling with a portable clothing steamer or travel steam iron, plus a small sewing kit. The Buttoneer ($19.95, www.buybuttoneer.com) is a handy and portable device that allows you to reattach buttons to almost any garment in seconds, with no sewing required.

PRESCRIPTION REFILLS

There are many pharmacies located in and around the nation's capitol, many of which are open 24 hours. If you need to have a prescription filled, refilled, or replaced, you'll need a copy of your original prescription or your doctor must contact the pharmacy directly. Be sure to travel with your doctor's contact information and your medical insurance card (if applicable). If you already have your prescription on file with your hometown Walgreen's, for example, go to the Washington, DC area location of that same pharmacy to save time and hassle. For a partial listing of pharmacies, refer to Section IX, "Personal Services."

REPLACING PRESCRIPTION EYEWEAR

Thanks to companies such as LensCrafters (www.lenscrafters.com) and Pearle Vision Centers (www.pearlevision.com), replacement eyeglasses can be created typically in one hour. These companies have multiple stores in the Washington, DC area. Some Wal-Mart stores (such as the location in Fairfax, Virginia, 703-631-6775) also offer inhouse vision centers capable of making prescription eyeglasses and replacing contact lenses quickly. For more information, see Section IX, "Personal Services."

In order to purchase replacement prescription eyeglasses, sunglasses, or contact lenses, you will need a copy of your current prescription from your eye doctor or the eyeglass company must contact your eye doctor directly. If this isn't possible, you can pay for an on-site eye exam. (This is something your insurance may or may not cover. Speak with your hometown optometrist's office before proceeding with the exam.)

MEDICAL OR DENTAL EMERGENCIES

See Section IX, "Personal Services," for contact and referral information for Washington, DC area doctors, dentists, and hospitals. Many doctors and dentists offer immediate appointments on an emergency basis, if necessary. The emergency rooms at the area hospitals are open 24 hours per day.

- To obtain a doctor referral, call Georgetown University Hospital's physician referral line at (202) 342-2400 or visit the hospital's web site (www.georgetownuniversity hospital.org). You can also call George Washington University Hospital's physician referral line at (888) 4GW-DOCS, or visit the hospital's web site (www.gwhospital .com/p5.html).
- To quickly obtain a dentist referral, call (800) DENTIST.

TIP
To see an up-to-date listing of the Washington area's best doctors, according to *Washingtonian* magazine, visit

HOTEL CONCIERGES SHARE THEIR SOLUTIONS

Part of the job responsibilities of a hotel's concierge is to help guests solve any problems encountered during their visit. Michael McCleary, assistant chief concierge at the Willard InterContinental, explained that one common problem business travelers encounter is trying to print out important documents using their laptop computer and the hotel's printers. "The problem typically occurs when a computer isn't configured with the proper drivers to work with our printers. One easy solution is that we have the guest e-mail either the business center or the concierge desk with the files they'd like printed, and we print them out," McCleary said. "We also help guests obtain tickets to different events and venues. If necessary, we can provide 'line standers,' who will stand in sometimes long lines to get tickets for a specific show, concert, event, or admission to an attraction. Tickets for the Bureau of Engraving and Printing or Washington Monument tour are distributed first thing in the morning, on a first-come basis. Our line standers can obtain tickets on behalf of our guests. We also have two notary publics on staff, so we can perform notary services for our guests after hours, when banks are closed. One other common problem we help with is assisting guests in replacing a cell phone charger they've either left at home or have misplaced."

Javier Loureiro, chief concierge at the Four Seasons explained that the biggest problem he helps guests overcome is making last-minute changes to their travel itineraries. "In this case, the concierge becomes the guest's personal assistant. We have contacts at most of the major airlines and even at some embassies that can help to expedite international travel difficulties. Most travel situations involve lots of patience on the phone working with the airline or travel arranger, since the rules that govern travel and ticketing between air carriers are complicated," he said.

Daniel Klibanoff, the concierge at the Mandarin Oriental, stated that the most common question hotel guests ask him relates to the fare system used by DC area taxis. Instead of using a meter, the DC area taxis use a zone system. "I always suggest asking the concierge or doorman what the fare should be based on your starting location and your intended destination. If you can't ask someone at the hotel, you can always ask the taxi driver what the fare will be before starting your trip. If you ask, the drivers are required to tell you in advance what the fare will be."

> Klibanoff added, "People don't initially understand all of the ways the hotel's concierge can help make someone's visit easier. We are really a catchall for requests. We can arrange for pet-sitters, in-room massages, and help you obtain items you might have forgotten to bring."

www.washingtonian.com/sections/health/topdoctors/index.html. This listing is categorized by medical specialty.

If you experience a medical emergency while in the Washington, DC area, dial 9-1-1 from any telephone or call your hotel's front desk or operator (dial 0). For non-emergencies, your hotel's concierge can provide personalized referrals for a wide range of medical specialists in the area. Some hotels even have a nurse or doctor on call who will come to your guestroom. In some cases, you may have to pay for medical services up-front and later apply for reimbursement from your insurance company.

TIP

If you see a doctor, dentist, or eye doctor, for example, while in Washington, DC, be sure to obtain copies of all new medical records to provide to your primary doctor(s) when you return home.

CELL PHONE-RELATED PROBLEMS

If your cell phone gets lost or stolen, call your service provider immediately to suspend your service. If you subscribe to a repair or replacement insurance plan through your service provider, you can arrange to have a new (refurbished) phone sent to you via overnight courier, typically within two business days.

If you lose or forget your charger or need a new accessory, there are Sprint/Nextel (866-438-1371), AT&T/Cingular (866-CINGULAR), T-Mobile (800-866-2453), Verizon (800-256-4646), and other cell phone stores located throughout the city. Many hotel concierges also stock a selection of chargers for popular cell phone models, or will send someone out on your behalf to purchase a replace charger for you.

EASY INTERNET ACCESS ... FROM ALMOST ANYWHERE

Apple iPhone, Palm Treo, and Blackberry users enjoy easy access to the internet from virtually anywhere using their handheld wireless device. This is extremely appealing to business travelers who know the importance of staying connected and require the ability to access their e-mail and the web whenever and wherever they happen to be.

The drawback to accessing the web using a cell phone or wireless personal digital assistant (PDA) is the small screen, limited keyboard, and dramatically scaled down web surfing capabilities these tiny devices offer. As a result, business travelers also tend to travel with a laptop computer, allowing them to access the internet from wireless (Wi-Fi) hotspots or from hotel rooms.

This solution also has its drawbacks. While most airports and hotels offer high-speed internet access, it comes at a cost. Airports, internet cafés, bookstores, and coffee shops (including Starbucks) throughout the country often charge a daily fee of between $6.95 and $9.95 to connect to the web via a wireless hotspot. Hotels typically charge between $9.95 and $19.95 per night to access the internet from a guestroom. For a business traveler constantly on the go, these charges add up quickly.

For budget conscious web surfers, it is possible to seek out free, public Wi-Fi hotspots and utilize them during your travels. The www.jiwire.com web site, for example, offers a listing of more than 150,000 free Wi-Fi hotspots worldwide. The www.wifi411.com web site also lists public Wi-Fi hotspots that offer free and paid access in cities across America.

The CyberCafes web site (www.cybercafes.com) provides an online directory listing thousands of internet cafes worldwide that allow users to access the web using supplied desktop computers for a low hourly fee, usually between $5 to $10 per hour. Most public libraries and Apple stores across America also offer free internet access to the public. Using this solution, there's no need to travel with your own computer.

There is another alternative. For between $49.95 and $79.95 per month, laptop computer users can subscribe to a wireless Broadband service offered by Sprint PCS, T-Mobile, AT&T, or Verizon. By connecting an inexpensive wireless modem to a laptop computer, true wireless, high-speed (Broadband) access is available from almost anywhere, especially within major cities. No phone lines or extra cables are required, plus you're not limited to Wi-Fi coverage areas.

APPENDIX

TRAVEL CHARTS AND WORKSHEETS

The following charts and worksheets will help you keep track of your expenses and time. Feel free to reproduce them for each trip you take to Washington, DC.

TIPPING RECOMMENDATIONS

SERVICE	RECOMMENDED TIPPING GUIDELINES
Bartender	Between 15 and 20 percent of bar tab or $1 to $2 per drink.
Bell captain (luggage attendant)	$2 per bag.
Concierge	$2 to $100 (depending on the service offered).
Curbside luggage check-in	You will typically pay a fee of $2 per bag for this service. Tip an additional $1 to $2 per bag.
Drink server	$1 to $2 per drink or 15 to 20 percent of the total bar tab.
Hotel housekeeper	$1 to $2 per night (leave the tip at the conclusion of your stay).
Limousine driver	15 percent of the total fare.
Personal shopper	15 to 20 percent of the total purchases made on your behalf.
Restaurant host/hostess	This is optional. Consider tipping $2 to $10 (depending on the quality of the restaurant, whether you've requested a specific table, or if the host/hostess reduced your wait time).
Room service	Virtually all hotels automatically add a 15 to 20 percent tip and delivery charge to the room service bill. It is optional whether you choose to give an additional tip.
Taxi driver	15 percent of the total fare.
Tour guide	10 to 20 percent of the total fee paid for the tour.
Valet parking attendant	$1 to $2 each time the car is parked or delivered.
Waiter/waitress (party of fewer than six people)	15 to 20 percent of the total bill.
Waiter/waitress (party of seven or more)	15 to 20 percent of the total bill (including alcohol). In many cases, the restaurant will automatically add a gratuity to the bill for large parties.

TIP CALCULATION CHART

AMOUNT	10%	15%	20%
$1.00	$ .10	$ .15	$ .20
$2.00	$ .20	$ .30	$ .40
$3.00	$ .30	$ .45	$ .60
$4.00	$ .40	$ .60	$ .80
$5.00	$ .50	$ .75	$1.00
$6.00	$ .60	$ .90	$1.20
$7.00	$ .70	$1.05	$1.40
$8.00	$.80	$1.20	$1.60
$9.00	$.90	$1.35	$1.80
$10.00	$1.00	$1.50	$2.00
$11.00	$1.10	$1.65	$2.20
$12.00	$1.20	$1.80	$2.40
$13.00	$1.30	$1.95	$2.60
$14.00	$1.40	$2.10	$2.80
$15.00	$1.50	$2.25	$3.00
$16.00	$1.60	$2.40	$3.20
$17.00	$1.70	$2.55	$3.40
$18.00	$1.80	$2.70	$3.60
$19.00	$1.90	$2.85	$3.80
$20.00	$2.00	$3.00	$4.00
$25.00	$2.50	$3.75	$5.00
$30.00	$3.00	$4.50	$6.00
$35.00	$3.50	$5.25	$7.00
$40.00	$4.00	$6.00	$8.00
$45.00	$4.50	$6.75	$9.00
$50.00	$5.00	$7.50	$10.00
$55.00	$5.50	$8.25	$11.00
$60.00	$6.00	$9.00	$12.00
$65.00	$6.50	$9.75	$13.00
$70.00	$7.00	$10.50	$14.00
$75.00	$7.50	$11.25	$15.00
$80.00	$8.00	$12.00	$16.00
$85.00	$8.50	$12.75	$17.00
$90.00	$9.00	$13.50	$18.00
$95.00	$9.50	$14.25	$19.00
$100.00	$10.00	$15.00	$20.00
$125.00	$12.50	$18.75	$25.00
$150.00	$15.00	$22.50	$30.00
$175.00	$17.50	$26.25	$35.00
$200.00	$20.00	$30.00	$40.00
$250.00	$25.00	$37.50	$50.00
$300.00	$30.00	$45.00	$60.00
$350.00	$35.00	$52.50	$70.00
$400.00	$40.00	$60.00	$80.00
$450.00	$45.00	$67.50	$90.00
$500.00	$50.00	$75.00	$100.00
$1,000.00	$100.00	$150.00	$200.00

TRAVEL ITINERARY WORKSHEET

Departure date: ___/___/___
Return date: ___/___/___
From: _____
To: _____

Hometown Ground Transportation to Airport
Service provider: _____
Phone number: _____
Reservation/confirmation number: _____
Pick-up location: _____
Pick-up time: _____ Drop-off time: _____

Airport Parking Information
Parking lot name/location: _____
Parking spot location/identifier: _____

Airline Information
Airline: _____
Phone number: _____
Airline frequent flier number: _____
Flight number: _____
Departure time: _____
Arrival time: _____

Connecting flight number: _____ Connecting flight city: _____
Connecting flight departure time: _____
Connecting arrival time: _____

Connecting flight number: _____ Connecting flight city: _____
Connecting flight departure time: _____
Connecting arrival time: _____

Rental Car Information
Rental car company: _____
Phone number: _____
Confirmation/reservation number: _____
Pick-up time/location: _____
Drop-off time/location: _____
Type of vehicle requested/reserved: _____

Washington, DC Ground Transportation from Airport
Service provider: _____
Phone number: _____

TRAVEL ITINERARY WORKSHEET, continued

Reservation/confirmation number: _____

Pick-up location: _____

Pick-up time: _____ Drop-off time: _____

Hotel/Resort Accommodations

Hotel resort name: _____

Phone number: _____

Address: _____

Confirmation number: _____

Check-in date: _____

Check-out date: _____

Washington, DC Ground Transportation to Airport

Service provider: _____

Phone number: _____

Reservation/confirmation number: _____

Pick-up location: _____

Pick-up time: _____ Drop-off time: _____

Airline Information

Airline: _____

Phone number: _____

Airline frequent flier number: _____

Flight number: _____

Departure time: _____

Arrival time: _____

Connecting flight number: _____ Connecting flight city: _____
Connecting flight departure time: _____
Connecting arrival time: _____

Connecting flight number: _____ Connecting flight city: _____
Connecting flight departure time: _____
Connecting arrival time: _____

Hometown Ground Transportation from Airport

Service provider: _____

Phone number: _____

Reservation/confirmation number: _____

Pick-up time: _____ Drop-off time: _____

EXPENSE TRACKER WORKSHEET

Page # ____ of ____

Expense Description	Date	Price	Payment Method* (circle one)	Receipt (circle one)	Expense Type** (circle one)
		$	$ CC TC	Yes / No	P B
		$	$ CC TC	Yes / No	P B
		$	$ CC TC	Yes / No	P B
		$	$ CC TC	Yes / No	P B
		$	$ CC TC	Yes / No	P B
		$	$ CC TC	Yes / No	P B
		$	$ CC TC	Yes / No	P B
		$	$ CC TC	Yes / No	P B
		$	$ CC TC	Yes / No	P B
		$	$ CC TC	Yes / No	P B
		$	$ CC TC	Yes / No	P B
		$	$ CC TC	Yes / No	P B
	Total Expenses:	$			

*Note: Payment methods include: Cash ($), Credit Card (CC), or Traveler's Check (TC)

**Expense types include: Personal (P) or Business (B)

APPENDIX / TRAVEL CHARTS AND WORKSHEETS · 241

TRADE SHOW MEETING PLANNER

Date:

Time	Location (Booth or Meeting Room Number)	Company	Contact Person	Purpose of Meeting	Notes

FREQUENT TRAVELER PROGRAM WORKSHEET

Airline					
Program Name					
Account/Member Number					
Membership Status					
Phone Number					
Web Site Address					
Username and Password					

INDEX

A

Accommodations in Washington, DC, 55–87
  Business Traveler Top 15 Business-Friendly Hotels, 60–85
  checklist of business amenities, 59
  choosing based on amenities and services offered, 57–59
  choosing your location, 56
  room rates, range of, 56–57
  using online booking services, 57
Airlines
  frequent flier programs, 39–42
  list of servicing Washington, DC, 2–7
Airport
  Baltimore/Washington International ((BWI) Thurgood Marshall, 28–33
  car rental, 37
  curbside check-in, 14
  Dulles International, 14–22
  ground transportation options, 33–37
  limousines, 37
  metro train service to and from, 34
  Ronald Reagan Washington National, 22–27
  security considerations and tips, 11–14
  shuttle bus service, 33–34
  taxi service, 34–36
Alcoholics Anonymous, 204
Amtrak service to and from Washington, DC, 37–38
Arlington National Cemetery, 145–146
Audiovisual equipment rentals, 180–181

B

Balloons, 181

243

Baltimore/Washington International ((BWI) Thurgood Marshall Airport, 28–33
- airline clubs, 33
- dining options, 32
- getting to Washington, DC from BWI, 30–31
- hotels and motels, 33
- map of, 28–29
- navigating, 28–33
- retail shops, 31
- terminal layout and services, 31–32
- ticket counters and baggage claim, 32

Banking and financial services, 181–182, 191
Bed-and-breakfast reservation service, 87
Ben's Chili Bowl, 123
BLT Steak, 107–108
Blue Duck Tavern, 108–109
Bodies, The Exhibition, 155
Bureau of Engraving and Printing, 146
Buses. *See also* Metrorail/Metrobus
- charters and shuttles, 102–104, 182–183
- service to and from Washington, DC, 38–39

Business amenities checklist for hotels, 59
Business services, 179–201
Business Traveler Top 15 Business-Friendly Hotels, 60–85
Buying a new business outfit, 229

C

Capital Grille, 109
Capital Hilton, 62–63
Capitol Steps, satire troupe, 139
Capitol, U.S., 152
Caterers, 183
Cell phone
- problems, 233–234
- services and accessories, 184

Charter and shuttle buses, 102–104, 182–183
Charts and worksheets, travel, 235–270
Chauffeured limousines and town cars, 96–97
Chiropractors, 204
City map, Washington, DC, 268
Cityzen, 110
Comedy, stand-up, 139
Computer rentals, repairs and technical support, 184–186
Concierge
- restaurant recommendations, 128
- services, 87
- solutions, 232–233
- tickets to shows, concerts and sporting events, 143
- top picks for tourists, 156

Convention and Tourism Corporation, Washington, DC, 86–87
Conventions or business meetings, attending, 163–178
Credit card companies, 186
Cruises, dinner/lunch, 123, 133–134, 135
Curbside check-in, airport, 14

D

Day spas, 210–213
DC Circulator Bus, 103–104
- map, 103

DC Guesthouse, 63–64
DC Improv, 139
Dental emergencies, 231, 233
Dentists, 205
Department stores, list of, 205–206
Dining options in Washington, DC, 105–129
- *Business Traveler* Top 15 Fine-Dining Restaurants in Washington, DC, 106–123

Dinner/lunch cruises, 123, 133–134, 135

Dry cleaning, 186–187
Dulles International Airport, 14–22
  airline clubs and lounges, 20–21
  fast-food dining options, 19
  hotels and motels, 21–22
  map of, 15
  navigating, 14–22
  retail shopping, 19
  sit-down dining options, 19–20
  terminal layout and services, 17–22
  ticket-counters and baggage claim, 20
Dupont Grille, 110–112

E

Embroidery and screen-printing companies, 188
Emergencies, help for travel-related, 221–233
Entertainment in Washington, DC, 131–162
ESPN Zone, 123, 126
Expense tracker worksheet, 240
Eyewear stores and optometrists, 206–207

F

FedEx Field, sports stadium, 142–143
Fedex Kinko's locations, 188–189
Fitness centers/gyms, 207–209
Florists, 189–190
Fondue restaurant, 127
Food-delivery services, 128–129
Foreign currency exchange services, 190–191
Four Points Sheraton, 64–65
Four Seasons, 65–67
Frequent traveler program worksheet, 242

G

Getting around town, 89–104
Getting to Washington, DC, 2

Golf courses, 144–145
Grand Hyatt Washington, 67–69

H

Hair salons/barbers, 209
Hard Rock Cafe, 124, 126
Holocaust Memorial Museum, United States, 152
Hooters, 124
Hospitals, 209–210
Hotels in Washington, DC, 55–87
  Business Traveler Top 15 Business-Friendly, 60–85
  chains, list of major, 85–86 (*See also* Accommodations in Washington, DC)

I

IL Mulino, New York, 112
Insurance, travel, 226–227
International Spy Museum, 146–147
Itinerary changes, last-minute, 222–223

J

Jet charter companies, 192
Jurys Washington Hotel, 69–71

L

Laptop computer, lost, stolen or damaged, 229–230
Lawyer referrals, 192
Legal Sea Foods, 124–125, 126
Lincoln Memorial, 147–148
Locksmiths, 192–193
Lost luggage, 225–228
Lost or stolen credit card, driver's license, and/or passport, 228–229
Luggage
  forwarding service, 227
  lost, 225–228
  repair and sales, 217–218

M

Madison, A Loews Hotel, 71–72
Magazines, local, 161
Mandarin Oriental, 72–74

Maps
- Baltimore/Washington International ((BWI) Thurgood Marshall Airport, 28–29
- DC Circulator Bus, 103
- Dulles International Airport, 15
- Metrobus, 100, 270
- Metrorail, 99, 267
- Ronald Reagan Washington National Airport, 23
- Washington Convention Center, 167–172
- Washington, DC, City, 268
- Washington, DC, Region, 269

Massage therapists, 210–211
McCormick & Schmick's Seafood Restaurant, 112–114
Media listings for Washington, DC, 160–162
Medical emergencies, 231, 233
Meeting and banquet room rentals, 193–194
Melting Pot, the, 127
Messenger services, 194–195
Metrorail/Metrobus, 97–102
- fares, 101
- system map of Metrobus, 100, 270
- system map of Metrorail, 99, 267
- tips for using, 102

Modeling agencies and temporary trade show personnel, 195
Mystery Dinner Playhouse, 125

N

Nail salons, 211, 213–214
National Archives, 148
National Cathedral, 155
National Gallery of Art, 148–149
National Mall, 149–150
National Zoological Park (aka the National Zoo), 150
Newspapers, local, 160–161

O

Occidental, 114–115
Office supply superstores, 195–196
Online travel services, 7–10, 86
Oval Room, the, 115–116

P

Packing for your business trip, 43–54
- before-leaving-home checklist, 54
- carry-on bag packing checklist, 51–52
- checked baggage packing checklist, 49–51
- luggage, 44–47
- optional items, 53
- products to keep you healthy while traveling, 53–54
- tips, 47–48
- TSA regulations, 47, 52
- Washington, DC weather, 48–49

Palm Restaurant, the, 116
Park Hyatt Washington, 74–76
Pentagon, the, 150–151
Personal services, 203–233
Personal shopping services, 215
Pharmacies, 215–216
Photography services, 196
Post office locations, 200
Potbelly Sandwich Works, 125
Prescription eyewear, replacing, 231
Prescription medication refills, 230
Public transportation-Metrorail and Metrobus, 97–102

R

Radio stations, local, 161–162
Regional map, Washington, DC, 269
Renaissance Mayflower, 76
Renaissance Washington, DC Hotel, 77–78
Rental car, 92–96
- companies, list of, 217

Ritz-Carlton, Georgetown, 78–79
Ritz-Carlton, Washington, DC, 79–80
Ronald Reagan Washington National Airport, 22–27
  airline clubs, 26–27
  fast-food dining options, 25–26
  map of, 23
  monorail, 24
  motels and hotels, 27
  navigating, 22–27
  retail shops, 25
  sit-down dining options, 26
  terminal layout and services offered, 24–25
  ticket counters and baggage claim, 26
Room service, ordering, 127–129
Ruth's Chris Steakhouse, 116–118

S

Scooter rentals, 104
Secretarial and temporary employment services, 197
701 Restaurant, 118
Shipping
  and freight services, 197
  supplies and boxes, 182
Shoe repair, 217
Shopping
  America!, 157
  Brooks Brothers, 157
  Burberrys, 157
  department stores, list of, 205–206
  Fashion Center at Pentagon City, 157–158
  Mazza Gallerie, 158
  opportunities for busy business travelers, 157–159
  Smithsonian Store, 158–159
  The Shops at Georgetown Park, 158
  Tyson's Corner Center, 159
  Union Station, 159–160
  White House Gift Shop, 159–160
Shuttle and charter buses, 102–104
Smith & Wollensky, 118–119
Smithsonian Institution Museums, 151
Sporting events, professional, 140–143
Stain removal, 230
Subway. *See* Metrorail

T

Tailors, 186–187, 218
Taxis, 90–92
Tea Cellar, 125, 127
Tea, meeting for midday, 125, 127
Television stations, local, 161
Theater and stage performances, 137–139
  comedy, stand-up, 139
  Ford's Theater, 138, 139
  list of area theaters, 137–138
  National Theater, 138
  Ronald Reagan Building Amphitheater, 139
  Warner Theater, 138, 139
Ticketplace discount tickets, 138
Theme and specialty restaurants, 123–127
Ticket brokers, 144, list of
Tipping recommendations/chart, 236–237
Tourist attractions, *Business Traveler* Top 15 Washington, DC, 145–156
Tours, Washington, DC, 132–137
  Bike the Sites, 132
  Boomerang Party Bus, 133
  Capital City Bike Tours, 133
  Capital SegwayTours, 133
  Dandy Dinner Boat, 133–134
  DC Ducks, 134
  exclusive tours for upscale business travelers, 136
  helicopter tours, 136
  Martz Grey Line, 134
  Old Town Trolley Tours, 134
  On Location Tours, 134

Private Limousine Tours, 134–135, 136
private yacht tours, 136
Scandal Tours, 135
Segs in the City, 135
Spirit Cruises, 135
Tourmobile Sightseeing, 135–136
Viator, 136
Washington Photo Safari, 136–137
Trade show
   and private security services, 198
   exhibit sales, installation, repair, and dismantling, 198–199
   meeting planner, 241 (*See also* Washington Convention Center)
Translators and interpreters, 199
Transportation, 89–104
Travel delays, 223–224
Travel itinerary worksheet, 238–239
Traveler's checks, 199–200
Tuxedo rentals, 218

U

Union Station, 38
   shopping and dining, 159–160

V

Verizon Center event venue, 140–142
Video production services and equipment rental, 200–201
Vietnam Veterans Memorial, 153

W

Walking around town, 104
Washington Convention Center, 164–178
   dining options at or near, 172–174
   directions to, 165
   driving from BWI Airport, 166
   driving from Dulles International Airport, 166
   driving from Reagan National Airport, 165–166
   exhibitor services, 177–178
   floor plans, 167–172
   hotel accommodations within walking distance, 174–175
   maps, 167–172
   Marc or Metrorail from BWI Airport, 166–167
   monorail from Reagan National Airport, 165–166
   navigating around, 167–172
   public parking lots, 167
   services and amenities, 175–176
   tips for attending a convention or trade show, 176–177
Washington Monument, 153–154
Washington, DC city map, 268
Washington, DC regional map, 269
Water shuttle, 104
Watergate Hotel, 80–81
Weather delays, 223–224
Welcome to Washington, DC, 1–42
Western Union electronic money-transfer services, 201
Wheelchair and scooter rentals, 219
Where to dine in Washington, DC, 105–129
Where to stay in Washington, DC, 55–87
White House, the, 154–155
Willard Intercontinental, 81–85
I Spa, 212–213
Willard Room, the, 119–120
Wine, tips on ordering at a business dinner, 121–122

Z

Zola, 120, 122

WASHINGTON, DC CITY MAP

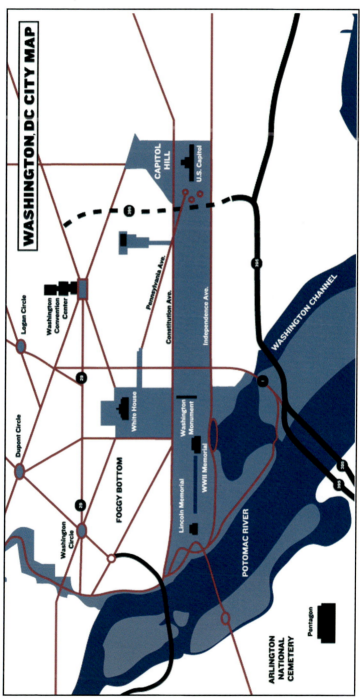

Map of Washington, DC area adapted from www.mapnetwork.com/mapspages/washington/DC_visitor_map_screen.pdf. Illustration by Amy Thomas.

WASHINGTON, DC METRORAIL MAP

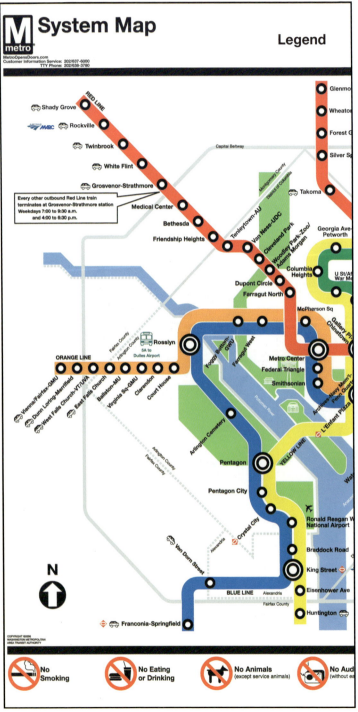

Courtesy of the Washington Metropolitan Area Transit Authority.

WASHINGTON, DC REGIONAL MAP

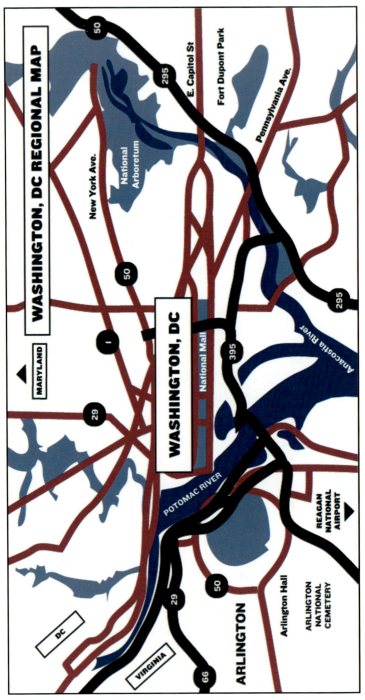

Map of regional area adapted from http://map.mapnetwork.com/destination/dc/.
Illustration by Amy Thomas.